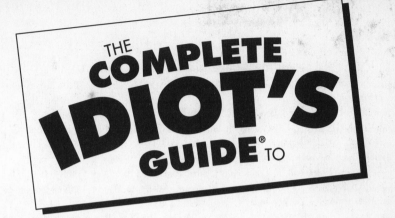

# THE COMPLETE IDIOT'S GUIDE® TO

# Closing the Sale

## *by Keith Rosen, MCC*

**ALPHA**

A member of Penguin Group (USA) Inc.

## ALPHA BOOKS

Published by the Penguin Group

Penguin Group (USA) Inc., 375 Hudson Street, New York, New York 10014, U.S.A.

Penguin Group (Canada), 10 Alcorn Avenue, Toronto, Ontario, Canada M4V 3B2 (a division of Pearson Penguin Canada Inc.)

Penguin Books Ltd, 80 Strand, London WC2R 0RL, England

Penguin Ireland, 25 St Stephen's Green, Dublin 2, Ireland (a division of Penguin Books Ltd)

Penguin Group (Australia), 250 Camberwell Road, Camberwell, Victoria 3124, Australia (a division of Pearson Australia Group Pty Ltd)

Penguin Books India Pvt Ltd, 11 Community Centre, Panchsheel Park, New Delhi—110 017, India

Penguin Group (NZ), cnr Airborne and Rosedale Roads, Albany, Auckland 1310, New Zealand (a division of Pearson New Zealand Ltd)

Penguin Books (South Africa) (Pty) Ltd, 24 Sturdee Avenue, Rosebank, Johannesburg 2196, South Africa

Penguin Books Ltd, Registered Offices: 80 Strand, London WC2R 0RL, England

## Copyright © 2007 by Keith Rosen, MCC

International Standard Book Number: 978-1-59257-603-6
Library of Congress Catalog Card Number: 2006932993

09  08  07      8  7  6  5  4  3  2  1

Interpretation of the printing code: The rightmost number of the first series of numbers is the year of the book's printing; the rightmost number of the second series of numbers is the number of the book's printing. For example, a printing code of 07-1 shows that the first printing occurred in 2007.

*Printed in the United States of America*

**Note:** This publication contains the opinions and ideas of its author. It is intended to provide helpful and informative material on the subject matter covered. It is sold with the understanding that the author and publisher are not engaged in rendering professional services in the book. If the reader requires personal assistance or advice, a competent professional should be consulted.

The author and publisher specifically disclaim any responsibility for any liability, loss, or risk, personal or otherwise, which is incurred as a consequence, directly or indirectly, of the use and application of any of the contents of this book.

Most Alpha books are available at special quantity discounts for bulk purchases for sales promotions, premiums, fund-raising, or educational use. Special books, or book excerpts, can also be created to fit specific needs.

For details, write: Special Markets, Alpha Books, 375 Hudson Street, New York, NY 10014.

**Publisher:** *Marie Butler-Knight*
**Editorial Director/Acquiring Editor:** *Mike Sanders*
**Managing Editor:** *Billy Fields*
**Development Editor:** *Nancy D. Lewis*
**Senior Production Editor:** *Janette Lynn*

**Copy Editor:** *Krista Hansing Editorial Services, Inc.*
**Cover/Book Designers:** *Bill Thomas, Trina Wurst*
**Indexer:** *Heather McNeill*
**Layout:** *Chad Dressler*

*To my wife, Lori, and my three children, Jessica, Jett, and Nicole (the greatest salespeople in the world), who continually remind me that at any age, "dreams really can come true." You keep my eyes focused on my priorities and the daily miracles in life that really matter.*

*You are all the center of my universe and will forever be my greatest source of inspiration. I am forever grateful to have you in my life.*

# Contents at a Glance

**Part 1:**    The Inner Game of Closing      1

   1  Never Close Again!      3
*Identify the most common myths and
limiting beliefs around closing. Turn the
model upside down so that you can bring
in more sales while never having to close
again.*

   2  The Anatomy of a Closer      21
*Confidence, self-doubt, control, fear. Tap
into your authentic power to choose to create what you want most in your career
and in your life. It really is your choice.*

   3  Cerebral Selling—Why People Will Buy
from You      43
*While the stars don't need to be aligned
for a sale to occur, certain things do.
Here's what you need to do to develop the
right foundation that a sale can be built
upon.*

   4  Get in Their Head and Get out with a Sale      59
*Enjoy the next best thing to becoming a
mind reader. Manage the intangible components of your sales process in order to
recognize when prospects are ready to buy,
without them actually telling you.*

**Part 2:**    Showing Up as the Sales Champion Your Customers Expect      79

   5  The Enemy Within—Barriers We're
Blind To      81
*Unfortunately, you're creating the very
objections that you are hoping to avoid.
Imagine developing a competitive edge
simply by getting yourself out of your own
way and removing the self-imposed barriers to more sales.*

6  Advanced Listening Strategies                    103
   *Discover how to use proven listening
   strategies as an active rather than a passive tool to close more sales, while eliminating the listening habits that destroy
   relationships and compromise your ability
   to hear the sale.*

7  The Myths of Presenting to Your Prospects    115
   *Never pitch again. The objective of a
   presentation is no longer about delivering
   information. Traditional presentations
   create more objections rather than overcome them. Stop dumping information
   and start a dialogue instead.*

8  Make Your Sales Presentations
   Objection-Proof                              129
   *Master the five steps of a Permission
   Based Presentation that stimulates a conversation with every prospect and gets you
   to closing the sale faster than ever before
   (with permission).*

Part 3:    Permission Based Closing: Get the Prospect to "Yes!"    153

9  The Top Ten Types of Closers                 155
   *Analyze the type of closer you are, to
   eliminate damaging communication practices. Model the behavior of the champion
   closer by upgrading your communication
   style based on your natural strengths, values, and personality.*

10 Planned or Canned? The Hybrid Closing
   System                                       179
   *Now that you've uncovered the type of
   closer you are, it's time to craft what
   you are going to say when attempting to
   defuse an objection at the closing table.
   Stop stumbling or getting tongue-tied
   when you hear an objection, and share
   compelling stories a prospect wants to hear
   that motivate them to buy.*

11  Closing the Sale—with Permission  203
*Most closing techniques need to retire.
Rather than reacting to every objection
with a statement, harness the power of
responding with questions. Use the I.G.O.
three-step system to defuse any objection
and watch prospects overcome their own
objections without you having to do so.*

Part 4:  How Top Producers Maintain Their Edge  215

12  Handle the Money or Lose It  217
*Get the money out of your way. Avoid the
most common blunders when handling the
price objection. Uncover the real reasons
for price objections and learn why dropping your price will lose the sale.*

13  Stop the Cancellations and Improve
Client Retention  233
*Here's what you can do immediately
to drive more repeat sales and prevent
cancellations, and how to use a proven,
step-by-step strategy to save a sale that's
on the rocks.*

14  Master the Basics: The Advanced Course  253
*Do you remember what made you suc-
cessful in the first place? Costly detours
from the basics lead to learning the wrong
lessons. If every sale is already yours for
the taking, learn what you can do to turn
your biggest competitor into your greatest
ally to maintain top producer status.*

Glossary  271

Index  275

# Contents

**Part 1:  The Inner Game of Closing**                                    1

**1  Never Close Again!**                                                 3

"I'm a Great Closer!" ...................................................... 5
No Closers, Please ........................................................ 6
What Exactly Is Closing? ................................................. 7
What Closing Is Not........................................................ 8
Why Traditional Closing Is Dead ............................. 10
Closing the Sale or Closing a Person ...................... 11
Turning the Model Upside Down ........................... 12
Give Value .................................................................... 15
Unlearning What You Learned ............................... 16
Why You Don't Have to Close .............................. 18

**2  The Anatomy of a Closer**                                          21

Confidence: What It Really Is ................................. 22
Fueling Self-Doubt....................................................... 24
Make Confidence a Choice..................................... 26
Are You a Control Freak? ........................................ 28
Control Is All Based in Fear ................................... 30
You're Either Creating or Controlling...................... 30
Be Creative ................................................................... 32
Enthusiasm ................................................................... 35
Sincerity and Authenticity Sell ............................... 37

**3  Cerebral Selling—Why People Will Buy from You**                    43

When Do People Make Buying Decisions? ............... 44
Why People Will Not Buy ...................................... 47
Handle the Fear or It Will Handle You ..................... 47
Get Emotional or Logical? ...................................... 49
The Dual Role of a Salesperson ............................. 51
Empathy or Sympathy? ............................................. 52
How Am I Perceived? ................................................. 54

**4   Get in Their Head and Get out with a Sale      59**

Adapt Like a Chameleon to Your Surroundings........ 60
The Simplicity of Selling ............................................. 62
Mirroring and Reflecting ............................................ 62
Sell Them Where They Want to Be .......................... 66
Ouch, That Hurts! Selling the Pain .......................... 67
Wants and Needs—What Is the Difference? ............. 68
I Am Almost Ready to Buy ......................................... 74

**Part 2:   Showing Up as the Sales Champion Your
          Customers Expect                            79**

**5   The Enemy Within—Barriers We're Blind To      81**

Don't Sell Like You Buy .............................................. 82
Stop Talking, Start Listening Deeply ......................... 87
You're Still Not Listening ........................................... 89
Eight Barriers That Prevent You from Listening ...... 91
Listening Through Filters—Selective Listening ........ 92
When a Prospect Stops Listening to You  ................. 97
Just the Facts, Please ................................................. 100

**6   Advanced Listening Strategies                103**

You're Prejudging, Not Prequalifying...................... 104
Encouraging Silence Closes More Sales .................. 104
  *Focus More on the Message Than on the Messenger.. 107*
Listening "to" Someone or Listening "for"
  Something.................................................................. 108
  *Make People Feel They Are Truly Being Heard........ 110*
  *Reflective Listening.................................................. 111*
  *Paraphrasing.............................................................. 112*

**7   The Myths of Presenting to Your Prospects     115**

Dangerous Knowledge ............................................... 116
The Paradox of Presentations.................................... 118
Questions That Gracefully Correct and Create a
  New Selling Opportunity ......................................... 119
Telling Isn't Selling—Asking Questions Is................ 121
How to Create More Obstacles to the Sale ............. 124

Process-Driven Selling—the Question Is the
Answer ...................................................................... 126
The Objective of Delivering a Presentation ............ 126

**8  Make Your Sales Presentations Objection-Proof    129**

The Five Steps to Delivering a Permission Based
Presentation ............................................................. 130
*Step One: The Introduction* ....................................... *131*
Customers Don't Want a Relationship with You ..... 134
*Identify the Knowledge Gap* ...................................... *135*
*Step Two: The Discovery* ............................................ *136*
*Use Segue Questions When Presenting* ...................... *140*
*Step Three: Clarifying* ............................................... *143*
*Step Four: Discuss Solutions* ...................................... *148*
*Step Five: The Close* ................................................. *149*

**Part 3:  Permission Based Closing: Get the Prospect to "Yes!"  153**

**9  The Top Ten Types of Closers    155**

Hopeful Harry .............................................................. 156
Pontificating Peter ...................................................... 158
Friendly Freddie .......................................................... 159
Hank the Hammer ....................................................... 160
Not-to-Blame Zane ..................................................... 161
Methodological Mike .................................................. 164
Paul the Perfectionist ................................................. 165
Stu the Yesaholic ........................................................ 168
Adrenalized Angie ...................................................... 171
Accountable Alice ....................................................... 174
Why Salespeople Fail .................................................. 176

**10  Planned or Canned? The Hybrid Closing System    179**

The Hybrid Closing System ........................................ 180
The "Exclusivity" Close .............................................. 181
The "Going Out of Business" Close ........................... 183
The "Price Increase" Close ......................................... 185
The Risk Reward Close ............................................... 188
No Budget, No Worries .............................................. 190
The Fear of Change Close ........................................... 192

The Why Close...............................................................194
The Shopping List Close..............................................195
Sentence Completion....................................................197
Negative Reversal.........................................................197
Pride of Work Close.....................................................198
With Your Permission ….............................................199

**11 Closing the Sale—with Permission** **203**

The Secret to Overcoming Objections—Don't.......204
Defusing Objections Head-On....................................206
Three Steps to the Sale—I.G.O.! Right to the
    Close ......................................................................207
    *Step 1: Isolate the Objection* .....................................*207*
    *Step 2: Get Permission*...............................................*209*
    *Step 3: Offer a Solution* .............................................*211*
Stretch Out Before the Close .....................................212
Turn Objections into New Opportunities...............213

**Part 4: How Top Producers Maintain Their Edge** **215**

**12 Handle the Money or Lose It** **217**

To Control or Not to Control—Money Issues........218
Dropping the Price Isn't Always a Good Idea .........219
How to Literally Build Your Value ..........................220
Always Justify Your Price Drop.................................221
Recognize When Your Prospects Are Testing
    You .........................................................................223
Think Again Before You Split the Difference .........224
Stop Creating the Objections That Kill Your
    Sales!......................................................................228
When the Salesperson Creates the Objection .........229

**13 Stop the Cancellations and Improve Client Retention** **233**

A Buyer's Hangover....................................................234
Don't Take Their Eye off the Value..........................235
Recognize a Cry for Help ..........................................235
Why Do People Cancel? .............................................236
Take Responsibility for the Breakdown....................238
Reconfirmation: The Pitch-Back ..............................238

When It Makes Sense to Save a Sale........................ 240
Seven Steps to Reducing Cancellations.................... 242
*Step 1: Get Neutral*..................................................... 243
*Step 2: Precall Preparation* ....................................... 243
*Step 3: Conduct an Exit Interview—Making the
    Call*.......................................................................... 245
*Step 4: The Rediscovery*.............................................. 246
*Step 5: Save Your Customer! Open Up a New
    Possibility*................................................................ 248
*Step 6: Offer Another Solution*.................................. 248
*Step 7: Ask for Referrals* ............................................ 249

**14  Master the Basics: The Advanced Course          253**

What's Blocking Your Sales Mojo? ........................... 254
The Wrong Lesson Leads to the Wrong
    Solution.................................................................... 255
Get Back to the Basics................................................ 258
Your Only Real Competitor........................................ 262
In Closing ... Final Thoughts from Your Coach..... 265
Exclusive Resources for CIG Closers ...................... 268

**Glossary                                              271**

**Index                                                 275**

# Introduction

Your heart starts pounding as you feel the room getting warmer. Your mind starts racing, searching for the words that would consummate the sale. That's right, you're ready to ask for the order and wrap up this sale.

Isn't this a bit melodramatic? I mean, do you really need to experience such an intense physical and emotional reaction every time you ask for or attempt to close a sale? Whether you're a salesperson, business owner, consultant, or sole practitioner, why is selling—and, more specifically, closing—such a painful proposition to take on?

Because we've been taught the wrong lessons! That's right, you've been duped into believing that closing is something you do during your sales process.

*The Complete Idiot's Guide to Closing the Sale* takes the traditional closing model and turns it upside down. The new truth about closing is this: having to close a sale is the result of a breakdown that exists in your selling process. In other words, if you find yourself having to "close the sale," it has nothing to do with what you're going to do and everything to do with what you've already done (or not done)!

This groundbreaking book brings new meaning to the phrase "closing the sale"—a definition that's going to make you more comfortable, more secure, and more confident than you've ever been before when it comes to asking for the sale and turning every prospect into a customer.

As we unravel and dispel the myths and misconceptions about closing, you will also be introduced to a new and more powerful, yet natural, proven step-by-step approach to closing more sales with truly less effort that will pay back huge dividends.

*The Complete Idiot's Guide to Closing the Sale* will give you the edge over your competitors, enabling you to align your selling approach with the prospect's preferred buying process and communication style. Now you no longer have to push, manipulate, or rely on generic or gimmicky closing techniques that have lost their effectiveness in today's rapidly changing marketplace.

## Practical, Organized Tools to Boost Your Selling Performance Today

This book is divided into four distinct parts, all of which are introduced to you in chronological order. Each chapter builds upon the previous one, providing you with the opportunity to continually reinforce what you have learned. I walk you through the natural progression of what it takes to become a master at closing the sale. It's like having me as your own personal sales coach in your corner to support you though this entire process.

**Part 1, "The Inner Game of Closing,"** explores the hidden secrets to closing the sale by first turning the definition of closing upside down and inside out. You'll soon find out why your mind-set rather than your actions can become either your greatest adversary or your greatest ally. We're going to dispel the myths of closing and why being a "strong closer" is more of a handicap rather than a complement to your selling efforts. You will discover how to eliminate self-doubt and boost your confidence by making it a choice and something you really can control. Once you've upgraded your thinking, you're ready to get into the mind of the prospect. The psychology of selling enables you to not only connect with prospects, but actually read them: how they think, how they buy, and what you can do to identify their decision-making process, which will then enable you to align your style of selling with the prospect's style of buying.

In **Part 2, "Showing Up as the Sales Champion Your Customers Expect,"** you will be surprised to find how much of your current behavior creates the very obstacles to more sales. You will quickly see the danger in selling the way you buy and imposing your buying strategy on each prospect. Your prospects don't buy the way you do, and if you're still wondering why more prospects don't come out and say "I'm ready to buy from you," maybe it's because you're really not listening to them. You will learn to recognize the filter in how you listen so that you can eliminate communication breakdowns that destroy sales and damage relationships. Finally, it's essential that we discuss the deep impact your presentation plays on your closing efforts. Ironically, most presentations create more objections rather than defuse them. The Five Steps to delivering a Permission Based Presentation enables you to have a conversation with each prospect rather than pitch someone. Doing so eliminates the objections you would typically hear when you ask for a prospect's business. Now you can close with your ears rather than your mouth.

Now that you've laid the groundwork, in **Part 3, "Permission Based Closing: Get the Prospect to 'Yes!'"** it's time for you to uncover the type of closer you are. Although there exist 10 different types of closers, the key here is to develop your own method of selling so that it's aligned with your values, strengths, personality, and communication style, while still incorporating the baseline strategies, behaviors, and techniques that need to be honored by every sales professional. So when do you say what you say, and how do you say it? Do you pitch a canned response to defuse an objection, or do you ask an artful question to gather more clarity and insight? Get ready for a groundbreaking, eclectic approach to defusing objections, The Hybrid Closing System, a pre-defined, well-languaged response to turn a hostile objection into a new selling opportunity. And to ensure that you have an infallible model to smoke out and defuse any objection, you will be shown the three-step I.G.O. approach that puts every objection to rest. If you want your prospects to overcome their own objections so that you don't have to, then it's time to start crafting better questions.

Are you 100 percent certain as to why your prospects buy from you? Does money ever seem to get in the way of a sale? **Part 4, "How Top Producers Maintain Their Edge,"** introduces you to the real reason behind price objections. If you believe that price is the only reason why your customers buy from you, you're placing a limit on your performance. Failure to develop your unique and compelling value proposition sets you up to spend the rest of your selling days handling the imminent and elusive price objection. If that's not painful enough, it's critical to ensure that you have taken the precautionary steps to solidify every major sale in order to prevent your happy new customer from having second thoughts or, worse, canceling. You are going to learn a seven-step system to handle a cancellation, what you can do to save the sale, and whether it even makes sense to invest the time in saving the sale in the first place! Finally, don't blame the game for mediocre results. Chances are, you're learning the wrong lessons! Before you start using your newly revised strategy for turning more prospects into clients faster than ever before, or, as the title implies, closing more sales, there's one thing left for you to do: identify and embrace your one true competitor (guess who!) and your continued strategy for mastering the basics in order to maintain your "A Player" status.

Finally, as a gesture of my unconditional commitment to your success, I invite you to a very special resource center designed exclusively for you, my dear reader. Templates, tools, and additional resources available only to CIG closers!

## Tips from Your Sales Coach

To make the learning and implementation process easier for you, I've included some tips, techniques, insights, inspiration, definitions, and red flags to watch out for that will support and complement your selling and closing efforts. The following sidebars will guide you through this journey and help you navigate your path to developing your own personal selling and closing system and approach.

### Closing Bell

We all make mistakes. However, the smart ones learn from other people's mistakes in order to flatten their learning curve and prevent these mistakes from reappearing. Here you'll find warnings, pitfalls, and minefields to avoid that will act as a barrier to realizing your potential and achieving bigger goals so that you can dramatically reduce the mistakes that can cost you many selling opportunities.

### Closer's Corner

This sidebar is chock-full of suggestions, innovative ideas, and observations that are sure to inspire you and accelerate your success. These words of encouragement will squash disappointment and frustration at its core. At the very least, they are sure to make you think and say "Hmmmm."

### def·i·ni·tion

These are definitions of words and concepts to expand your knowledge base as it relates to closing the sale. These definitions add clarity to the process, providing you with a deeper understanding of what it takes to excel at selling.

### Closing Thoughts

In these sidebars, you will find quotes and tips that complement and expand upon the concepts you are learning while positioning you to become a selling superstar.

Before you jump into this book with both feet, keep the following three points in mind. In my effort to prevent any potential confusion, there are some words that I use interchangeably throughout this book.

1. *Product* **and** *service*—Whether you sell a tangible product or an intangible service, I've used these words synonymously throughout the book. So if you see me use the word *product* more than the word *service* when discussing your deliverable, please note that it's not because I'm biased toward selling tangible products. I am simply using it generically to refer to both products and services.

2. *Clients* **and** *customers*—The same rule applies here; I'm using these two words synonymously.

3. *Closing* **and** *opening*—My commitment is to hand-deliver a selling system to you that is so effective you will never have to "close" again. The objective of your selling system is to eliminate and defuse any objections before you ask for the sale. As such, I have introduced the phrase "opening or reconfirmation" to change your mind-set about the traditional definition of "closing." I still use "closing" throughout this book, since people are most familiar with this term when referring to this activity. Besides, referring to "closing" as "the reconfirmation step" or "the opening step" certainly makes it more palatable.

## Acknowledgments

Taking a dream and bringing it to fruition could not have been possible without certain people in my life. I feel incredibly fortunate to have the unconditional support and generosity of my family, my wife, my mom and dad, and my sister, Jocelyn, who will forever be deeply appreciated. I only wish to be able to do the same for my children that my parents have done for me.

A sincere thank you to my clients who have provided me with a unique and valuable opportunity to continually learn and evolve. I am always in awe of what they achieve. I appreciate each client and the opportunity I've had to work with every one.

A heartfelt thank you to the entire team at Alpha Books who were so incredibly supportive, helpful, and understanding, and an absolute joy to work with.

I'd like to send a special thank you to you, my dear reader. Your voice has been heard. This book is my response to your request to find a practical, no-nonsense solution to closing the sale—one that you're comfortable with, one that's aligned with your style of selling and communicating, and one that doesn't require memorizing some fancy close in someone else's words that don't even work in today's marketplace! Stay authentic and keep it real! After implementing the strategies outlined in this book, please feel free to share your successes with me. I'd love to hear about all of them.

## Trademarks

All terms mentioned in this book that are known to be or are suspected of being trademarks or service marks have been appropriately capitalized. Alpha Books and Penguin Group (USA) Inc. cannot attest to the accuracy of this information. Use of a term in this book should not be regarded as affecting the validity of any trademark or service mark.

# Part 1

# The Inner Game of Closing

How confident are you in a selling situation? Do you know why your customers buy from you? Does self-doubt erode your selling efforts? What some salespeople perceive as a gift or a natural ability to convert a resounding "No" into a "Yes" or a reluctant, resistant prospect into a happy customer is less about what they do or the actions they take to close the sale; it has everything to do with who they are and how they come across to the prospect. This part of the book begins your development of the essential characteristics of the permission-based closer. In other words, it's time to make sure you get your head in the game with the winning attitude you need. Once you get out of your own head (and your own way), you're prepared to get in the head of the prospect so that you can uncover how your prospects make a purchasing decision. Mastering the inner game of closing will enable you to identify and remove the greatest psychological barriers to the sale so that you can then sell prospects where they want to be.

# Never Close Again!

## In This Chapter

- ◆ Dispel the myths and misconceptions of closing
- ◆ Expose the weak link in your sales process
- ◆ Understand the limitations of a canned pitch
- ◆ Discover the new definition of closing
- ◆ Learn why you will never have to close again
- ◆ How to deliver real value

Todd began his meeting with Mr. Smith 2 hours ago. The conversation was flowing effortlessly. Todd delivered a stellar presentation and did a wonderful job aligning his product's benefits with the prospect's needs. Todd even confirmed with Mr. Smith that his product was a perfect fit for him.

As Todd moved toward the end of his presentation, he noticed something happening. His heart started pounding faster. He felt the room getting warmer. Todd's mind started racing as he searched for the words that needed to leave his lips to consummate the sale. That's right, Todd was ready to ask for the order and wrap up this sale.

Although Todd realized that it may be time to bring the sale to its conclusion, something had gripped him. Todd froze as he started questioning his actions and next steps in his head. "Should I ask for the sale now? Will the customer feel like I'm pressuring him? I don't want to be perceived as one of those high-pressure sales types. And I certainly don't want to scare him off or blow the opportunity for a future sale. Maybe I'll wait a little longer. Maybe I'll wait for the customer to tell me when he's ready. Maybe I'll tell him to call me when he's prepared to make a decision. Maybe I'll check to see if there's any additional information he needs from me. Maybe I should call my wife and ask her if she wants me to pick up dinner."

Maybe Todd isn't exactly sure what *closing* is, let alone how to do it. Maybe Todd is doing a better job teeing up this prospect for his competition to take away from him.

**def•i•ni•tion**

> **Closing** is an organic process rather than a planned one. Since the close can happen at any point during a conversation with a prospect, it needs to be a fluid and natural component that evolves from a well-designed and well-executed sales process.

"Maybe" doesn't bring in new sales. "Maybe" is a lot like using "hope" to close more new business. ("I hope one of the prospects I met with this week turns into a sale.") Neither of these is an effective selling strategy.

In this first chapter, I coach you on developing a new meaning for the phrase "closing the sale"—a definition that's going to make you more comfortable, more secure, and more confident than you've ever been when it comes to asking for the sale and turning that prospect into a customer.

As we unravel and dispel the myths and misconceptions of closing, you will also be introduced to a new and more powerful, yet natural approach to consummating the sale that *will pay back huge dividends*.

# "I'm a Great Closer!"

I remember years ago when I owned another business. We were in recruiting mode again and on the search for talented salespeople. The ad started running in Thursday's newspaper and ran throughout the weekend. "Full-time sales position. Salary plus commission. Please send resumé to …" was how the ad read.

By Tuesday morning, I had completed reviewing all of the resumés. After combing through about 40 resumés (sorry, the handwritten resumés were immediately disqualified), there were 10 applicants I wanted to meet.

My sales manager began scheduling the interviews with these 10 candidates. After several hours on the telephone, he was able to schedule an interview with 8 of the 10 people who had sent me a resumé. It looked like Friday was the day for me to conduct all of my interviews.

Friday morning, 9 A.M. The first candidate arrived a few minutes early. She thought it was an inside sales position. No fit.

10 A.M. The second candidate arrived more than 30 minutes late and without a valid excuse. I cancelled the interview. C'mon, if you can't even be here on time for the interview, the proverbial writing is already on the wall. It only gets worse from this point!

11 A.M. As I was waiting for my next interview, the phone rang. It was my 11 A.M. appointment. "Hi, I am so sorry, but I totally forgot about my meeting with you. Can we reschedule?" I don't think so. Instead, I tried to help. "Here's the name of my competition. I think they are hiring. Try giving them a call."

It was now 12:00 in the afternoon. My next candidate was waiting in the lobby. Before we sat down to discuss the position, she told me how difficult it was for her to get to my office by bus. "Don't you have your own transportation?" I asked, wondering how she had missed the minimum requirements needed for this position, clearly stated in the ad. "No, we don't provide you with transportation. You'll need to have your own car and your own license. No, you can't take a bus to and from your appointments." No fit here, either.

1 P.M. My assistant put a call through about the position. "Hi, I'm calling about the job? Do you guys do any background checks or drug testing?"

"As a matter of fact, we do," I replied.

"Click." They hung up.

I glanced at my clock. 3 P.M. Still no qualified candidates. It was beginning to look bleak.

I stayed positive. I still had a handful of candidates to meet with. It was now almost 4:00 in the afternoon. I pulled out the resumé of the next candidate, in preparation for our interview. "Frank Stone. Hmm. Solid experience. This one looks really good," I thought. I walked into the lobby and introduced myself to the fifth candidate of the day. Well presented, looks the role. A definite maybe.

Our conversation couldn't have gone better. Frank was an extrovert all the way. He was funny and good natured, and spoke well—the type of person you want to have representing your company. So far, Frank seemed to possess all of the characteristics of a top salesperson. It was time for us to discuss his sales experience and training.

And that's when he said it. The four words that made my stomach knot up. The four words that the promising salespeople of yesterday used to tell me. The four words that every sales manager thinks he wants to hear. The same four words that have become a gauge to help me assess the potential of every candidate.

"I'm a great closer."

Another 10 minutes passed. We exchanged more pleasantries, and I concluded the conversation. I shook Frank's hand and thanked him for coming out to meet with us. After Frank left, I reluctantly crossed his name off my list of potential candidates and continued my search for the next sales champion that I could bring aboard to join our team.

# No Closers, Please

Now, dear reader, I hear you thinking, "C'mon, Keith. It's too early in the book for you to try that Jedi Mind Trick on me. Why title your book *Closing the Sale* if you're telling me this is not what I'll be learning how to do? Don't you want to be a closer? I mean, isn't that the point? Aren't companies looking for strong closers when they hire salespeople?"

Let me clarify, to reduce some confusion. By using the strategies outlined in this book, you will learn how to turn more prospects into clients than you ever have. That, I promise you. You will learn how to convert more prospects into clients better than any self-proclaimed "great closer" without any pressure, manipulation, confrontation or old-school closing techniques. You are going to discover exactly what you need to do to bring in more sales. However, you're not going to have to "close" the prospect in order to do so.

# What Exactly Is Closing?

"I'm a good closer."

I've heard this or some variation of this claim countless times from salespeople. "I'm a strong closer." "Just call me the hammer." "One call does it all." "I can close anyone." "I will close hard when I need to." "I start closing as soon as I begin talking with a prospect." "My salespeople call me in when they need to close the deal."

These statements suggest that closing is a good thing—something you do, a pitch you deliver or a skill you have that enables you to maintain top producer status. At the same time, these phrases suggest that the act of closing involves the use of force or control in order to push the sale through. It's no wonder why the majority of salespeople feel they could never become the great closer they need to be. Their clientele would never tolerate such a caustic approach from a salesperson.

### Closing Bell

Don't let old perceptions of what it takes to be a great salesperson mislead you. For example, not being a good closer can be viewed by some people as a sign of weakness, saying things like, "You can't even close a door!" Don't fall victim to this philosophy. Instead, consider this: it is a sign of strength if you are able to achieve your sales goals without having to become a great closer.

Besides, if I were to hire a "great closer" (which, by the way, I've made the mistake of doing in the past), what does that even mean? What exactly am I getting? Based on this antiquated definition of closing, it is an action, the final step in your sales process. If that is the case, then what about the steps that precede the closing step? If a salesperson claims to be a great closer, which is the last step in their sales process, then how good can they be at performing all of the other steps in their sales process? Can I surmise that this candidate may be in need of some serious help in the areas of presenting, listening, asking questions, prospecting, and communicating?

Let me tee this up in a different way. Let's say you visited my website at www.profitbuilders.com and decided that you wanted to work for my company, marketing and selling my training and coaching services. So you called me in response to the career opportunity we had posted. Of course, one of the first questions I may ask you would be, "So what makes you a top producer?" Now you could respond by telling me that being a great closer is what makes you the right candidate for this position. In this case, the conversation would be pretty much over. On the other hand, you could respond to this question in a different way. "Well, Keith, for me it's being a master at asking the right questions at the right time and then listening for the appropriate response that will help me determine whether there's a strong fit. Only then will I guide the prospect toward making a purchasing decision. This is what makes me a sales champion." I'll tell you straight: this type of response would be exceedingly impressive.

There is also the more generic use of the words *closing* or *close* that muddies the definition of "closing" even more. Similar to how we use the word *aspirin* to generically describe a tablet that relieves pain, people use the word *close* as a way to let someone know that they've made a sale. For example, the sentences "I closed two deals today" and "I should close that sale tomorrow" and "That last customer took a while to make a decision, but that sale finally closed" do not suggest the same negative connotation as the other phrases I mentioned earlier; instead, they use *close* as a synonym to the word *sold*. The use of force or pressure is less apparent when using the word *close* in this context.

# What Closing Is Not

I remember sitting through a training program for one of the sales positions I had during college. My manager's required reading was Zig Ziglar's book *Secrets of Closing the Sale*. I remember reading the captivating stories that Zig told about him and his Redhead (a.k.a. his wife).

I can still picture myself taking the time to memorize some of those closes that Zig had in his book.

Now, Zig is an icon in sales training, there's no question. I have nothing but respect for the man. And there are times that a canned response to an objection or a prospect's concern can certainly come in handy. However, many people, like my old sales manager, took this to a very literal level. "Closing" is not defined as memorizing someone else's predefined cookie-cutter script that you regurgitate all over the prospect at the slightest hint of an objection. You have to speak your language and develop a response to an objection that feels authentic and real for you so that it fits your style of selling and communicating.

Just look at what happened to Harold. Harold sells networking and technology solutions to small businesses. He knows technology. He's on top of his game and is an expert in his field. As Harold finished presenting the solutions to Jane, one of his newer prospects, he knew that the next step was to ask her for her business. After Harold delivered all of the information that Jane needed to make an informed decision, he asked her if she had any additional questions.

Beads of sweat began to form on Harold's forehead. Finally, Harold mustered up enough courage to ask Jane for her business. He asked, "So Jane, should we discuss an installation date?"

The prospect looked at Harold and responded with, "Well, this all sounds good, but let me think about it, okay?"

Harold paused for a moment. "Absolutely, Jane," is what he reacted with. Harold thought about all of the things he could have said to this prospect. All of the closes he read about in the books. For example, he could have used the "Make Your Decision When the Facts Are Present" close or the "Win or Lose" close or the "Incentive Today" close. Instead, Harold froze. The only thing that closed was his mouth.

Finally, Harold got out of his head. He looked at the prospect and said, "So should I call you back next week or just wait until I hear from you?"

What's that, you say? Oh, I know what you may be thinking. "What a spineless jellyfish. That was pretty lame. I would never be that spineless when it comes to asking for the sale. I'd at least find out why Jane wanted to think about it." Or maybe you would be more empathetic.

**Closing Bell**

If you are relying solely on your powerful ninja closing abilities or a canned closing statement to do the selling for you, then you've already lost the sale.

"That poor guy, Harold. I totally understand where he's coming from. I've been in that same uncomfortable position countless times. He tried to do the right thing. Besides, what else could he have done? He might still have a chance for a sale, right?"

# Why Traditional Closing Is Dead

Whether you've been selling for a while or are just starting out, you may have experienced a situation similar to that Harold went through. Maybe you felt that you lost a sale because you drew a blank and couldn't find the words to move the sales process to its conclusion. Maybe it was because you felt like you couldn't say what you wanted to say or use one of the closes you memorized, in fear of insulting a prospect. And you certainly didn't want to come across as a slick salesperson or, worse, a "canned" salesperson. Maybe it was because who you are wasn't being fully expressed in your selling strategy. That is, you were not allowing your natural strengths, personality, values, and talents to surface so that you could reorient your selling approach around them.

Or just maybe you started empathizing with your prospect, feeling, "I wouldn't want someone doing this to me."

Regardless of the reason or the story, the one common denominator is this: if you're focusing on the close, then you are stuck in your own head. And if you're stuck in your own head, then you are making the sales process about you and not your prospect. As a result, you can't be focusing on the prospect and how you can best fill his or her needs.

If it's not a bug in your mental operating system that's causing the breakdown, then look at the external forces at work that affect the way you and your company sell and market your product or service.

Consumers today are savvier than ever and are aware of certain sales tactics that would have them running in the other direction and toward your competitors. The Internet dispatches immediate information at the click of a button, enabling consumers to gather the information and data they need to make an educated purchasing decision.

As such, the salesperson's role has evolved. Instead of taking the time to educate the prospect about their products and services, salespeople are finding that their prospects are already aware of the options available to them. In response to this, the top salespeople are using their time with prospects to first uncover what the prospect already knows about their products. Then the salesperson can help sift through the mounds of data the prospect has already collected about their industry, their company, and their products to make the best decision.

 **Closing Thoughts**

Instead of making the selling process about you and how much you might be able to gain from the sale (money, recognition, and so on), make it about the prospect: how much value you can deliver and what's in it for him or her. Shift the focus away from you and onto that person.

Consequently, the salesperson's role has evolved to become more of a consultant, guiding and assisting the prospect throughout the decision-making process instead of limiting the role to an information provider who simply brings the prospect up to speed on the available options.

This subtle shift in the role and expectations of a sales professional is changing the way salespeople are being trained, coached, and developed. To stand apart from their competition, salespeople are moving away from the old model of becoming a strong closer and instead are evolving into more of a trusted advisor and an expert in their field.

## Closer's Corner

The days of relying on the close to do all of the selling for you are over. Shall we forget the old Smith & Wesson Close? A sales trainer reminded me about this comical close he used to tell his sales team. (Note: I'm hoping I don't have to say this, but don't actually try this yourself!) As the salesperson holds a gun close to the prospect's head, he says, "Mr. Prospect, there's going to be one of two things on this contract: your brains or your signature. You decide." Talk about an extreme example of a high-pressure close.

# Closing the Sale or Closing a Person

Salespeople have a tendency to look at their prospects and customers through the wrong set of lenses. Look at the traditional definition of "closing." Closing is an action. It's the final step in your selling process, where you ask for the prospect's business and, if necessary, convince a prospect to purchase from you. In essence, it means being persistent enough to turn a "No" into a "Yes."

Let's look at this through a different set of lenses. Closing is not an event. Closing is not an action you take or a step in your process that happens in some type of sequential order. Most important, closing is not something you do to someone.

Do you notice something here? Salespeople are taking their eye off the goal and objective of what professional selling truly is. What happened to providing beneficial solutions or solving the challenges and problems through the service or product you sell? When did it become more about closing the customer and walking away with another order than delivering measurable, rewarding results? In this model, salespeople are making the sales process more about them and what they can get (another sale) than the value they can give. They have distilled the sales process down to a numbers game, making the prospect more of a statistic than a person.

**Closing Thoughts**

Closing the sale describes something you may have done, but closing is not something you do to a prospect. Rather, it is something you collaboratively achieve naturally.

Now that we've torn apart the old definition and mind-set of closing, let's build a new, improved one that inspires you to want to go out and sell.

# Turning the Model Upside Down

If closing is not an action or a step, or a fancy canned pitch that we memorize, or a thunderous event of unprecedented proportion, then what is it? Here's a new, healthier definition of closing that will upgrade how you think about it and subsequently redefine the approach to use when converting a prospect to a client.

Closing is the natural evolution of your selling process when your prospect becomes your customer. Closing is the art of creating new possibilities and solutions that may not have been presented before.

That's it. Short and very sweet. Notice I didn't say the natural conclusion of your selling process. The reason why closing is more of a natural evolution than a conclusion is because while you may have converted a prospect into a client, the sale is still far from over. We discuss the post-sale process in Chapter 13.

Evolution is, by definition, natural and ongoing—the word *conclusion* implies "termination, finish, end" and, of course, "close."

Closing is not about trying to control the sales process or forcing a prospect into saying "Yes" (which you can't effectively do, in case you didn't realize that—more on this later). Closing is more about recognizing the right opportunity and waiting for the right time when the prospect is ready to become a client.

Closing is less about "ending, shutting, or terminating" and more about "creating, collaborating, inquiring, and coaching." It took me a while to realize this. Although I was always a successful salesperson, I was never a great closer. Instead, I was great at opening up and creating new selling opportunities that may never have existed. The bottom line was, I was a great opener, not a closer. Chapter 11 breaks down, step by step, this new model of closing—I mean, opening—for you so that you will never have to close a sale in the traditional sense again. Instead, it will happen naturally.

Finally, the sale or the close can be initiated by either the salesperson or the prospect!

A little personal history about your author. I was one of the first sales and business coaches to hang my shingle, a true pioneer in the coaching profession, if you will, and one of the first Master Certified Coaches to get credentialized. (Okay, enough shameless plugs—for now.)

**Closing Thoughts**

The greatest salespeople realize that in order to achieve incredible success at selling, you need to become a strong opener rather than a strong closer.

As you can imagine, I was certainly ahead of the curve. Being an innovator and a leader in this now rapidly growing profession of life and business coaching, I had to create my own road to achieve success because there was no other proven path to follow. Being a leader in such a young industry certainly had its advantages. However, it also came with some tall challenges that needed to be eliminated.

At this point, I had sold my business (of course, with the unwavering support of my wife, as nervous as she may have been.) So here I was, with no income stream coming in as I launched full steam into an unproven and unknown profession with only my experience in managing and owning several other businesses to help guide me.

One thing was for certain. I had a very strong sales and marketing background. After all, when I had owned my other businesses, I had been the one responsible for the recruiting, hiring, training, managing, and coaching of all our employees.

In an attempt to apply my wisdom, I came up with some best practices and developed what was to be my first of several attempts to put my new selling strategy together.

I started doing what I knew how to do: pick up the phone and start making cold calls. And to my surprise, I was very successful at getting through the door and into an appointment with the decision maker. Without minimizing my efforts and results, I encountered that, when meeting with these prospects, most of the time, they wanted to meet with me out of sheer curiosity. After all, at this point, no one had ever heard of coaching outside athletic or sport coaching. So I had the advantage of positioning business and life coaching as something new and unique.

A month later, I wasn't even making enough money to stay broke. Pitch after pitch, presentation after presentation, I kept hearing the same thing. "It sounds really interesting, Keith, but I just can't see how we can apply this to what we're doing right now. Let's stay in touch, and maybe sometime in the future we can look at this again. But hey, it sounds real cool what you're doing now. Good luck!"

**Closing Thoughts**

Regardless of when the close happens or who initiates it, this is the time when your prospect becomes your customer.

# Give Value

With all of the prospects that I had generated over the last month and the results I had experienced from my lackluster selling efforts, it was time to re-evaluate. So I did what any new, intelligent, humble, and highly evolved coach would do. I called my coach for help.

And after I shared with her what I had gone through, do you know what she told me with all of her years of wisdom? "Keith, you have to stop presenting and just give value."

"What the heck does that mean?" I thought. I had no clue what she was talking about. Give value? Well, I took her coaching and put forth my best effort in deciphering what I thought she meant. I started thinking about how I could, as my omnipotent coach said, "give value."

A funny thing happened. I stopped talking and started listening more. I stopped pitching and presenting, and started asking better questions. Since my coach didn't share with me a strategy to give value, by default, I had to figure out and uncover what "value" meant to each prospect I spoke with. And the only way to uncover each prospect's perception and definition of value was to ask more questions.

Talk about one of those "Aha!" moments! My coach knew exactly what she was doing. Rather than telling me to deliver the same presentation or a revised presentation to every prospect, she opened up a new possibility for me to find out what value looked like from the eyes of every prospect instead of from my own. What evolved was a process of inquiry and a defined set of questions I used when meeting with each prospect. (Don't worry if you don't have this developed yet. We tackle the art of presenting in Chapter 7.)

You see, the gem I discovered very quickly when it came to selling my training and coaching services was totally counterintuitive. That is, you can't sell coaching. Or at least not in the traditional sense of selling. Talk about your paradoxes.

Let me say this another way. Because coaching is about the investment in yourself and your own personal or professional development, the client has to be ready and willing to be coached.

Either you are ready to generate substantial unprecedented results in both your life and your career, and are willing to be accountable and honest and to do what is necessary (in your integrity, of course) to achieve your goals, or you are not.

Luckily, none of my early closing techniques worked on any of the prospects I saw thus far. Because if they did, then you can bet I would be working not only with fewer clients, but also with clients that I would probably be much better off without. (If I didn't ask questions, then how would I know if there's a good fit?) Discovering this inspired me to develop an entirely different model that went against traditional selling.

I stopped trying to close and I started opening. The point I want to drive home is this: I've never had to close another sale again.

# Unlearning What You Learned

Now that we have established a new way of looking at closing, here's a story I'm certain you'll find entertaining because it relates to learning the wrong lessons. I had just completed a keynote presentation in Manhattan on the topics of prospecting and the art of delivering powerful presentations. Being someone who embraces learning as a lifestyle, I'm always interested in receiving feedback from my audience. And as I typically do at the end of every seminar I deliver, I graciously requested that each person take a moment to complete the evaluation form on the last page of the handbook I had created for them. As they were completing their evaluations, I began packing up my bag to head home. A group of people approached me after my seminar with some questions.

By the time I had finished coaching them around their biggest sales challenges, the majority of the audience had made their way out of the auditorium. I began walking through the auditorium, collecting the remaining evaluation forms that people had left on their chairs. A young woman approached me and asked if I had a moment to talk. "Of course," I responded genuinely.

Her name was Lucy. She was a recent college graduate and had just changed jobs, taking a sales position with a jewelry design company in Manhattan.

"First, I have to thank you so much for your seminar. It was absolutely fantastic and exactly what I needed to hear."

"Well, thank you so much for your kind words, Lucy. It sounds as if we both got what we needed to hear today," I responded, smiling.

"No, Keith, you don't understand," Lucy said. "Do you want to know how I was trained in my first sales job right out of college? You wouldn't believe it."

Lucy continued, "It was my first job as a salesperson. I had never sold anything before. I got a job working for a well-known and well-respected jewelry designer in California. During the interviewing process, the owner of the company told me they would provide sales training, which was something I clearly expressed that I definitely needed.

"Well, it was the first day on the job. As part of my training, I was scheduled to meet with my sales manager and spend the day with him. What an experience. We spent about half the day together, going from one appointment to the next. This provided me with the opportunity to learn more about the company and silently observe his style of selling to see how a sales call should be conducted.

"When we got back to the office, I thought we would take some time to review what had occurred throughout the day—you know, go over each sales call and discuss what had happened so that I could learn from them. Afterward, I figured we would do more one-to-one training. Well, that wasn't exactly what happened.

"Instead, he took a DVD out of his desk drawer. It was the movie *Glengarry Glen Ross*." (I must say, it's a fabulous movie with an all-star cast, including Alec "Second prize, steak knives!" Baldwin, Jack Lemmon, Al Pacino, Ed Harris, Alan Arkin, and Kevin Spacey.) "'Here, take this movie. Watch and study this movie and the salespeople in it a few times when you go home tonight,' he ordered. 'This movie will teach you everything you will ever need to know about selling and how to close.'" Oy.

Folks, it's situations like these that keep my company very, very busy. Although this sales manager's "training program" may be more of an exception than the norm, the unfortunate truth is, the norm isn't that far removed from how this sales manager trains his salespeople.

> ### Closer's Corner
>
> If you want to see some examples of what not to do when selling and closing, several classic and entertaining movies tell different stories about salespeople and their struggles to close the big deal. Aside from *Glengarry Glen Ross*, some movies include *Tin Men*, *Boiler Room*, *Cadillac Man*, *Death of a Salesman*, and *The Big Kahuna*. We can make this a box-set titled "Training for the Ethically Challenged Salesperson."

# Why You Don't Have to Close

If you eat healthfully and take care of yourself, then you will never need to go on a diet. A sound and practical philosophy, regardless of how challenging it may be at times to consistently do so.

This same philosophy holds true when it comes to selling. If you honor a well-balanced sales process, which includes everything from first contact to how you qualify a prospect, as well as how effectively you deliver your presentation, then you will not have to close.

Look what was being taught in the old school of selling. The old school taught salespeople to close, close, close. Salespeople were told to spend most of their time closing the deal. Trainers taught salespeople fancy closes to handle and overcome objections. Over the years, a new school of thought has evolved: the school of possibility. Imagine what would be possible if all the objections you typically hear at the "closing table" were prevented and defused throughout the course of your presentation.

There exists a choice a salesperson has to make. The first choice is spending minimal time on your presentation and spending the rest of your time attempting to close the prospect. The second choice is investing most of your time up front on a masterful presentation infused with well-crafted questions that defuse the most common objections you hear. This results in the prospect essentially closing himself, with minimal effort. Which school do you choose to be a student of?

Do you run into the same objection over and over again? If you see a pattern, wouldn't it make sense to plan for or master a way to defuse these objections by preventing them from surfacing before they actually arise? Wouldn't it make your job easier to put these objections or concerns to rest throughout your presentation? The end of your presentation should simply be the natural evolution of the selling process: earning the business of a new prospect.

If you can overcome an objection during the course of your presentation when it is still in its fetal stage, as opposed to waiting until the end of your presentation when it becomes a full-grown obstacle, you will find yourself spending less time closing and more time posting new sales. Consider this: if you were building a brick wall, what would be easier—removing a broken brick that has just been laid or waiting until the wall is fully constructed? If you wait until the end, you have to tear down the entire wall just to get to the broken brick, and then spend the rest of your time reconstructing it. The same holds true with your selling process. Remove the defective bricks or objections first in order to avoid having to do so later, when it just might be too late to do anything about it.

## The Least You Need to Know

- Closing is not something you do to a person; it is something that happens naturally with a person.

- The greatest salespeople are not great closers. Instead, they are skilled openers of new selling opportunities.

- Become more of a consultant and advisor to your clients than simply being a salesperson.

- Deliver value to your prospects rather than delivering a presentation.

- The more time you invest asking well-crafted questions, the less time you will spend overcoming objections.

- A well-organized templated response can come in handy, but learn to speak your own language of selling rather than someone else's.

- The more you align your selling approach with your values and style of communicating, the more authentic you will come across.

# Chapter 2

# The Anatomy of a Closer

## In This Chapter

- ◆ Develop the core characteristics of a sales champion
- ◆ Get off the emotional roller coaster when selling
- ◆ Build your confidence, permanently
- ◆ Eliminate self-doubt
- ◆ Become more creative than controlling
- ◆ Sell authentically from your heart, not from your head

At this point, we've introduced a new model and philosophy to closing the sale. Although I wish I could say that simply changing what you do regarding your approach to selling and closing will yield the results you are looking for, I can't.

Here's the reason: it takes more than upgrading what you do to achieve incredible success in your career. You also need to change how you think, as well as the way you come across. Just think about the salespeople you like to do business with. I'm sure it's more than just their sales acumen that made you comfortable enough to want to purchase from them. After all, when you think of a salesperson you like to do business with, how do you describe that person? Chances are, it would sound like, "She is great! She is very attentive and caring. She really takes the time to find the right solution for you. She is a very nice person." How often would you describe a salesperson by saying, "Wow, she is very well trained." Don't think so.

This chapter focuses on the anatomy of a closer and the attributes needed to ensure your long-term success.

# Confidence: What It Really Is

"So I guess you could sense a change in the tone of my prep form that I sent you for our sales coaching call today?"

It was Denise calling in for her 7 A.M. coaching call. Prior to each coaching call, clients e-mail me their objectives for the call and their week in review. This way, they stay focused and accountable to their commitments, and have the opportunity to celebrate their wins each week.

She was right. "If you are referring to the sentence where you wrote, 'I feel like getting out of sales completely and getting a mindless job somewhere else, maybe the government,' or the sentence 'Maybe I'm not cut out for this,' then, yes, I do sense something else may be off here."

Denise and I had been working together for about seven months now. She had made incredible breakthroughs in both her performance and her attitude. As a result, she had been offered a promotion from Regional Sales Manager to National Account Manager. With this promotion came a territory change, as well as a new type of prospect. Where her average sale used to be about $10,000–$20,000, now her average sale was approximately $250,000.

"What triggered this sudden change in attitude?" I inquired.

"Well, you know how we've been talking about the prospects that I've been filling in my pipeline? At this point in time, many of those prospects should be converting into sales. So I started making my follow-up calls as scheduled. Nothing but 'Call me next week' or 'Now's not a good time' or 'If you would like to leave a message ....'

"I guess you could say that I'm getting a bit antsy. I want some of these deals to close already so that I can post some positive sales numbers toward my quota. As you can probably hear, I'm a little nervous. What if these deals don't close?"

"You tell me, Denise. What if these deals don't close?"

"I can tell you this, Keith. It won't be a good thing! Maybe I never should have taken this national account position. I knew it was going to be a big change from regional sales, but I didn't anticipate such a change in the length of my sales cycle."

"Maybe? Am I sensing some doubt in you?" I asked curiously.

"Oh, absolutely," Denise exclaimed.

"And what, may I ask, are you doubting?" I responded.

"Myself," Denise said quietly in a deflated voice. I could hear her *confidence* waning. It was as if someone had reached inside her soul and ripped all of the self-worth out of her.

She continued, "And I know it's just a matter of time until Lewis—you know, my boss—calls me with some bad news, like, 'Denise, we really expected a lot more out of you. We thought you'd be much further along than you are. Denise, you're fired!'"

**def•i•ni•tion**

**Confidence** is an unwavering belief in yourself and in your abilities without needing the evidence to support it.

I always find it amazing how creative our minds can be when it comes to visualizing our consequences and fears.

I shifted gears. "Denise, I'm curious about something. Didn't you recently start this position?"

"Yes, about 4 months ago."

"And isn't it true that you've already closed and up-sold some big accounts?"

"Well, yeah, but that was, like, a month ago, and I haven't sold anything since. Besides it …."

Before the next excuse came out, I interrupted with, "And isn't it also true that you've gotten at least two deliberate and intentional accolades from both your new boss and his boss about how thrilled they are with what you have achieved so far?"

Silence.

"I'm sorry, Denise, but can you speak up a bit? I wasn't able to hear you," I said sarcastically, yet in a way that still made Denise feel empowered and supported.

"Denise, what are you hearing in what I've just shared with you?" I asked.

"That maybe I'm being a bit too hard on myself," she reluctantly admitted.

"Does that feel true for you?" I reconfirmed.

"Yes, Keith, this is right on the money."

"Well, are you ready to hear a little more that may also be right on the money but just a bigger pile of money?"

"Hit me!" She exclaimed. "I'm ready for it."

# Fueling Self-Doubt

I continued. "You had mentioned that your confidence, your self-worth, your self-esteem—however you want to refer to it—has been deflated as a result of what you perceive as low productivity. Because you haven't brought in any new sales recently, you doubt yourself and your abilities. Is that accurate so far?"

"Yup."

"So can I then conclude that you measure your self-worth by what you produce? That is, if you are closing new business practically each week, then your confidence would skyrocket to an all-time high?"

"That is for sure!" Denise exclaimed.

"Conversely, where you feel like you are now, where you haven't sold, it's affecting your confidence and the faith you have in yourself."

"No question there."

"Denise, what does the word *confidence* mean to you?"

I could hear her thinking. "I don't know. I guess confidence means being in control. It's when I have control over something. It's a feeling of control and a belief in what I can do," she replied.

"So in essence, you are worth only as much as you've sold recently? Wow! That must be an interesting roller-coaster ride of emotion you're on."

"You can say that again, Keith!"

I continued. "So basically, if you sell, you're feeling great. You're in a positive state of mind. You are in a good mood and feeling a strong sense of worth about yourself. Conversely, if you don't sell or don't get the appointment or don't get in touch with a certain prospect that you've been attempting to connect with, you're feeling pretty lousy about the day and about yourself. Denise, is this strategy of yours working for you?"

"Well," Denise began, "I don't know if I would necessarily say this is working for me. After all, it's certainly causing way too much stress, anxiety, and overwhelm. And it also keeps me from enjoying my family and maintaining my peace of mind."

"So would you be open to hearing what I'm seeing and a new way of thinking that would remove your self-doubt as well as the stress that follows, permanently, so that you can start enjoying your life more?" I inquired, getting permission to continue our conversation and share some truths with her that I see.

"C'mon, Keith. We've been down this road before. Just lay it on me. I'm open to another way of thinking if it's going to keep me sane, happy, and employed."

"Of course. Consider this: do not allow external situations to dictate your internal condition."

"Wow, that's heavy. Is this another Keithism?"

I smiled, "Let me explain. You mentioned earlier that confidence is a belief in yourself. Where do we adopt these beliefs we have about ourselves? From our experiences and from other people. At some point during our life we learned the wrong lesson based on an experience we had. And the lesson was, if you want to be successful, you need to acquire things. You need to prove yourself and your self-worth. And those things you can acquire can be anything: money, cars, homes, toys, clothes, and, in this case, sales. If we acquire these things, if we create these things or work hard to achieve them, then we will be successful based on our current definition of success. And if we're successful, we've proven ourselves. And if we've proven ourselves, then, boy won't our level of confidence continue to rise.

### Closing Thoughts

Let your peace of mind, happiness, confidence, and self-worth be a choice you make consciously rather than surrendering your power by allowing external situations to dictate your internal condition for you.

"Now, keep in mind that, based on this model, your level of self-worth and confidence has become conditional. That is, it goes up and down, depending on what you've achieved or produced rather than what is truly important: who you are."

"That's pretty much true for me," Denise said.

# Make Confidence a Choice

"Conversely, what if we don't allow external situations to dictate our internal condition? What if your confidence is simply a choice you make about yourself? A belief in yourself?"

"Let me say this in a different way. What if you could choose to be confident, choose to have faith in yourself and adopt an unwavering belief in your abilities, regardless of the outcomes of each day? Consider for a moment that you have already proven yourself and that all of your future accomplishments are achieved as an expression of who you are, what you value, and the value you want to deliver to others, instead of playing the endless game of justifying your self-worth to feed your insatiable ego."

"If you can believe in this, your confidence now becomes unconditional because it is based on who you are and the quality of the person you are, not simply what you do or what you produce."

"The value you deliver isn't reflected only in the number of sales you make. Your value isn't what you do, but who you are and the quality of person you have become and are continually evolving into. Who you are is consistent, who you are is a choice, who you are is something you control 100 percent. That's why who you are is always more important than what you do."

**Closing Thoughts**

Who you are is always more important than what you do and is not defined by the results you produce. Instead, who you are is a choice. So, be who you want!

"For this reason, the true definition of confidence is having an unwavering faith or belief not only in yourself, but in each experience you have. And that belief is this: regardless of the situation, regardless of how bleak it may look or difficult it may be, it will all work out in the end without the evidence to support this belief. It's trusting in yourself without any proof to back up your conviction."

"Hmm, interesting," Denise said after a few moments. "I can see how this makes sense, but you can't sit there and tell me that your attitude doesn't change when you're making sales each week!"

"I can certainly understand that, Denise, and you are right. For most salespeople, meeting or exceeding sales goals has a very clear and measurable effect on their attitude. Yet doesn't this support your old model of thinking? You're putting yourself back into the confidence trap, surrendering your ability to control your level of self-worth by choice and, instead, allowing your experiences to dictate how you feel about yourself.

"Besides, does the feeling of satisfaction you experience from closing the sale last, or is it fleeting until the next sale?"

"It's addicting, if that's what you mean. And you're right. The sense of achievement you get when closing a new sale is only a temporary feeling you experience until the next sale. You can bet that I'll continue to keep pushing to get more sales. I'll just have to do a better job at controlling the process and each sales call I go out on."

"That's interesting. Do you believe that a sales call or your sales process is something you feel you can actually control?"

"Well, I'll certainly try harder to do so!"

"Really?" I paused for a moment, reflecting back to the beginning of our conversation. "You said earlier that confidence equates to control. May I ask, what's the relationship you have with control?"

# Are You a Control Freak?

"If you mean I'm a control freak, then the answer is a resounding 'Yes,' and I'm proud of it," Denise answered.

"Are you familiar with the paradox of control?" I asked her.

"No, please share."

To give you some background, the word *paradox* is Latin for "beyond opinion." A paradox is a seemingly contradictory statement that may be true. They are a way to test and challenge reality, or the limiting or general assumptions we have made that stall our evolution.

*The more we try to maintain control in our lives, the less freedom we create for ourselves* illustrates one of the many paradoxes in life. While we may strive to maintain control over our lives, our careers, and even over other people in order to produce certain outcomes, this desire to control creates rigidity or resistance to change. We feel that if we control certain things, it limits risk and error.

This lack of flexibility creates friction in our lives, especially in the face of adversity.

The result? As we continue to put our energy into preventing change, or staying within what we know is safe and comfortable, control becomes the very thing that limits the progression, inhibiting the ability to create or recognize even better opportunities. As we let go of the need to control, greater possibilities unfold naturally.

Paradoxes such as this illustrate how the very actions we take to generate desired results often slow us down and diminish the quality of the outcome we want to achieve. (Another paradox!)

---

### Closer's Corner

You can determine whether you are attempting to control something that you can't by asking yourself the following questions.

- ◆ Are my efforts and actions enhancing my life or consuming my life?
- ◆ Do I want to continue doing things the way I am doing them now for the next 30 years?
- ◆ Is this my agenda or someone else's agenda?
- ◆ Do I have an attachment to the outcome?
- ◆ What am I afraid of? (What's the fear?) What am I trying to avoid?
- ◆ What am I trying to do or create perfectly? What result am I hooked on achieving?

In other words, consider what would be possible if you responded to the events in your life, both in action and in opinion, in the exact opposite manner in which you would normally respond to them. (If you're a *Seinfeld* fan, you may remember the episode in which George made better, more successful decisions by doing the exact opposite thing he would normally do.)

Once explored, these contradictions open up new possibilities by challenging certain beliefs that we may have initially thought of as true.

This exploration into contradiction is evolutionary, since it immediately creates alternative opportunities and paths to travel upon.

Here's the bottom line. There are only three things that you have any real control of:

1. Your actions

2. Your responses to your experiences

3. Your thoughts and beliefs

**Closing Thoughts**

Evolution's paradox: embracing what we resist or try to avoid (chaos, change, conflict, failure, vulnerability) is our greatest source of growth and progress.

That's it. Everything else that we think we can control is an elusion. The irony is, most of us spend our time trying to control the things we can't rather than focusing on mastering the things we can, these three areas that we truly do have control over.

"That is so true," Denise declared when I had finished explaining this to her. "Hmm. I can't help but think of the countless hours, days, even years I've wasted trying to control the things I can't! Well, today is certainly the start of a new day for me and a new approach to selling. Any other jewels you want to share today?"

# Control Is All Based in Fear

"Funny you should mention that," I responded. "Here's something else that may be outside of your line of vision. Control is all based in fear."

"What do you mean?"

"Well, you said that you want to do your best to control as much as possible. What would happen if you weren't able to control what you feel you need to?"

Denise took a deep breath and said, "Life would end as we know it, of course. No, but not too far from that. I'd lose my job, be on the street with my family, lose the house—you know, all the worst stuff you can imagine."

"So can you see here how your need for control is rooted deep within your greatest fears?"

"Explain, oh omnipotent guru," she requested, jokingly. (But who am I to argue with that?)

# You're Either Creating or Controlling

Well, said another way, we try to control as many things as possible to reduce risk. And by definition, risk is synonymous with "danger, hazard, or threat." What is fear? A sense of apprehension or panic. So by default, if we reduce risk, we reduce our fear.

As such, we believe that the more we attempt to control our risks in any situation, whether it is the risk of losing a sale or the risk of having our children grow up without the right guidance, ethics, or values, we then can keep at bay that which we fear happening most. As mentioned in the paradox of control, the myth is, the more we attempt to control things, the more we can eliminate our greatest fears from coming to fruition.

Unfortunately, this paradigm and philosophy comes at a cost. You see, if you are trying to control, for example, a sales call and the outcome you desire, there is one thing that you cannot be doing. And that is, you cannot be creating. And the ability to be creative is one of the most important attributes of a sales professional. After all, it is your job to create new and better solutions for your prospects!

Said another way, control and creation are polar opposites. Here's why:

| Control | Creation |
|---|---|
| Control is an attempt to generate predictable, expected results. | Creation is open to new possibilities and generating unpredictable results. |
| Control is rigid. | Creation is fluid and evolving. |
| Control is based on achieving a certain outcome in the future. | Creation can happen only in the present moment. |
| Control is focusing on a known outcome. | Creation has no agenda to the final outcome. |

As you can see, if you are attempting to control the outcome or the sales call, then you cannot be creating new possibilities in the moment. As such, if you are focused on what you want to control, then you will miss out on uncovering or recognizing a new and better opportunity to turn a prospect into a client. Conversely, if you are in a constant state of creation, then you are going to allow new possibilities and solutions to surface naturally.

"But, Keith, if I'm in a constant state of creativity, don't I need some structure to support it? I mean, should I toss out my entire sales process, routine, and goals?" Denise asked.

### Closing Thoughts

Selling is the art of creating new possibilities and solutions. Salespeople are responsible for the creation rather than the controlling of solutions for their prospects. As such, if you are a highly creative salesperson, then there is no need for you to attempt to control the outcome.

"Not at all," I responded. "However, I can see where the confusion is. Remember, just like any belief or process, the proverbial pendulum can swing to either side as an extreme rather than a balance. You certainly want to honor your daily routine, your sales process, and your goals. However, you are not going to do so to the point that they have you gripped and are controlling you. Said a different way, when things outside of your control change (whether it's the market, your career, your prospects, your product or service, and so on), that's when you want to be flexible and adaptable to this change so that you can adjust your processes and strategies accordingly.

"After all, if you were working for a company that sold pagers, and you had a great presentation that allowed you to continually attain your sales goals, would you still be using the same approach when selling mobile phones? In essence, your marketplace would have changed along with the needs of your clients and the way in which you would present to them."

At this point, Denise was evolving at light speed. I could hear her getting it.

"Well this has certainly been a productive and enlightening call!" she exclaimed. "Thanks a million, coach! I feel better already."

"Wonderful!" I declared. "I'm looking forward to our call next week and the success that will follow from today. Good-bye, Denise."

At this point, we have discussed the importance of developing the right mind-set of a sales professional. We are now ready to uncover several other characteristics of a closer, starting with the importance of becoming a creative salesperson.

# Be Creative

It is 3 P.M. on a lovely fall day. You are on your way to work. As you walk by a school, you notice all of the children playing outside. You pause and watch them for a second. A flood of emotions and memories intoxicate your mind as you remember yourself as a child. You admire their youthful exuberance, their unlimited supply of energy, their fervor for freedom, their passion for knowledge, their desire to learn, and their boundless creativity.

You listen to their conversations as they play. Some are talking about the planets they are visiting. Others are envisioning the castle in which they are playing. They see this vividly, down to every detail, including the moat around the castle. Some pretend to be presidents, firemen, astronauts, even doctors.

**Closing Thoughts**

Become a create freak rather than a control freak.

How creative children are! How powerful their minds are. Full of ideas, with no inhibitions or limitations to restrain them. Children have the ability to visualize or imagine their true dreams. They bring their dreams into their reality and make them real.

The most creative time in a person's life is from birth to the age of around 11 years old. This is the time when they are not constrained by rules or regulations. Children are not concerned with what is supposedly acceptable in thought or behavior and what is not, what is practically right or wrong, proper or improper, fact or fiction.

In a child's eyes, there exist no boundaries. There is nothing to regulate them or inhibit their level of creativity. Everything that children see and experience is new and exciting. (Just imagine driving over a bridge, going to the beach, or riding on a train for the first time!) They are constantly absorbing information and expanding on their ideas. The more they learn, the more children want to express themselves. They want to share what they have learned. They have no fear of rejection, of being wrong, or of the unknown. Why? Because they have not experienced it yet!

The years begin to pass. The people in a child's life, such as teachers and parents, begin to instill their values and ideals in the minds of their children.

- "No, that is not appropriate for a child of 12 years old (or 15 or 17, and so on)."

- "No, you can't act like that anymore."

- "No, you can't spend all of your time playing. It is time to start thinking about your future and get serious."

- ◆ "You can't do that (wear that, say that)."

- ◆ "That is wrong."

- ◆ "Doing that is unacceptable."

- ◆ "No, Santa and the Tooth Fairy really don't exist."

As children get older, they begin to experience what it's like feeling embarrassed, being wrong, having people put down their ideas and dreams, and being punished for doing the "wrong thing."

The creative boy now becomes a man. His eyes no longer see the dreams and visions he had as a boy. He becomes serious, more focused on the perceived role he has to play in society and the pressures from his family. He concentrates on what he thinks he wants and needs. The thoughts and desires that he had as a child become clouded with every passing day, only to be replaced with more and more responsibilities: a mortgage, a job, a family.

He begins to lose sight of what was especially important in his life. The simple things. Freedom of expression, having fun, peace of mind, living simply, appreciating his surroundings, treating every day as a new adventure and not getting caught up in the minutia that blinds us from appreciating the beauty around us. All of the visions and dreams are put on a shelf, where they begin to collect dust.

The man begins to forget what it was like to be creative, to dream, and to imagine. Lack of creativity breeds complacency. He now becomes just like everyone else: another face, another number.

Imagine if we never lost our creative edge. Imagine what would be possible if we didn't feel compelled to have to change due to other people's beliefs, perceptions, or rules. Now imagine if you had the ability to share your visions and dreams with those around you.

Before you can assist a prospect in opening up their mind to change, you must open up your own. Know what it is like to sit on a cloud. Can you see yourself sitting way up in the sky? Do you smell the crisp air? As you look down, do you see the whole world? Imagine that there is nothing to restrain you. Look at the root of the word *creative*. Create. Take action to create your own destiny. Go back to a time in your life when you were most creative. Take your dreams off the shelf and wipe away the dust. Once you can envision the possibilities you can create, you are ready to take the prospect with you.

Anyone can study and memorize a presentation. But if you truly want to determine if your presentation is the reason why you're selling, then ask someone why they actually purchased from you. Will they say it was because you had the most beneficial package or product? They might. However, most of the time they will say it was because of you and the solutions you proposed. After all, you can't fake creativity.

# Enthusiasm

Think about something that excites you, something that you feel passionate about. It can be a hobby, sports, music, your significant other, your family, even your career. It can be anything that you strongly believe in that delivers an abundance of joy, satisfaction, or a sense of accomplishment. Now close your eyes for a moment and harness that feeling. Picture yourself engaging in one of your favorite pastimes or activities. Experience the emotion you have when doing so. Feel your energy level increase and your well-being, your clarity, and your purpose become stronger and more vivid.

Remember how passionate you can talk about something that you live to love and love to live? Can you envision the feeling of driving a golf ball 350 yards, or making that three-point shot at the last second of the basketball game? How about the feeling you experience when listening to your favorite song, or playing a musical score without error? Even if someone has a different opinion than your own on something you truly believe in, you can make that person see your point of view because of your level of enthusiasm, passion, and belief. After all, the intense level of conviction that you are displaying in what you are saying offers something intriguing and compelling, and creates interest in others, even if they don't share the same mind-set or philosophy that you do.

How do powerful people become powerful? By enrolling other people in their beliefs and ideas. Sharing their thoughts, ideas, excitement, and energy empowers

## Closing Thoughts

Show me a salesperson who can harness what he or she feels most passionate about and can bring that feeling into a sales call, and I will show you a salesperson who is unstoppable.

others. People will want to be in your presence. This creates an atmosphere for other people to want to share in your dreams. How else were companies like Microsoft and Google created? At Microsoft, it was founder Bill Gates who shared his idea with others. He enrolled other people to envision and become part of creating a company that would revolutionize the way we conduct business and manage every area of our lives.

Now think about selling and what you sell. Do you sell with the same passion, belief, and conviction? Do you carry that same feeling and electricity into every sales appointment? Is the feeling about your career, your product or service, and your desire to serve others as intense as the feeling you possess over the things that excite you the most?

This does not mean you need to stand up on your soapbox and preach the gospel to anyone who will listen. Your enthusiasm can be apparent in the way you deliver your information. A prospect can feel your energy and become excited because enthusiasm is contagious. Having the greatest product, company, or service is no longer a possibility or something that's said by every salesperson the prospect meets with. Instead, it comes across to the prospect as factual based on how you deliver this information and your unwavering confidence. In essence, you are the embodiment of your product.

This is what enthusiasm is all about. To be inspired. A strong warmth or feeling. A keen interest. The state of exuberance in which all things seem possible. Elicit that same powerful feeling of belief that you have around what you sell and share it with your prospects so that they can experience that feeling as well. Learn to transfer that feeling into the hearts of your prospects. It is this feeling, this passion that drives each one of us to pursue something that we love. It is your inspiration and keen interest in serving each prospect that becomes contagious on a sales call. If you can harness this special power, you have dramatically reduced the time needed to close more sales. After all, your prospects are going to want whatever it is you have that has inspired such a high level of conviction and confidence!

### Closing Thoughts

The word *enthusiasm* stems from the Greek word *entheos*, which means "possessed by a god or other superhuman power."

It is imperative to tap into the prospect's emotions when selling. Think about the role of a professional coach of a football team. Before each game, does the coach sit and quietly explain to the players the technique or logic of winning? Does he have a discussion about the results he is looking to obtain? Is this done in a passive, relaxed environment? Of course not. Before every game, he focuses all of his energy on getting the athletes "pumped up" and passionate about winning. When the players go out to the field, they are motivated by the feeling of winning, of teamwork, of success (as well as wanting to crush the other team).

The coach's job is to get his players "fired up," to get their blood pumping and their hearts racing. A great coach motivates his players to reach deep within themselves in order to put their heart on the playing field and into everything they do. It is often during an athlete's heightened state of emotion and passion when their efforts will shine on the field and their true potential is unleashed.

> **Closing Bell**
>
> Enthusiasm comes from your heart, not your head. If your heart is empty, then what is inside your head and what comes out of your mouth are meaningless.

> **Closer's Corner**
>
> Unless the prospect is an impulse buyer who buys solely on emotion, many prospects will first process the information needed to make a purchasing decision in a logical, rational order. However, when it comes time to make the purchasing decision, they will do so during a heightened state of emotion.

# Sincerity and Authenticity Sell

Sincerity is being free from hypocrisy. It is being authentic and honest. Being sincere means being genuine or real. Your conviction and sincerity about your career and your product come across as a fact, an indisputable reality. Just like the fact that you are holding or reading this book right now. There is no disputing it. Why? Because you are.

Leslie, a consultant for a marketing firm, was very effective at setting up the second meeting with her prospects to conclude the presentation and wrap up the sale.

Interestingly enough, Leslie did not have the strongest presentation in the company, nor did she claim to know any more than the other consultants within her organization. Leslie's product knowledge was average, at best. When other consultants asked Leslie what her secret was, she responded with, "Creating honest and open communication with every prospect."

### Closing Thoughts

The old adage that you are not only selling your product, but you are also selling yourself still rings true today. People are buying not only what you are selling, but they are first buying your integrity and sincerity. You are selling yourself based on your belief and conviction in the product or service, and are transferring this feeling to the prospect.

In other words, they trusted her. Leslie gave a convincing reason as to why the prospect should meet with her for a second time. People read the integrity of a salesperson fairly well.

Do you take a strong stand for delivering the most effective solution to every prospect, even when the solution may not be delivered by you or achieved by using your product or service? Do your actions support your beliefs?

Being truly sincere ...

◆ Avoids sounding like a salesperson

◆ Instills a strong belief within the prospect about what you are selling

◆ Fosters stronger relationships with people

◆ Transfers your feelings and beliefs into the hearts of the prospect

◆ Is being who you are and what you stand for (your vision, goals, integrity, desire to deliver value, and so on).

Do you know who the best salespeople are (besides children)? Religious leaders. This is said with the utmost respect and is meant as a compliment (for those leaders who are not the fanatics causing pain and suffering throughout the world). Their beliefs have motivated thousands if not millions of people to follow them. They are their religion and embody the standards and practices unconditionally. To the members of their congregation, these leaders' word is law and carries more weight than anyone else's word.

Sincerity is power. Your belief is contagious. Caring is an attitude that you bring into the relationship, showing that you are sincere about your motives and your agenda, which should be aligned directly with the prospect's agenda. Learn how to be sincere about everything you do, and people will begin to follow you, too!

**Closing Thoughts**

People do not care how much you know until they know how much you care.

To illustrate the power of sincerity, here's one experience I had with a very sincere salesperson. Several months after moving into my newly constructed home, I noticed some trees that were dangerously hanging over my house. As much as I hate to cut back any tree, it had to be done for the safety of my family. So I called in a tree expert to remove some very large and overgrown limbs jetting over my house.

The first visit was from the salesperson, who quoted me a price. I thought it was a fair price and instructed him to begin the job as soon as possible.

That happened to be the following day. At around 10:00 in the morning, several workers and the boss arrived with their trucks and equipment. Before they began working, the owner rang my bell and needed to talk with me. I walked outside with him and into my backyard, where the trees were that needed to be trimmed.

There was a strange look on his face. I knew something was up.

"Keith," he began reluctantly, "I need to talk to you about the price that my salesperson quoted you."

"Here it comes!" I thought to myself. He's going to hit me with a higher price. After all, if he wanted to talk about money, it was a safe bet he wasn't calling me out to tell me, "Good news! My price is going to be lower."

Now, as a sales coach, you can imagine how very sensitive I was to situations like this. I bit my tongue and listened to what he had to say. Typically, I would frown heavily on any salesperson who would attempt to use this tactic (and then kick him off the job). This sales tactic (also known as the *bait and switch*) would sound something like, "Well, we underbid the job and it's going to be a bigger job than we thought, so I'm sorry, but the price is now going to be higher."

I was ready to get self-righteous and pounce all over him. But something else happened. Here's what Bill, the tree man, said.

"Listen, Keith. I know my salesperson quoted you one price. This is really hard for me to do, and I hate doing it, but he screwed up on the price he gave, to the point that I can't make a dime, and here's why. I have five guys out here to handle this job, which I guarantee is going to take up half my day. So between paying them, my equipment, and my insurance, and trying to make a buck for myself, the price he quoted you would essentially make me work for free. And I don't want to work for free today. So while I know that this job isn't going to be my top moneymaker of the week, I was hoping that you would understand this. So rather than having me pack up and leave because I really wouldn't be able to do the job for the price we quoted you, could you still do it for an additional $150 bucks? And listen, to be fair, if I can get out of here faster, I won't even charge you. But I'm telling you, I will definitely be here for half the day."

Now, Bill has had no sales training, ever. He didn't even finish high school. He's been working in this industry since he was a kid. However, Bill had something that I valued deeply, and it came across in the conversation I had with him. Bill had sincerity. He was being his authentic self, and I got that flat when talking with him. Bill spoke from his heart.

Sure enough, Bill was there for a large portion of the day, just like he said he would be. He did a great job. I paid him his money, the additional amount as well, and went around to each one of his guys to give them a tip, a token of my appreciation of their good work.

Here's what solidified my belief in Bill and why I knew he was a stand-up guy. Before he left, I went to give him a tip as well. He wouldn't even hear of it. Bill wouldn't take my money! I couldn't believe that I was now selling him on taking more money from me! Finally, I closed the deal when I told him to use the money and buy his guys lunch. He agreed, and we both continued with our day.

## The Least You Need to Know

♦ Rather than measuring your self-worth based on what you produce or achieve, let who you are, the person inside, and your qualities become your gauge.

♦ Developing a high level of confidence is a choice you make rather than something conditional.

♦ There are only three things that you can control: your beliefs, your actions, and your responses.

♦ Rather than attempting to control the sale, create it. Unlike control, which is having an attachment to the future, creation can occur only in the present moment.

♦ You can't fake authenticity or sincerity. It's the same as lying.

♦ If your prospects pick up on the strong feeling of sincerity and enthusiasm you emulate, you will become unstoppable.

Chapter 3

# Cerebral Selling—
# Why People Will Buy
# from You

## In This Chapter

- ◆ How your prospects make a purchasing decision
- ◆ Uncover the greatest psychological barriers to the sale
- ◆ Find the balance of using logic and emotion when selling
- ◆ Learn how the sales funnel will help you
- ◆ Distinguish between using empathy and using sympathy when selling

What motivates someone to make a purchasing decision? How do some salespeople so eloquently convert a reluctant, resistant prospect into a happy customer? Why do some salespeople possess what seems to be a gift or the natural ability to change a resounding "No" into a "Yes"? Are these prospects making a purchase because of the price, the need, the desire, the benefits, the salesperson, persistence, pressure, voodoo, mind control, or a combination of these factors?

Countless books and resources offer you a glimpse into the minds of consumers and the process they go through when making a purchasing decision. As you can imagine, this one topic can easily fill an entire book. However, in the spirit of providing you not only the psychology behind moving a prospect to "Yes!" but the step-by-step strategies and the proven, tactical approach you need to close more sales faster, in this chapter I've summarized the most important concepts that you need to know in order to get into the minds of your prospects and tap into their decision-making process. This will then enable you to align your style of selling with the prospect's style of buying.

# When Do People Make Buying Decisions?

If you were to poll all of the customers who purchased something from you regarding why they bought from you, they would respond with a variety of reasons. What follows are the most common reasons people buy.

People make a purchasing decision when …

- ◆ It is the right product or service that they are looking for.
- ◆ They want to buy.
- ◆ They are comfortable with the price of the purchase.
- ◆ They are comfortable with the company that is representing the product or service.
- ◆ They like and trust the salesperson.
- ◆ It is affordable to them.
- ◆ They like the advantages the product or service has to offer.
- ◆ They visualize the positive changes/benefits of the purchase.
- ◆ They see the urgency in taking action to minimize or eliminate a problem.

◆ They are comfortable making a buying decision.

◆ They think they have gotten a "great deal."

◆ The timing is right for them to make the purchase.

◆ The value derived from the investment outweighs the cost incurred.

◆ They are impulse buyers (motivated by the emotional aspect of the sales process and the product's potential).

### Closer's Corner

If I put together a success formula for what needs to be established during a sales call to motivate a prospect to buy from you, here's what it would look like.

Decision makers + Rapport + Trust + Uncovering their want + Uncovering their need + Urgency + Pain + Establishing the value/measurable benefits + Price + Affordability + Timing − Risk/Concern/Fear = $ale

What follows is a visual interpretation of moving the prospect through your sales cycle and the factors you need to address to make the prospect comfortable enough to make a purchasing decision. Since selling is not an exact science, there may be situations in which you made a sale without addressing each component of this success formula.

As I mentioned earlier, if you sell waterproofing solutions and walk into a home that is flooded, the homeowner may be less concerned about the price or rapport they have with you and more concerned about getting the foot of water out of the home. The timing, urgency, and need are clearly established, along with the desire for an immediate solution.

Regardless, approaching a sales call with these factors in mind will make your selling strategy bulletproof.

### Closer's Corner

When determining the length of your sales cycle or how long it takes for you to turn a qualified prospect into a customer, consider this rule of thumb. The larger the price of your product or service and the more complex it is, the longer your selling cycle will be.

Decision Makers, Rapport, Trust, Want, Need, Urgency, Pain, Value, Price, Affordability, Timing, Risk/Fear

Rapport, Trust, Want, Need, Urgency, Pain, Value, Price, Affordability, Timing, Risk/Fear

Trust, Want, Need, Urgency, Pain, Value, Price, Affordability, Timing, Risk/Fear

Want, Need, Urgency, Pain, Value, Price, Affordability, Timing, Risk/Fear

Need, Urgency, Pain, Value, Price, Affordability, Timing, Risk/Fear

Urgency, Pain, Value, Price, Affordability, Timing, Risk/Fear

Pain, Value, Price, Affordability, Timing, Risk/Fear

Value, Price, Affordability, Timing, Risk/Fear

Price, Affordability, Timing, Risk/Fear

Affordability, Timing, Risk/Fear

Timing, Risk/Fear

Risk/Fear

=

*–Sale–*

*The Sales Funnel.*

### Closing Thoughts

When it comes to making a purchase, people do what makes them comfortable rather than what makes the salesperson comfortable. Now, that doesn't mean they are comfortable with the solution or even want to spend the money and make the purchase. (Just ask anyone who had a flood in their basement and needed to spend thousands of dollars investing in a waterproofing system for their home.) However, it does mean they have a level of trust and comfort in the salesperson, the sales process, and the solution.

I remember something that my daughter did one day when she was five years old. We were getting ready to leave the playground on a chilly fall afternoon. She stood next to me as I opened the car door. Suddenly, she said, "Dad, I don't feel well. My tummy hurts." A few seconds later, she put her head in the car and vomited all over her car seat and the car floor. Of course, my first reaction was, "Honey, are you okay?" She responded, "Yes, Dad, much better. I think it was something I ate." I then had to ask her, curiously, "Baby, why didn't you just put your head down and throw up right in the street outside the car rather than inside it?" Her response: "Oh, Daddy, it's too cold outside. It's much warmer in the car." Starting at a very early age, people do what makes them comfortable.

# Why People Will Not Buy

Now, for the same reasons that people decide to make a purchase, here are the reasons people will not buy.

Prospects may feel that ...

- It is *not* the right product or service.
- They are *not* comfortable with the price of the purchase.
- They are *not* comfortable with the company.
- They do *not* like or trust the representative.
- It is *not* affordable to them.
- They do *not* see the value of what the product or service has to offer.
- They are *not* comfortable making a buying decision.
- They do *not* see any special incentive to buy.
- They do *not* understand what you have shown them.
- They do *not* see the urgency to make the investment, nor the cost or pain they will experience by not buying from you.
- It is *not* the right time to make this purchase (other bills, projects, no money right now, and so on).

# Handle the Fear or It Will Handle You

With all of these reasons I have listed, the greatest obstacle in making a purchasing decision is fear:

- Fear of making the wrong decision
- Fear that the product or service will not perform up to their expectations
- Fear of being ripped off (no trust)
- Fear of putting their money into something that will not benefit them (not getting the full value from their investment)

- Fear of tying up their money in another project

- Fear of loss of savings in the bank or budget in case of emergencies

- Fear of the outcome or repercussions (from a supervisor, partner, spouse, or family)

- Fear of making any type of decision

- Fear of not being accepted by their peers if they make a poor purchasing decision (looking bad)

- Fear of spending too much money

- Fear of losing out on a better deal elsewhere

Fear can manifest itself in a variety of ways and forms, but the greatest fear we experience when making a purchase is the fear of change.

Think about what prevents you from purchasing a product or service. People fear any change; they fear the unknown. Quite often, although the problems we experience may be causing some discomfort, they may still be easier for someone to tolerate than making a change. We may be able to recognize the problem, but we may not always be able to visualize or solidify in our mind what the change (the solution) may bring.

There is a natural resistance to change. Embracing any new idea, option, or solution begins with a level of resistance when it is first introduced. Think back to when these innovations were first introduced: fat-free foods, compact discs, the fax machine, e-mail and the Internet, voice mail, pagers, mobile phones, and, of course, life and business coaching, to name a few. The companies and people who pioneered and introduced these innovations were initially confronted with a great deal of resistance. However, over time, through public awareness, education, and a very strong marketing and sales campaign, these advancements in technology and in our society that were once considered new and unproven are now a part of our everyday life.

Consider the person who has a fear of changing careers. They know what to expect at their current job, but they aren't exactly sure what to expect in a new position at a new company. Your prospects experience the same feeling when making a purchase. That is, they often have a fear of leaving their comfort zone or what they are currently used to in their life or in their business.

This leads to another discussion. Do people buy based on logic and fact, or do they make a purchasing decision based on their feelings and emotions?

# Get Emotional or Logical?

It has been a source of discussion and controversy for years. Do people make purchasing decisions based on logic or emotion? Some consumers use logic or reason to process the information they have received before making a purchasing decision, and rely solely on what they perceive as the facts.

Others believe that people are motivated by their emotions and how they feel at the time, which determines whether they will buy.

The fact is, the prospect uses a combination of both logic and emotion to come to a conclusion on whether to buy. When you are giving a presentation, you are getting the prospect emotionally involved with what you are selling to create ownership of your product. That is, you want your prospects to experience the feeling they will have as a result of using your product or service. Prospects are motivated to take action through physical and emotional involvement during your meeting with them.

Although some prospects draw upon logic and data to make a decision, the way in which we deliver the advantages of what we are selling and how it will enrich their life or career triggers the emotional response. This, in turn, motivates the prospect toward the purchase.

**Closing Thoughts**

The professional salesperson knows that logic will enable a prospect to "think" but emotions cause a prospect to take action.

**Closing Bell**

Don't forget to put the *e* into *motion*. If you don't use emotion when selling your product or service, then you are simply going through the mundane motion of selling. And if you don't get excited about what you do, then how can you expect your prospects to?

Emotions create the excitement and urgency to take action. Therefore, sales professionals need to formulate a precise balance of both logic and emotion during their presentation. The type of prospect you are dealing with determines whether you accentuate more emotion or logic and facts. What happens if a salesperson uses only one method? Take a look at what happened to our friend Ted.

Ted spent hours every week reviewing the technical information of the products that his company markets. He is responsible for selling computer systems direct to businesses. Ted performs very well on the sales calls that were initiated by the prospect—that is, the appointments generated by people who take the initiative to call Ted's office expressing a need for his services. In these instances, the prospect has already expressed a need.

Unfortunately, Ted did not have the luxury of running into prospects who needed the work done immediately and were ready to buy. The majority of Ted's appointments were generated through cold calling, where he had trouble. Although Ted could effectively deliver all of the technical information, these prospects were not pressed to make changes overnight, especially with the high monetary investment required to do so. After all, since it was a cold call, a purchase like this may not have even been on his prospect's radar. This is where the emotional aspect enters into the selling paradigm.

Ted was hoping that his technical information alone would move the prospect to take action. However, the word *action* is a power word, whereas *logic* is a passive word. The degree of action that prospects take is closely related to how much emotion and conviction you put into your conversation with them.

Imagine what would happen if there was no emotion or feeling during motivational seminars or religious sermons. Religious leaders cause people to take action by moving them into a heightened state of emotion. At that time, they can ask for a charitable donation. A speaker during a seminar motivates the audience by eliciting the feeling that success is imminent. He or she creates enough excitement to cause the audience to take the necessary actions to better themselves.

Ted finally realized he needed to change his approach. He started listening to prospects' feelings rather than focusing on and delivering raw technical data. Ted focused on what excited the prospects as it relates to the benefits they would realize from installing his products. He accomplished this by asking better questions that triggered an emotional response rather than a logical one. (More on the types of questions in Chapter 7.) After tuning in to the emotions of the prospect, Ted saw a dramatic change in his performance.

# The Dual Role of a Salesperson

Salespeople possess an advantage that, if leveraged correctly, enables them to better connect with each prospect they speak with. That is, aside from being a salesperson, you are also a consumer and a prospect.

Think about what goes through your mind when you make a buying decision.

- Is this something that I truly want or need?
- Am I getting the best deal?
- Is there a real, identifiable value in the product or service?
- Is the price fair in relation to the value?
- Should I spend a little more money for better quality?
- Is this salesperson being up front and honest with me?
- Is this salesperson sincerely looking out for my best interests?
- Can I afford to make this purchase now?
- Should I shop around and see what other companies are offering?
- Should I hold on to my money in case I need it for something else, like a real emergency?
- Do I clearly see the benefits of making this purchase?
- Is it going to cost me more in the long run if I don't make this change (as a result of buying this product/service)?

These are the same questions that run through the mind of the prospect who is listening to you and what you have to offer. By keeping these questions in the forefront of your mind, you will be better equipped to defuse the concerns and resistance that would otherwise stall your sale.

# Empathy or Sympathy?

It had been two hours since Lisa began her presentation discussing insurance for C.D.I. Incorporated. She was sitting at the table with the two people responsible for making the decision on which insurance carrier to use. After explaining in detail all of the terms and types of coverage available, she paused and asked for some input. They said that they would need to think about it. Lisa had a feeling that she was blowing this sale. She realized that she may have overloaded these prospects with too much information.

Lisa then remembered what had happened to her previous customer, Mrs. Smith, when she went out to purchase insurance for her company. Lisa remembered Mrs. Smith explaining how confusing it was trying to choose the policies that gave her the most value and coverage for her money. Lisa began to empathize with these two prospects, realizing that they were in the same position Mrs. Smith was in when she was looking to purchase insurance.

With this in mind, Lisa replied to the prospects, "You know, one of my previous clients was in a similar situation. Her name was Mrs. Smith. She, too, was out shopping for a new insurance carrier within a specific price range. After speaking with several different carriers, I had the fortunate experience of meeting with her last. Confused and exhausted, Mrs. Smith expected me to give her my pitch. Instead, I asked her some questions. After Mrs. Smith explained her situation, I responded with several additional questions that none of the other salespeople had even bothered to ask.

- What is the most important factor in your decision?

- How do you typically go about making a decision like this?

- What are some of the concerns you have about making this decision?

"Mrs. Smith and I talked a little longer so that I could better understand her situation before offering her a policy that would be a fit for her. It turned out that Mrs. Smith was paralyzed by all of the information coming at her. She wasn't exactly sure how to go about sifting through the data in order to compare the policies available and determine the one that delivered the most value for her. So we took the time to review all of the policies she was considering. I made it clear to Mrs. Smith that if my policy was not the best one for her, I would certainly let her know, since I'm more concerned about my clients having the right coverage than having an unsatisfied client.

"After comparing the policies, it turned out that there was one policy offered by another company that actually fit Mrs. Smith's needs a little better than mine. Since Mrs. Smith needed several different insurance policies, Mrs. Smith wound up purchasing that policy from the other company and the other insurance coverage from me.

"Listen, I know how confusing all of the different policies can be, and so do many of my other customers who have been in a similar situation that you're in. Why don't we spend a couple of minutes breaking down each policy to ensure that my policy is, in fact, the right one for you, just like I did for Mrs. Smith? I will also

**Closing Thoughts**

Prospects relate better to situations and salespeople when they know that someone else shares the same feelings they are experiencing.

show you what some of my other customers in your situation said and why they finally decided to utilize my services in some instances, and another insurance carrier for other coverage that I do not specialize in."

It turned out that the prospects were hesitant because of their lack of understanding of the product they were going to invest in. Lisa also showed these prospects some testimonial letters from other customers that expressed the same concern that these particular prospects shared. When these decision makers realized that they were not alone in their thinking and realized that other people shared their concerns, they were in a more comfortable position to make their purchasing decision and explore the best solution with Lisa. Lisa got the order.

Lisa was very empathetic with her prospect's needs. She shared a similar experience she'd had with another client, enabling her to relate better with these prospects.

Many people, however, confuse being empathetic with being sympathetic. There is a slight difference between *empathy* and *sympathy*.

*Sympathy* is defined as the inclination to think or feel alike, the act or capacity of entering into or sharing the feelings or interests of another. Sympathy is being sensitive to another person's feelings.

As stated in this definition, you might be sympathetic to those who are poor or who are living in the streets. However, you have never lived in such a fashion, so you can only imagine what it might be like. You can only try to imagine the emotional state that a poor, less fortunate person might share. "I sure feel bad about that person having to live in the street," you might say, as you return to your home.

If you were empathetic to this situation, you might have been someone (or known someone) who had lived on the streets in poverty and found your way out of that lifestyle and into a better one. You had the hands-on knowledge and experience of being in that unfortunate situation. You actually lived through this.

"I sure feel awful about that person having to live in the street. When I was younger, I lost my family and was forced to live without a home. Luckily, I was strong enough to persevere and get myself off the streets by finding employment and a place to live," you might say.

**Closing Thoughts**

Empathy is a more powerful attribute to possess than sympathy.

When you are on an appointment, demonstrating feelings of empathy and sharing stories of other customers who have been in similar situations will enable you to bond closer, creating a stronger feeling of camaraderie and trust. Share situations similar to those of the prospect. Everyone can sympathize and try to imagine what it may be like being put into a different situation, but few empathize and share the same or similar feelings that the prospect has by actually having "been there before."

# How Am I Perceived?

Do you ever wonder how people actually perceive you? Chances are, it is very different from the way you perceive yourself. You might view yourself as a diligent, hardworking, responsible person. Others, however, may view you as obnoxious, arrogant, curt, or quick-tempered. You might consider yourself to be relaxed, soft-spoken, and calm. Others might see this as lazy, insecure, and indifferent.

It is important to understand how your actions can be perceived differently by different people. This can have a detrimental effect on your future and on your performance.

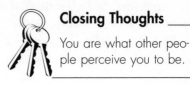

**Closing Thoughts**

You are what other people perceive you to be.

Ask yourself these four questions:

♦ How do you view or describe yourself?

♦ How do people (friends, family, employer) actually perceive or describe you?

♦ How do you want to be viewed or perceived?

♦ How do you want to come across to others?

It is intriguing how the answers to these questions often conflict each other, depending upon who you ask. You may feel that you are a noble, down-to-earth, modest, nonmaterialistic person. However, if you are driving around in a flashy new sports car and are having dinner at The Four Seasons, that may paint a different picture in the eyes of other people. How do you think others are going to perceive you? Affluent, materialistic? Do your actions and lifestyle represent the attributes that you feel you hold or possess? Do you *mirror* or *reflect* the disposition you are striving for?

**def•i•ni•tion**

Mirroring and reflecting are two techniques salespeople use to better align their style of communication to that of the prospect's. Aligning how you speak, as well as the physical gestures and disposition, with that of each prospect enables you to establish a more common ground with people. As such, it will make your prospects more comfortable doing business with someone who appears to share similarities in both their speech and action.

Make sure you are portraying the image you want your clients to see. Your friends and family have known you for years and know who you are, but a prospect does not have this luxury. If prospects see you driving an expensive car, they may judge you immediately, regardless of what type of person you truly are. Now, this may not be a bad thing. In fact, depending upon your industry, profession, and client base it may practically be a requirement to do so, if that is the image you want to portray. Hey, if that's the type of client you want to attract then that may be one way to establish either your credibility ("he must be successful if he's driving around in that car") or common ground ("hey man, I've got the same ride").

Conversely, prospects may become jealous of your possessions, and no matter what you say or do, they will not buy from you. Unfortunately, you would never know that this was the reason why they didn't buy unless the prospect actually told you. A similar incident happened to an aspiring young salesperson named Kelly.

Kelly was excited about winning the year-end sales contest. The prize that she had received was a new BMW. She already had a reliable car, but, hey, this BMW was much nicer. She decided to start using her new car when going on sales calls. During her first month of doing so, Kelly noticed that her selling percentages dropped a bit, and she couldn't figure out why.

She then began noticing and hearing some of the reactions people had when she drove up to her scheduled appointment. One morning while on an appointment, one of her prospects made a comment that caused Kelly to re-evaluate whether to use this car on appointments. "That's a really nice car you have. You must have to sell a lot of business in order to pay for it."

Kelly realized that because of the clientele she was selling to and the product she sold, people perceived her as being pretentious. Many of the prospects felt that their money was paying for her car payment. Needless to say, Kelly stopped driving her BMW to appointments and used her older car instead.

In some selling environments, having an expensive car can imply that you are a successful businessperson. People want to do business with others who are successful. In other environments, it can unknowingly become detrimental your selling performance. What type of dress code is indigenous to your industry? Casual or formal business attire? Become aware of the type of prospect that you will be selling to. It is imperative that you understand your market as well as your audience.

> ### Closing Bell
> If you sell face-to-face, the first impression a prospect will have of you is based on your appearance. Therefore, make sure that your external features and characteristics are aligned with your internal ones and who you are. Otherwise, the visional presentation of yourself can overshadow the authentic you. People may form an opinion about you before they discover who you really are. The result? Your prospects may have already made their decision about whether to buy from you!

## The Least You Need to Know

- The greatest barrier to prospects buying from you is the fear of change.

- Logic and facts validate making the purchase; emotion and the desire for a future gain cause the prospect to act.

- The faster you can connect with each prospect, the easier it will be for that prospect to purchase from you.

- The first impression prospects have of you is based on your appearance, which often dictates whether they will buy from you.

- Empathy forms a deeper connection with people than sympathy.

- If you can understand how, when, and why each prospect makes the buying decision, then you are either choosing to adapt and become a sales champion or choosing to stay the same and fail.

# Chapter 4

# Get in Their Head and Get out with a Sale

## In This Chapter

- Adapt to each prospect while staying the same
- Pain and the cost of not making a change cause action and sales
- Sell the prospect where they want to be
- Turn a want into a need
- Recognize when the prospect is ready to buy

Yes, we've established the fact that this book is not for idiots and this title denotes the farthest thing from the truth. In fact, the polar opposite is true; this title is simply one way to levitate a very heavy and difficult concept for many people to grasp.

This chapter proves it. Here's where you start developing your sixth sense when closing. We go deeper than the words you can use to close a sale, and less obvious than putting on a clean suit or changing your clothes in order to make the right appearance.

We are going beyond superficial change. We are going right into the mind and heart of the prospect. You are going to discover how you do so using your gut, your heart, your intuition, and your understanding of psychology as tools to fine-tune your selling approach to improve your odds of selling.

Understanding the psychology of how your prospects buy and then adapting your communication style to complement it provide you with a huge competitive edge over your competition's generic and traditional style of selling. I can assure you, the bulk of your competition is not spending time developing aptitude and proficiency in the psychological art of selling.

The psychology of selling enables you to go beyond what it means to connect with prospects. We're talking about being able to *read* them: how they think, how they buy, and what you can do to adapt your approach so that it is well received by the prospect without the typical resistance. Here's how you can deliver information in a way each prospect likes and wants to hear.

# Adapt Like a Chameleon to Your Surroundings

Great salespeople have the ability to adapt their personality to that of the prospects.

"So now you are asking me to become a lizard." In a sense, yes. However, please do not slither to your next appointment, or stick out your tongue to the prospect in order to get the sale. Learn to develop the attributes of a chameleon.

What does a chameleon do? A chameleon is a small lizard whose skin changes color according to the surroundings. Chameleons adapt and physically change with their environment. Whether a chameleon is hunting for food or avoiding a predator, the ability to go through a physical metamorphosis allows him to capture his prey and avoid being preyed upon. The color of his skin is a controlled function of his torso. His prey never knows he is there until it is too late. By then, the chameleon has captured and devoured his prey. For the same reason, he is a difficult adversary to hunt down. He knows when he needs to take a step back, be quiet, and become an observer. This is one reason the chameleon has outlived many species of life on our planet; this reptile has been around since the age of the dinosaurs.

A professional sales consultant adapts to the surroundings. The sales consultant goes through a metamorphosis or level of change. After uncovering the personal experiences of the prospect, you will learn to take on both physical and verbal similarities. Like a chameleon, you will learn when it is appropriate to pursue a prospect and when to take a step back. Although you need to develop an awareness of the techniques that enhance your selling performance, experience will be the one tool you need to develop on your own.

It is important that you recognize the different personality types of consumers and adjust your demeanor accordingly. When you initially enter an appointment, you are there to observe and explore. Yes, your prime objective is to earn the business of a new client. However, if you fail to adjust your personality and your presentation to that specific prospect, chances are you will miss an opportunity to sell.

Learn how to read people quietly. Do not stereotype people by their race, age, sex, employment, or past experiences with other customers. Conversely, some cultures within our society have certain buying habits that you need to recognize.

### Closing Thoughts

A skilled salesperson knows when he needs to take a step back and be quiet, listen, and observe.

Some base their buying decisions through the bartering or haggling system. This may be prevalent within their culture. Others need to build a personal relationship with the salesperson. This type of prospect believes in building a business relationship with someone before buying. How do you find out? Ask better questions.

As stated before, prospects determine whether they want to purchase something from you within the first several minutes, unless you have a monopoly in your market and your prospects have no choice but to purchase from you. If a prospect feels that you are not the person he wants to purchase from, giving the job away for free will not make him more receptive.

### Closing Thoughts

We have all heard the expression, "There is no second chance to make a first impression." Live by this phrase when selling.

# The Simplicity of Selling

Many salespeople overlook four simple tasks:

1. Question

2. Detach

3. Observe

4. Listen

So what replaces these critical sales activities? You guessed it: talking, talking, and more talking. Most salespeople get so caught up in whether the prospect is going to buy that they fail to recognize what the prospect is actually communicating. Why? Because they are too busy talking! It is the simplicity in the selling process that salespeople forget about, the basics of selling.

What follows are several techniques you can use to assist you in becoming a chameleon so that you can more rapidly connect and build a relationship with every prospect you meet with.

# Mirroring and Reflecting

There's nothing you do when looking in a mirror that your reflection will not imitate. In other words, mirror the actions of the prospect. Become the reflection of the prospect's actions. This is done both physically and verbally. Often what the prospect does not say is the information you need to be aware of and understand.

**Closing Thoughts**

Prospects prefer to buy from people who are like them and who share similar values, backgrounds, interests, and beliefs.

*Reflecting* refers to the form and timing in which you discuss information. This can be based upon which method of communication the prospect utilizes to process information. In other words, do they focus more on the spoken word and what they hear, or do they process new information better visually, such as in writing? Finally, they may like to touch, feel, and experience your product or service firsthand before making a decision.

*Mirroring* refers to acting subtly similar to the other person in physical ways. There is a difference between this and mimicking. Instead of copying every gesture, which would come across as annoying and phony, follow the other person's lead in relation to the following three factors:

1. **Disposition**—Mirror the formality or casualness of the prospect based on personality type. Is the prospect relaxed or intense? Professional or casual? Business oriented or relationship oriented? Adapt to the prospect's style and demeanor.

2. **Body language**—If the prospect is physically expressive (talking with the hands), do the same. Does the prospect place her hands in her lap or on the table? Are her arms at her sides, or are the arms crossed as she talks with you? Casually mirror how prospects physically present themselves through their gestures, posture, and overall presence.

3. **Verbal acuity**—This refers not only to the tone, speed, or volume in which prospects communicate, but also to the language or vocabulary they use. If you sell over the phone, then you may not always have the luxury of identifying their disposition or body language, which makes it even more important for you to be hypersensitive to how they come across over the telephone. If the prospect talks slowly, calmly, and in a monotone, do the same. If the prospect talks fast and loud, slightly increase the tone, speed, and volume of your voice.

If a prospect is detailed oriented, become detailed oriented. If a prospect is a straight shooter, then do not pull any punches; lay it on the line. If the prospect likes to tell stories of the past, then be cordial and quiet, and listen! For this type of person, it would be appropriate for you to also share stories that would foster a closer connection. If the prospect enjoys spending time developing a relationship by joking around and getting to know you, then go with it. Like the chameleon who adapts to his environment, you are to do the same in your approach, attitude, communication style, and disposition.

People are quick to develop close relationships with those who seem similar to themselves. Think about the people you surround yourself with. Two people hit it off when they share similar thoughts, needs, opinions, and feelings. People are more receptive when they are treated the way they want to be treated, not the way *you* want to be treated.

Do you feel that techniques contradict what I said earlier about being fully authentic when selling? Not exactly. Do not interpret this as being a phony. Instead, what you are doing is becoming sensitive to others regarding how they like to communicate.

**Closing Thoughts**

Align your style of selling to the prospect's style of buying.

Dave, the sales manager at Copy Express, approached this sales call with care. He was aware of the importance of adapting his style of selling to each individual prospect.

It seemed that three other representatives from his company had tried to earn a work order from this particular prospect. It had been established that Creative Graphics, Inc., was in desperate need of a new copying machine. The only deterrent, however, was the decision maker. It seemed he had a bit of an attitude, to put it mildly. When Dave had asked the other representatives why they couldn't get the order, they all had stated that the owner, Carl, was so abrasive, obnoxious, and arrogant that they could never get into their presentation. "All he did was yell and scream," proclaimed one of the representatives who had attempted to speak to Carl. It seemed that Carl did not like hearing presentations. It was clear to Dave that he had to take an entirely different approach when meeting with Carl.

Dave greeted Carl with a handshake. Dave began by asking, "How can we help you this afternoon?" "How can you help me?" barked Carl. "You can start by giving me your bottom line on what a new copier will cost. Then you can help me by leaving my office." Although Dave had

**Closing Bell**

Do not mistake mirroring and reflecting as mimicking and parroting. These techniques refer more to the style of communication you use and how you deliver your presentation than becoming a clone of the prospect.

tried to prepare himself for this type of prospect, theory and practice are always two entirely different entities. Dave, who was normally a calm, soft-spoken man, became a bit irritated.

No one enjoys being yelled at. A wave of energy and adrenaline caused the blood in Dave's veins to start pumping. After several more minutes of being verbally abused by Carl, Dave exclaimed, "You know, Carl, I am the fourth person from our company to come out and attempt to offer you a solution for your old copier, as well as a solution to some of the headaches you are currently experiencing. It seems my other representatives were not able to assist you. Was there something that you did not approve of in their approach?"

"Listen," Carl grunted, "They all came in here trying to give me their presentation and tell me what I really don't want to hear. All I want is a price and for you to be on your way. If you can't do that, then don't waste my time."

"You know something, Carl?" Dave said sternly. "If you even listened to the first representative I sent out here, your company would not only have made more money in the last couple of weeks from the installation of our new copier, but it probably would have helped the morale and productivity of your employees, since they wouldn't have to hear you whining anymore about the problems you experience with your copier!"

Dave began to smile.

"Wait one second," Carl said in a more controlled tone.

"Finally, a person who knows what I am looking for. Let's see which machine you have that will best fit my need."

Driving home that afternoon, Dave could not believe he had gotten the order. He had remembered reading somewhere that if you present the prospect with the same attitude he is giving you, it will help in the sale. "I can't believe it actually worked," Dave kept repeating on the ride back home. "I just can't believe it." All Carl wanted was someone similar to him to tell him how it is—the bottom line, the facts.

Bringing Carl's drama or disposition into consciousness actually disarmed him and prevented him from continually being aggressive. Dave uncovered Carl's style and exposed it by giving it right back to him.

There are many situations in which mirroring the prospect will assist you during a sales presentation. Although Dave was not able to control the situation, he was able to control the way in which he responded to the situation. Dave responded to this unwanted situation by mirroring the tonality, pitch, and communication style of the prospect. Carl, who subconsciously witnessed similar attributes in Dave, identified better with Dave and, concurrently, felt comfortable with him.

Now, please understand: I'm not telling you to go out and start to verbally abuse your prospects. That would be the extreme. However, subtle changes to adapt to the prospect's style and personality will give you the edge over the other salespeople you are competing against.

# Sell Them Where They Want to Be

One of the first questions I ask my clients when I begin working with them is this: "So what exactly is it that you sell?" As you can imagine, most of the time, they respond with either the product name, the type of product or service they sell, or the process in which they deliver their product or service.

This may be the final deliverable, but it's not exactly what you are selling. The fact is, the product doesn't always, as the old adage goes, "sell itself." Instead, consider that the prospect is actually purchasing the end result of your product or service, or, said another way, their desired state of where they want to be. (I dedicated an entire chapter to developing your compelling reasons in my last book, *The Complete Idiot's Guide to Cold Calling*.)

Here are some examples that advertisers use to paint a visual picture of the desired state that their target audience wants:

- Lose 20 pounds in 2 weeks.
- Look younger in 30 days.
- Cut your debt in half.
- Find your ideal relationship.
- Discover your dream job today.
- Fill your practice in less than 3 months.

Now, painting the vivid picture of the end result your prospects will experience from buying your product is only half the equation. While you may be able to communicate a clear benefit that prospects will experience from your product, that doesn't mean the benefit is strong enough for them to make a change. Let me say this in a different way. The current product or service the prospect is using may be "just fine" or "good enough." And if it's good enough, then why should the prospect spend money to make a change? As we discussed, the fear of change is the biggest fear of all when it comes to making a purchasing decision of any magnitude.

# Ouch, That Hurts! Selling the Pain

Before you can enroll someone in purchasing the desired state you can deliver on, there has to be enough pain or discomfort in the present state that would motivate the prospect enough to want to make a change and take action.

Therefore, you need to uncover what their current pain is and the cost of *not* making a change. What does it cost your prospects by not changing their current condition and keeping things just the way they are? Does it cost them money, time, stress, productivity, lost sales, a potential hazard, a great employee, their health?

**Closing Thoughts**

Help prospects visualize the advantage of moving from their present state to their desired state.

**Closing Bell**

In order for a prospect to buy from you, the cost of not changing must be greater than the cost of making a change.

When you can uncover what their pain is through the use of well-crafted questions (see Chapter 7), then and only then can you paint the picture of moving the prospect from their "painful" present state or condition to their desired state of benefits.

If you're sick, you want to get better. The pain associated with being sick encourages you to seek help to become healthy again. If you are miserable at your current job or are unemployed, this pain may be the driving force that is pushing you to find a new job in order to pay off your debt or start enjoying your life and career again.

There is a story of an officer in the army who did a fabulous job enrolling the new recruits in the government benefits available to them.

Officer Murphy was assigned to the induction center, where he advised new recruits about their benefits, especially their GI insurance.

It wasn't long before Captain Miller noticed that Officer Murphy was having a staggeringly high success rate selling the government insurance policy to nearly 100 percent of the recruits he advised. Rather than asking him about this, the captain stood at the back of the room and listened to Officer Murphy's presentation.

Murphy explained the basics of GI Insurance to the new recruits. "Nothing different here," thought the captain.

After Officer Murphy explained the basics, he shared the following insight with the new recruits. "If you are killed in a battle and have GI Insurance, the government has to pay $200,000 to your beneficiaries. However, if you don't have GI insurance and get killed in the battle, the government has to pay only a maximum of $6,000.

"Now," he concluded, "which group do you think they are going to send into battle first?"

As you can see, Officer Murphy did a great job extracting and then sharing the pain or cost of not purchasing the GI insurance in a way that the new recruits could understand and certainly relate to. The cost of not purchasing the insurance was now greater than the cost of purchasing the policy.

Pain is a greater motivator than pleasure. If you are in good health, you do not visit the doctor (unless you go to the doctor for annual checkups in order to prevent a future pain from occurring). If you are currently employed and happy with your job, chances are you are not actively seeking new employment.

# Wants and Needs—What Is the Difference?

Many people feel that these words are synonymous. They possess, however, very different meanings. For example, the basic necessities and needs for survival are as follows. The *need* for …

- ◆ Food
- ◆ Clothing
- ◆ Shelter

Without these basic necessities, survival within our society would be extremely difficult. With this in mind, let me share with you a story about someone I know. Her name is Jill. Like many of us, Jill certainly appreciates the finer things in life. Because of this, Jill may *want* …

♦ A cook to prepare the most fabulous gourmet meals for her.

♦ The latest in expensive, high-fashion clothing.

♦ A mansion with a swimming pool and a tennis court.

This goes beyond the things we need for survival. These wants or desires are items of luxury or comfort, more than what is needed to simply exist. Although these three wants still represent the model for basic necessities, they are the extreme reflection of them.

Let the purchase of a new car illustrate this point. The only way for Jill to get to work every day is by driving a car. There is no other source of transportation for her. In other words, Jill *needs* a car in order to get to her office. However, when Jill went shopping for a car, she *wanted* a convertible Mercedes. Unfortunately, Jill was able to afford only an economy car. As you can see, there is a dramatic difference between what someone may *want* and what that person actually *needs*.

I remember coaching a young man named Harry who recently started selling home improvements for a large remodeling company.

The appointments Harry went on were generated through telemarketing. Harry knew that when a telemarketer sets an appointment, he sells the appointment by offering the homeowners in the neighborhood a "free product demonstration." In Harry's mind, if a prospect can be sold over the phone on taking the estimate, then that prospect can be sold in person.

When Harry got to Mr. Jacobson's home, he noticed that the windows in the home were in very poor condition. After Harry heard the typical "You are wasting your time—I do not want new windows" from Mr. Jacobson, he managed to get the prospect seated at a table, where he began building a rapport with small talk. Harry then asked the prospect what he didn't like about his present windows. The prospect explained to Harry that he has been living with these windows for 10 years, so why change them? Besides, Mr. Jacobson *wanted* to purchase a new fishing boat for next summer's fishing season. In other words, Mr. Jacobson did not feel he *needed* new windows.

Harry got up and went to inspect one of the windows in Mr. Jacobson's home. Here's what Harry uncovered:

- The windows were in desperate need of a paint job.

- They needed to be cleaned.

- They were leaking a considerable amount of air, causing higher energy consumption.

- The lock was broken.

- They did not open very easily.

- When Harry finally opened one, it came slamming back down, almost catching all of Harry's fingers.

- One of the panes of glass was cracked.

In Harry's mind, this prospect needed new windows. However, it was up to Harry to enroll the prospect in feeling this same way and to make this enough of a priority for Mr. Jacobson to want to invest in new windows. Although Harry had already outlined in his mind the advantages Mr. Jacobson would realize with his new replacement windows, he knew it would take more than simply stating benefits. He needed to uncover the pain that Mr. Jacobson was unknowingly experiencing and the cost he would incur by not changing these windows. Harry needed to have the prospect want to take action to change his current condition. The advantages of Harry's product were as follows:

- Since Harry's windows were all vinyl, the prospect would never have to paint them.

- The sashes tilt in for easy cleaning. This way, the prospect would not need to risk death by climbing on a ladder to clean his second-story windows.

- Because of the high-efficiency double-paned glass in the window, Harry can guarantee in writing a percentage of savings on the prospect's energy consumption.

◆ Because safety is of paramount importance to most homeowners, the locking system is reinforced. This way, no one can easily pop the lock out of the sash and break into the home.

◆ The windows are also guaranteed never to stick. When the double-hung window is opened, it stays open.

◆ Because of the double-strength tempered glass in Harry's window, he can guarantee that the glass will not break under normal wear.

Harry continued by asking the right questions. He was able to elicit all of the disadvantages that Mr. Jacobson was currently experiencing with his windows. Doing so painted the pain Mr. Jacobson was experiencing by keeping these windows in his home. More important, Mr. Jacobson expressed the additional level of pain he would experience if he does not take action. Here's what the conversation sounded like.

Harry: "Mr. Jacobson, what are your current utility bills?"

Mr. Jacobson: "About $425 a month, on average."

Harry: "Mr. Jacobson, take a look at this utility chart that was given to me by the utility company. Notice what it is saying. Since you told me that you do not plan on moving any time in the near future, look how much money you will be spending over a period of 7 years on energy consumption alone. Gee, that is as much as a new fishing boat, isn't it?"

Mr. Jacobson: "Wow, it sure is."

Harry: "Now notice how much money you will be putting back into your pocket in energy savings alone once these windows are installed in your home. Mr. Jacobson, let me ask you what may sound like a silly question. Would you rather continue to pay the utility company all of this money, which I'm sure they would love, or put the money back into your biggest investment, your home? The best part is, with the amount of money you will be saving on your heating and cooling bills each year, you can use this savings to purchase and enjoy a nice new fishing boat."

Mr. Jacobson: "I see what you are saying. Now, how much money did you say I can save? Let me take a look at what you've got."

Harry: "Great. Let me go get my sample."

Harry knew he was walking away with a work order. He was able to uncover the current pain that Mr. Jacobson was experiencing. Initially, Mr. Jacobson looked at these windows as a costly expense. Harry enrolled Mr. Jacobson in realizing that the real cost was not taking action and making this investment. Harry moved the prospect away from the fear and cost of spending the money on new windows (an initial pain) to the cost he would incur by not doing so (present state). Finally, Harry clearly communicated the advantages of having them installed (desired state). The needs were so strong that it caused the prospect to want to take action.

### Closing Bell

It's not enough to uncover the want, since a want may not be strong enough for a prospect to make a purchase. The big difference between wants and needs is that needs often take longer to uncover.

It would not have been enough to simply list the advantages of having the new windows. The prospect may agree that he *wants* the new windows, but that does not mean that the *need* is strong enough for him to spend several thousand dollars. Conversely, Mr. Jacobson may still not want the new windows, but he realized as a result of Harry's presentation this is a need that must be filled.

A company may want to have a $50,000 computer system installed in the office to make it more efficient. However, the owner may feel that for $50,000, he can live with his current system and save the money. In other words, it is not enough to simply state the want. You must turn the want into the need or desire of ownership.

### Closing Thoughts

You need to build enough measurable value in the prospect's mind that the advantages of getting the product or service far outweigh the cost involved.

Prospects must feel that they will experience even more pain if they do not take action. The idea of taking no action will actually cause more pain for the prospect than taking the necessary action to change their condition and make the investment.

**Closing Bell**

Avoiding pain is often a greater motivator than gaining pleasure. Otherwise, there wouldn't be a market for selling insurance. After all, why do we spend thousands of dollars each year on insurance? So that in the unlikely event something bad happens, we are protected. Since using our insurance would suggest that something undesirable has happened, we certainly hope that we never have to use it.

Here are a few examples of needs that would cause a prospect to want to take action:

- I will be getting this done this year.

- I need a product that will help reduce my overhead.

- I want to make my employees more efficient with the help of a more powerful network and software program.

- I am looking for specific coverage and service that will enable me to protect my family.

- My sales team has to start using a universal selling process that's going to enable them to consistently reach their goals.

Keep in mind that when you uncover the need, it must be strong enough for the prospect to want to change.

1. A need may start out as a small want, problem, inconvenience, deficiency, or weakness that the prospect may have simply grown accustomed to and, as such, has learned to accept or work around it.

2. The salesperson must then bring this defect to the surface by stating the pain and cost involved if no change occurs.

3. This *want* will now become a *need* in the prospect's eyes, causing him to take action and change his current condition (moving from the present state to the desired state).

It is not enough to have prospects simply admit that they have a problem. It is up to the salesperson to be proficient enough to ask the right questions in order to uncover their pain. The prospects must perceive that the situation or problem is large enough to cause them to take action and change the current condition for a better future.

On the other hand, excitement in the prospect's voice, along with certain questions a prospect may ask, can act as buying signals.

# I Am Almost Ready to Buy

I've come across many salespeople who, although talented, have done a remarkable job selling themselves right out of a sale. They've been able to do so because they do not take the time to recognize when the prospect is comfortable enough to want to explore how they can make what you are selling become theirs. In other words, it's critical to be able to identify the buying signs so that you don't overtalk or oversell your product.

Buying signs are communication signals that suggest the prospect is now ready to discuss how they can take ownership of your product and how it would specifically benefit and work for them. In other words, they are now proverbially sold on your product or service and are ready to discuss what it would look like if they, in fact, did purchase from you.

If you fail to recognize the buying signs, you run the risk of overselling your product and missing out on the window of opportunity when the prospect is most receptive to becoming one of your clients. So if you continue sharing information or delivering your presentation to a prospect who has already sent out some buying signals, the prospect can interpret this as, "You are not listening to me. You are giving me information that I'm no longer interested in, so I'm shutting down and turning off my listening."

Buying signs can show up as early as the first few minutes of a conversation with a prospect, as well as at the very end of your meeting. Basically, they can show up at any time during your conversation. It's up to you to home in on these signals so that you can adjust accordingly and begin moving closer to asking for their business.

Here is a list of questions that would suggest to you that the prospect is interested enough in your product to want to gather more information regarding how it would fit.

1. Are there any other styles or colors to choose from?

2. How quickly can you get this project underway?

3. How long would it take to complete this project?

4. How much money do you need to begin this service?

5. Do you offer financing?

6. Have you done any work for other companies (neighbors) in this area?

7. Can I speak to one of your customers that you did work for?

8. What type of warranty comes with this product?

9. What type of service does your company offer?

10. Are there any other types of warranty coverage available?

11. Do I have to do the whole project now, or can I do it in stages?

12. Are there any other discounts available?

13. What sort of monthly installment can you offer me?

14. How will this work regarding my situation? (What type of results could I expect?)

Questions on turnaround time, integration, installation, delivery, date or start of service, available features, expected results, questions on product, and questions on installment terms should be interpreted as a sign that you are closer to earning a sale. Other questions a prospect may ask can be drawn from past purchasing experiences. Prospects who have had bad experiences in the past with either a company or a product need to know they are making the right purchasing decision this time. This can manifest itself as *support-building questions* asked by the prospect. Questions about problems from past experiences let you know that the prospect may be a bit timid and skeptical, and does not want this to happen again. These prospects are looking for the reassurance and support in knowing that, this time, they will be making the right decision in using your services.

**def•i•ni•tion**

**Support-building questions** are questions prospects ask that suggest they are looking for reassurance that they are making the right decision and will avoid any past unfavorable experiences they had.

Here are some examples of a prospect utilizing support-building questions:

1. I purchased this computer one year ago. When I called the company for a service call, I found out they have already gone out of business. I certainly do not want to go through that again. What's your company's background?

2. The last coverage I purchased from another insurance agent led me to believe that I had more coverage than I actually had. I need to know that I am going to be fully covered in case of an emergency. How can I be so sure that your policy is going to offer me this protection?

3. Is this for me?

4. Are you sure this is the best price you can give me?

5. So if I do make this purchase, this will be the last time I will ever have to worry about (this situation)?

6. Will this warranty cover any possible problems I may run into with your product?

7. What doesn't this warranty cover?

8. You don't think that your competitors can offer me something better?

You may find yourself in a situation in which the prospect has repeated the same question several times. Do not become annoyed. Using *repeat questions* is the prospect's way of telling you they just want a little more assurance before they make the purchase. The prospect may simply want to hear the answer he or she is looking for more than once. It can also mean the prospect hasn't fully grasped all of the information you have laid out for them, and needs to hear it once more.

**Repeat questions** are questions that prospects ask you, to suggest that they need more reassurance in making the right purchase this time around. Asking the same or a similar question more than once, as long as the salesperson responds with a consistent message, reinforces to the prospect that it is safe to move ahead with the purchase.

1. Can you review one more time what the warranty and service policy will cover?

2. Can you show me how your product works again?

3. Will you go over those financing terms once more?

4. How quickly is the turnaround time for account servicing?

5. So what this includes is ….

6. And you are sure that once I start using this ….

If you just open your eyes and ears, all the answers you're looking for that will enable you to close the sale are right there in front of you. And these answers to solidifying a sale are drawn from the utilization of powerful, thought-provoking questions.

## The Least You Need to Know

- Adapt your style of selling so that it complements each prospect's style of buying.

- Learn to recognize the buying signs that your prospects send you other than "Yes, I'm ready to buy."

- In order for a prospect to buy from you, the cost of not changing the current situation must be greater than the cost of making a change.

- Wants may be easier to identify than needs, but needs will motivate the prospect to take further action and buy from you.

♦ Pain, fear, risk, and consequence are always a greater motivator than pleasure.

♦ Adapting like a chameleon and, more specifically, harnessing the power of mirroring and reflecting enables you to align your communication style to how your prospects like to communicate and how they like to be sold.

# 2

# Showing Up as the Sales Champion Your Customers Expect

It's time to eliminate the barriers to the sale that your presentation, as well as your listening, actually create. In this part, we take time to ensure that you are not leaving any holes unplugged during your conversations with prospects that would prevent you from uncovering, addressing, and defusing all of their concerns and objections before you even ask for the sale. Here's your opportunity to become the powerful, authentic communicator you can be. When you stop the constant pitching and replace your pitch with a conversation infused with questions that prevent and defuse objections, you can listen for the sale rather than close it.

# Chapter 5

# The Enemy Within—
# Barriers We're Blind To

## In This Chapter

- ◆ Why you are still not listening
- ◆ Keep creating your own objections
- ◆ Remove the filter in your listening
- ◆ Stop selling the way you buy
- ◆ Change the way your prospects listen to you
- ◆ Eight barriers that prevent you from hearing the sale

I love paradoxes, mostly because our lives revolve around them. Over the years, I've compiled a list of my favorite paradoxes that have evolved into a set of universal principals for successful living that I share with my clients.

One of my favorite paradoxes is, we create the very problems that we hope to avoid. This chapter illustrates how we do so, especially as it relates to the way we listen to others.

I'm going to tell you straight. You're not listening. (You know by now that I don't pull any punches. However, I am told that they land very comfortably and softly most of the time.) I know that sounds really presumptuous, given the fact that we're only in Chapter 5 and I'm already talking to you like you're an old friend. (We should wait until at lest Chapter 10 when we get to know each other a little better, right?)

Now, I'm not referring to the listening you think you're doing, the way most of us interpret what it means to listen—that is, hearing the words out of the other person's mouth and understanding their spoken message. You may believe that you do this exceptionally well. However, there exist self-imposed barriers in our listening that we are not even aware of (until you read this chapter). The same obstacles prevent even this basic level of listening from being accomplished.

Here's your chance to permanently remove these barriers that pollute the listening process; what you can do to become a masterful listener.

# Don't Sell Like You Buy

I was almost at the end of the keynote I was delivering to an audience of Internet service providers in Tampa, Florida. As I brought the program to its natural conclusion, I let the audience know that I would open the floor to them to answer any questions they had.

Several hands went up. The third person I called on made a statement rather than asking a question.

"Keith, that sounds too salesy. I could never do that with a prospect." He was referring to the four qualifying questions that I claimed are guaranteed to bring in more sales when meeting with any prospect. (Don't worry, I wouldn't tease you like that. We unpack these questions in Chapter 8.)

"Sounds too salesy?" I wanted to confirm I heard him correctly. I responded to this gentleman with a question. "To whom?" I wondered.

"To me!" the person replied. "Those questions that you suggest we ask every prospect sound way too salesy to me. There's no way that would work with my prospects." (Said a different way, "There's no way I could ask those questions. I'm scared!")

I responded, "Well, I can certainly appreciate the fact that these questions may sound a bit different—or, as you say, salesy—to you (especially if you don't ask the prospect any questions, ever). But what about your prospects? How do they sound to them?"

"Huh?"

"When you ask these questions to your prospects, do they tell you that it sounds salesy to them?" I clarified.

"Sure."

"Really? Is that what they told you?"

"Not exactly," the person said, and then continued with, "I really don't know. I've never used these questions."

"Oh, so if you did use these questions, you're assuming that they would come across as salesy or unfavorable to your prospects. Is that what you're saying?"

"Yes."

I thanked this person for his comments and clarification, and then asked the entire audience how many people felt similar (that is, if they actually took the time to ask the questions—which they never did—they would feel that it wouldn't be something that would work for them). A majority of hands went up.

I then asked a question to the audience. "How many people have heard of the Sahara Desert?" Most of the hands in the audience went up. I then asked, "How many people here have actually had the firsthand experience of visiting the Sahara Desert and experiencing it for themselves?" No hands went up.

"So then, how do you know it even exists?"

Silence. I then continued, "If you've never experienced it, then how do you know it's real? Just like the questions I suggest that you start using, to make your sales efforts pay off more than ever. If you've never used these questions, then you really have no idea whether they will work or how they will be received by your prospects."

I was building my case. I then turned to the audience and said, "Do not sell the way you buy."

Now, you may feel at this point that I'm contradicting myself. After all, we discussed how important it was to empathize and sympathize with your prospects and clients.

However, there's a very fine line between understanding and respecting someone's decision-making process and assuming that everyone makes a purchasing decision in the same manner and using the same criteria that you do. Moreover, there is the faulty assumption that your prospects respond in a similar fashion to the type of sales approach and the type of salesperson that you respond to and would buy from.

 **Closing Bell**

The belief that "People buy from people who they like" doesn't mean you should sell the way you buy. Learn to draw a clear separation between a proven permission-based sales process and your buying process/how you buy.

I then shared a personal example of the dangers of selling like you buy. "Folks, if I sold in the same manner in which I make a purchase and then, in turn, transferred those values and beliefs to each prospect that I speak with, I could tell you with great certainty that I would not be up here talking with you today."

Here's the reason: When I make a purchase of any substantial amount, I take the time to research my options and learn about the different products or services available. By the time I'm ready to actually make the purchase, whether it's something for my home, a television, a car, or a computer, more often than not, I know more about the product, the competition, and the marketplace than the person who is attempting to sell it to me.

My point is, if I started selling the way in which I make a purchasing decision, I would be putting my values, thought process, and beliefs on the customer, assuming that they purchase the same or in a similar way that I do. The result? More objections, fewer sales.

Besides, what if I was talking with an impulse prospect who was ready to buy? I would be talking myself right out of the sale!

The old adage of putting yourself in their shoes is really a costly assumption that destroys many a selling opportunity. Why? Because when you "look through their eyes" or attempt to see things how you assume they see them, it is still really what you see, not what they see.

The result? You develop a sales process based on how you think they buy rather than how they actually make a decision. Why? Because how you think they buy is really how *you* buy. Is your brain twisted enough yet?

If you truly want to wear their shoes, then you need to know how they think and what is important to them. Therefore, the only way to uncover how prospects like to process information and make a purchasing decision, and the criteria they use to do so, is by asking better questions.

Now, let's take this same ineffective model of selling like you buy and turn it around for a moment. If this belief of selling like the way you buy is getting in the way of taking certain actions or asking certain questions when on a sales call, then what about other things that you are doing or saying that you think are safe to you but, in fact, are not safe or comfortable for the person you are speaking with because you're still operating off the same tool: costly assumptions!

Salespeople who sell in the same manner in which they buy are sure to have a lower number of satisfied clients. Take a look at some different scenarios in which utilizing your own beliefs, assumptions, and value system can have a detrimental effect on your performance and income.

 **Closing Thoughts** ___

The lesson: don't believe everything you sell, I mean, tell yourself.

1.  Since Carol usually shops around before choosing which company to buy from or which product to buy, she accepted the prospect's reason for doing the same. Like herself, she couldn't expect people to make a decision during the initial consultation.

**Closing Bell** ___

Putting yourself in the prospect's shoes and selling like the way you buy is a collapse of two distinct and different ideas. Consider this. What does it feel like after walking around all day in a pair of shoes that are two full sizes too small? Selling the way you buy operates off assumptions, while putting yourself in their shoes operates off the powerful use of well-crafted questions. Otherwise, you know you're bound to be walking in a pair of shoes that do not fit.

2. When Mike makes a purchasing decision, he usually purchases the least expensive item available. He thinks you can get the same top value at a lowest price. Although he represents one of the highest-quality products in his industry, the amount of money he sold for was always at the lowest profit margin. Mike had a hard time asking for more money, even though he was offering the consumer the highest in value.

3. Robert hated hearing sales presentations. When he went out on his appointments, he was always done within 30 minutes. In order to effectively cover all of the necessary information and provide the right solutions for the prospect, the average time a representative should invest during an appointment was between 2 and 3 hours.

4. Dana was very indecisive when it came to making a purchasing decision. Because this was inherent in her personality, she offered her customers many different alternatives. The end result was confusion on the consumer's end and on Dana's end, and no work order. Some salespeople out there are even more indecisive than their prospects. Can you see it? "I'll ask for the order now. No, I'll wait a little longer. No, I might miss the opportunity to do so later, so I'd better do it now." This can clearly put a damper on your performance as well as your mental health.

5. There was never a "right time" for Bob to purchase a new car. When prospects explained to Bob that they had other commitments, he totally understood and told them that he would call them back when the time was right.

6. Rhonda always bought from salespeople who were overzealous and aggressive. She tried to emulate that same disposition on every sales call she went on.

### Closer's Corner

People make purchasing decisions based on their style of buying, not yours.

Sell in the manner in which you were trained to sell, and stick with the proven selling sequence that works for you and within your industry. You cannot expect prospects to purchase in the same manner as you do.

If you sell in the same manner as you buy, you are instilling your beliefs in other people. Since every person's beliefs and buying habits are different, every prospect processes information differently. What is important to one person may not be important to another. Therefore, there will never be two presentations exactly the same.

As you will discover in the next chapter, you must learn to adapt your presentation around the values of each specific prospect. One prospect might weigh company stability and the quality or value of the product as the most important aspects in making a decision, but another prospect might weigh price as the most important.

We now shift our focus to another area that will have a profound impact on your ability to close. You can further remove toxic and poor communication and selling habits by sharpening one of the most critical skills in selling: your ability to actively and deeply listen. Doing so will enable you to actually listen the sale right out of your prospects.

# Stop Talking, Start Listening Deeply

Later in this guide, we discuss how selling is not telling. Asking questions and getting feedback from the prospect is selling. If that's the case, why do salespeople insist on talking more than the prospect? Salespeople feel, psychologically, that if they are talking more, then they are the ones in control. Salespeople also feel that if the prospect allows them to continue to talk, then that prospect must be interested in the product or service and, therefore, must be close to buying. Wrong interpretation.

Studies have shown that the most effective sales professionals have the biggest egos or highest level of self-confidence. As such, these salespeople have the need to be in charge or the center of attention. This is why some salespeople love delivering presentations. They feel as if the energy and spotlight is focused on them. However, this causes more collateral damage than it assists in closing more business. Only the insightful sales professional realizes that he must take a step out of the spotlight in order to place the prospect under it.

> **Closer's Corner**
>
> Salespeople lose more sales for the simple reason that they do not know when to stop talking and start listening!

The fact is, the prospect should be the one doing most of the talking. If we were to divide it into percentages, the prospect should be talking approximately 70 percent of the time, and the salesperson should be talking or responding to what the prospect asks or says about 30 percent of the time.

**Closing Thoughts**

The person who talks may dominate the conversation, but it is the person who listens who controls the situation.

Most of the time, salespeople think that they are actually listening to what the prospect is saying. In reality, they are too busy planning what they are going to say in response to a statement or an objection the prospect made.

Have you ever been to a social engagement where you are listening to someone else's story, only to wait for the person to finish the story so you can begin your own? This is not an example of active listening.

Active listening requires focusing and paying attention in order to hear the value in every message. As a salesperson, you need to concentrate on the prospect's words and the message behind the words, and then let the prospect know that you not only heard, but correctly interpreted what the prospect said. Whew!

**Closing Thoughts**

During a sales call, a salesperson does not learn anything from listening to his own talk.

The greatest skill or talent worth exploiting and continually strengthening that always pays a huge return is the ability to listen deeply—not only to what the prospect is saying, but also what the prospect is implying or not saying.

We think we listen, but in reality, we do not. If we did, then the leading cause of failure in the selling community would not be the inability to effectively listen.

There exist hidden messages or meanings behind the words the prospect uses to communicate with you. It is ultimately your responsibility to effectively interpret what the prospect is actually saying. A salesperson can learn and master certain precautions and skills in order to listen more deeply. First, we take a moment to uncover some of the myths, barriers, and destructive listening habits salespeople have.

# You're Still Not Listening

I'd like you to read the following article that I found online at Realtor. com. I figured that mortgage rates and homeownership are something that many of us have in common.

> Mortgage Rates Continue Climbing Upward—The 30-year mortgage rate jumped this week to a 16-month high of 6.31 percent, according to the latest Freddie Mac report.
>
> The 1-year adjustable mortgage rate rose as well, reaching a 3 1/2-year high of 5.09 percent, while the 5-year hybrid ARM climbed to 5.76 percent from 5.03 percent in January.
>
> Freddie Mac chief economist Frank Nothaft attributes the gains to higher energy costs and unexpectedly strong economic growth during the third quarter, which sparked concerns about inflation.
>
> Housing affordability has been pinched because increases in ARMs have outpaced fixed rates since the start of the year, according to Mortgage Bankers Association chief economist Doug Duncan.
>
> Source: *USA Today*; Sandra Block

Now, without referring back to this article, do your best to answer the following questions. (No peeking!)

1. When did the 30-year mortgage rate jump to a 16-month high? What was it?

2. How about for the adjustable rate?

3. What was the source of this article?

4. What's the name of Freddie Mac's chief economist?

5. According to Mortgage Bankers Association chief economist Doug Duncan, housing affordability has been pinched. What was his reasoning?

If you can't answer these questions, that's perfectly normal and illustrates my point. The fact is, listening is not a passive activity. It's something you have to do actively, with a conscious level of practice, effort, concentration, and focus.

It is said that more than 70 percent of all problems within the workplace and with your customers are a result of faulty communication.

So the question is, "Are you really listening when you think you are?" According to several studies, people who think they are good listeners are actually listening at only 35 to 45 percent of their listening capacity—that is, their ability to truly listen to the entire message, both verbally and nonverbally.

So if good listeners are operating at only around 40 percent of their listening capability, imagine the capability at which those people who feel they are poor listeners are truly listening? And if you feel that you're a good listener, consider what new opportunities are available for you if you're still operating at only 40 percent effectiveness as it relates to your listening potential.

During the communication process, there is always a point at which a failure to actively listen can result in mistakes and misunderstanding, especially with our co-workers and clients, dramatically affecting the results you seek to achieve during a conversation and throughout your selling efforts.

Failure to identify or confirm with a client the next step in the selling process, unfulfilled expectations, or the inability to actively listen for what the client really needs can dramatically affect the results sales professionals seek to achieve—the very same thing that limits our ability to sell more.

Now, if we know that effective listening makes a dramatic difference, why don't we listen better? Probably because it takes hard work, patience, the ability to interpret other people's ideas and recap them, concentration, open-mindedness, the ability to separate logic from emotion, and the ability to identify nonverbal voice tones, gestures, and body language.

Listening is a very complex process as well as a learned skill that requires conscious effort. It requires the utilization of all of our senses. Active listening or listening deeply is an organic, ever-evolving process involving both our intellect and our emotions.

The ability to actively listen has been proven to dramatically improve relationships and performance, and is, ironically, the least-developed skill in communication and among salespeople.

Often we simply get tired of listening, and much of this is due to the constant bombardment of stimulation we receive from the media. Words come at us every day, and much of this takes the form of advertising, in which someone is pushing us to buy something or try something or do something. Soon screening out this outside noise becomes a habit, further adding to the challenge of being able to tell the difference between what is important and what isn't.

What blocks our ability to fully listen? Why don't we listen? Let's begin by looking at the following situations and roadblocks to masterful listening to determine whether any of these behaviors describe you.

# Eight Barriers That Prevent You from Listening

What causes a salesperson not to listen? Here are the top eight barriers to clear and powerful listening.

1. Are you doing something else while the client is talking? Are you thinking about the next call, how much money you will make if you sell, or what you will be eating for dinner?

2. During your conversation with a client, do you wait for a pause so you can spit something out?

3. How difficult is it for you to stay quiet? Do you say something without thinking first?

4. Are you faking your listening to the client just so you can get in your comments?

5. Do you practice selective listening? Do you hear only the things you want to hear?

6. Are you aware of the message the person is sending other than the words, through body language such as facial expressions, eye contact, and vocal intonation?

7. Do you allow background noise or your environment to hinder your ability to listen?

   If any of these behaviors seem familiar, you are creating a huge barrier that limits your ability to fully listen.

Although we have mentioned various factors that limit our ability to fully listen, there exists another barrier we have created in our listening that we aren't even aware of: the *filter* we've created in our listening.

8. Do you listen through filters? Yes, whether you realize it or not, we all do. When you listen through a filter, you are listening based on a past experience or belief or based on some type of anticipated future outcome. When you pass judgment on people by their age, success, or how they look, and when you invalidate people based on what you see or based on a similar situation with another client, you build a wall between yourself and the other person that prevents clear and unrestricted communication and understanding of the message being received.

## def•i•ni•tion

You may use a filter when you make your coffee every morning. Or you might use a filter to remove any impurities in water you want to clean, like the filter in your refrigerator or in your home drinking water. The **filters** that exist in our listening are already embedded in our listening, preventing us from being able to listen beyond our past beliefs and experiences and our future expectations. Since a filter prevents this, you cannot recognize or create new selling opportunities because you will continue to re-create the past.

# Listening Through Filters—Selective Listening

Have you ever met someone and, based on their appearance, passed judgment on them? When you walk by a homeless person on the street, what do you say to yourself? Would you take the advice of this person as quickly as you would from someone you respect and admire? The information might be just as valuable, yet too often the person delivering the message determines whether we will listen to what they are saying.

Unfortunately, because we pass judgment based on what we see, what we *hear* is not always the message that is being *said*. People's age, their disposition, what they look like, how much money we think they have, how successful they are, their voice, the car they drive, or the house they live in all act as barriers to effective listening. When we validate or invalidate people based on what we see or perceive, it prevents clear and unrestricted communication and understanding.

Here's a story that illustrates this point. I remember attending a financial seminar with a friend of mine. The last one I went to was very informative. However, my friend's experience was different. He remembered that the last seminar he had attended was a waste of his time. He felt that the speaker had not imparted any new knowledge to him. As we were walking into this seminar, think about the internal dialogue he had with himself: "I'll bet this will be a waste of time also. I'm probably not going to get anything out of this but lunch."

At the end of the seminar, my friend walked away from the seminar feeling uninspired (yet full), while I had gained a good amount of valuable information.

Both of us heard the same information yet listened to two entirely different messages.

And what about the client who, based on appearance or attitude, you were certain wasn't going to buy from you no matter what you did? Maybe you felt that this person couldn't afford your product or service or was not the decision maker.

You then come to find out a week later that the prospect purchased something from your competitor—and at a higher price, to boot, and with not as much value. Ouch.

The fact is, we listen differently to our spouse, our boss, a stranger, children, our customers, a store clerk, and our friends, evaluating the messenger over the message.

That's why the greatest barrier to listening is the filter we created in the way we listen.

When you listen through a filter, you are listening based on a past experience or belief or a future expectation. Another way of saying this is, you are already listening to the message before you even hear the message. You've anticipated what the

## Closer's Corner

The polar opposite of filtered listening is pure listening. As such, how adept you become at listening actively and deeply will be clearly reflected in the results of your closing efforts.

other person is going to say or how the person is going to react based on a set of judgments you have that, for the most part, are grossly inaccurate.

**Closing Thoughts**

"Treat people the way you want to be treated" is a common phrase of wisdom. Here's another version by Keith Rosen:

"Listen to people the way you want to be listened to."

Everyone has a gift to give. Believing so refocuses you to start recognizing the value in every message.

Because we pass judgment based on what we see, perceive, or have experienced in the past, what we *hear* is not always the message that is being *said*.

For example, have you ever spoken with a customer and, based on that person's appearance, race, sex, age, or disposition, already begun listening from a past experience about another customer in a similar situation?

Let's do a quick exercise to uncover a few of the filters in your listening. I will begin a sentence and you finish it by saying out loud the first thing that comes to your mind, okay? (Unless, of course, the environment in which you're reading this book is not conducive to yelling out a gut reaction. Make sure you do this in a quiet space, away from people who may be offended by your behavior.)

After each question, pay close attention to your first reaction, the initial adjectives, thoughts, or assumptions (right, wrong, good, or bad!) that come to mind regarding how you perceive each topic. Pause briefly after each question to give yourself some time and space to recognize how you instinctively respond. Complete the following sentences:

Politicians are:

1. _____

2. _____

3. _____

My prospects and customers are:

1. _____

2. _____

3. _____

My boss is:

1. _____

2. _____

3. _____

My family is:

1. _____

2. _____

3. _____

Salespeople are:

1. _____

2. _____

3. _____

Take note of your visceral reactions to appreciate the value of this lesson. You are listening from a certain place. That is, you have identified several filters in your listening! As a result, these filters in your listening are all you are going to tune in to and hear. That selective listening you have around these people will actually tune in to what you want to hear based on your assumptions, and beliefs, preventing you from listening to the full and intended message.

To further illustrate this, let me share a quick story with you.

It's about the most important woman in my world, my mom. (Okay, I got clearance from my wife to write this—are you happy now? Let's continue.)

As I've mentioned, we all are constantly listening from a certain place. That's our filter. With my mom, I was listening from a place of, well, "My mom's a little annoying."

Don't get me wrong, I love my mom dearly. She's the greatest person in the world and has been a wonderful role model. It's just that, even years later with no evidence to support my feelings (well, a little evidence), when I would talk to my mom on the telephone or in person, I was already listening from past experiences.

Now, these past experiences probably are ones that happened when I was a kid or an adolescent (and from my understanding, I was not the easiest kid). So based on some decision I may have made years ago in terms of how I will relate to my mom, I, in turn (we all do it), carried this with me in how I related to her to the present day. This manifests itself in the way we listen and communicate with people.

Then I discovered this concept of filtered listening. And I had a breakthrough. You see, it really wasn't that my mom was annoying (see, Mom, I got to talk myself out of this here). It was more the fact that she loved me, she cared about me, and she wanted to be a part of my life even when we lived in different states.

So the million-dollar question is, "Did my mom change?" Did she suddenly become coachable? Not exactly. You see, my mom didn't change at all. What changed was the way I listened to her.

Once I was aware of the filter I had regarding how I listened to my mom, I was able to recognize it, choose to remove it, and adjust how I listened to her, which is now coming from a place of love, family, and understanding. This, in turn, made our conversations and our relationship richer and stronger.

### Closing Thoughts

It was how I listened to my mom that changed, nothing else. So if you want other people to change how they listen to you, you must first change how you listen to them. Imagine what would be possible if you applied this in every area of your life.

Later on, you're introduced to a new concept that's going to affect, once again, how you think. That is, we actually assume how and what people think and what they will do.

To take this concept to another level, I'm suggesting that we also assume what people will tell us or what we will hear and, as a result, react accordingly!

During a conversation, have you ever heard someone say, "I know what you're going to say"? And then cut you off in midsentence to continue with a rebuttal to what they think you are going to say? If this is how you communicate, then what do you need the other person in the conversation for? Just kidding. However, these types of communicators seem to be very effective having a conversation by themselves. But I don't suppose you know anyone like this, right?

Learn to focus on *how* you listen. These negative listening habits salespeople demonstrate act as a catalyst to poor communication between the salesperson and the prospect. In other words, these habits can cause a prospect to *stop listening to you.*

**Closing Thoughts**

We have all been given two ears and one mouth. Therefore, we can surmise that it is more important to listen than it is to talk.

# When a Prospect Stops Listening to You

There are many reasons why someone would stop listening to you. Ironically, other than either hanging up the phone or walking away, most people miss out on the subtle cues that should tell you the other person is no longer listening to you.

Here are some of the main reasons people stop listening:

- ◆ They have formulated an opinion, belief, conclusion, or response.

- ◆ They have been turned off or felt invalidated by the salesperson.

- ◆ The salesperson is not saying anything that the prospect wants to hear, is interested in, or asked for.

- ◆ The prospect was not asked for any feedback, comments, or questions within a certain time frame. Communication is two way. You must get feedback from the prospect every minute or so, to ensure that the person is maintaining focus, interest, and understanding.

- ◆ They decide to interrupt the salesperson in order to say something. In other words, they are tired of listening to you!

Aside from listening to the verbal communication of the prospect, physical actions and gestures from the prospect will communicate what the prospect feels. Here are some examples of what to look out for (if you have the luxury of being in front of them, that is.)

- Clock watching
- Yawning
- Perspiration
- Irritability
- Wandering eyes
- Body movements

What does it mean when the prospect is yawning or watching the clock? It is time to either get the prospect more involved or energize your presentation. It could also mean that the prospect has some other engagement or responsibility that you are taking him or her away from.

If you see a bead of sweat forming on the prospect's brow, he may be experiencing some type of anxiety or nervousness, possibly the pressure to make a purchasing decision.

Is there eye contact, or are the prospect's eyes wandering around the room? This could be a result of a loss of interest or focus. The prospect, believe it or not, may also be lying to you! (Be careful! In some cultures, direct eye contact is disrespectful.)

Here are some questions to determine when you are listening through a filter:

1. Do you give everyone you speak with the same respect and gift of your listening? Do you feel that you are supposed to value the message differently depending upon who is delivering the message?

2. Do you listen differently to your spouse, your boss, a stranger, a prospect, a customer, or a friend?

3. Do you judge people when you are listening to them? Rich or poor? Status? Looks? Age? Dress? Sex? Race?

4. Do you stop listening when you think you know and can anticipate what the person is going to say? In many instances, a salesperson may feel that he already "knows it all" because he has "heard it all." So the salesperson jumps to a conclusion and interrupts the person speaking because he feels that he knows what the person is going to say.

5. Do you pass judgment based on regional or ethnic accents? When a phone call to a company is answered by a receptionist with a British accent, that person is likely to convey an image of being intelligent and better organized, creating a positive impression of the company.

6. (Here's another example of filtered listening.) How good are you at remembering people's names? You may have been in a position in which you were introduced to someone and two seconds later realize that you forgot their name. Why do you think that is so?

   It's not a result of a bad memory, but the fact you weren't listening. And if you weren't listening, chances are, you were doing something else, such as prejudging, passing judgment, and evaluating the person you were speaking with.

C'mon, you all had a certain perception of your humble and authentic coach and author when you first read my bio, saw my picture, or visited my website.

And when you found out that my follow-up book to my first best-seller, *The Complete Idiot's Guide to Cold Calling*, was going to be entitled *The Complete Idiot's Guide to Closing the Sale*, you may have had a certain reaction as well!

That reaction could have sounded like, "Why an idiot's guide? I'm not an idiot! Oh, I get it—he's poking fun and making a tough topic a bit lighter. Duh." Or "Another book on closing? What can Keith teach me that I don't already know?" or "I am so pumped to get into this book! Keith's last book rocked and made me a ton of money!"

Now, that reactive assumption and judgment, which we all hand over too much power and credibility to, would have changed if I was standing in front of you delivering a seminar, or if I was older or younger, richer or poorer, of varying perceived status, a different sex, a celebrity, and so on.

Because we judge people when we are listening to them based on what we see, it prevents us from giving everyone we speak with the same respect and gift of our listening.

I mentioned earlier in this book the concept of making learning a part of your lifestyle. Regarding the ability to listen deeply, we talked about embracing the message in every experience and in every conversation or interaction with a prospect or customer.

However, if you are busy passing judgment or not respecting other people's opinions or points of view, then you can't learn from them. At any point in time, you can be given a solution that would better your situation, but because of the filter in your listening, because of your judgment, you cannot to hear it.

Somewhere during our development we were taught to listen to and communicate in a different fashion depending upon who we were talking with—your staff, your family, your co-workers, even your customers.

> **Closer's Corner**
>
> Guess what? Your prospects are forming their own conclusion the minute you open your mouth, which is *whether they will buy from you.*

The next time you're on a sales call, rather than assuming the objection, how the prospect makes a buying decision, what the prospect knows, or what the prospect wants to hear, follow these suggestions to create more selling opportunities.

To sharpen your ability to listen and remove your filter, here are a few things you can do immediately, starting with boosting your awareness and sensitivity to the truth—or, I should say, the facts. (We confuse the two.)

# Just the Facts, Please

When clients ask for help in closing more sales, I ask them to list the objections they are hearing that prevented the sale. It's when they start stumbling over their response that I ask, "Are these the objections you are hearing directly from your prospects or what you're assuming is the reason they don't buy?"

"I told a prospect that I'd follow up within a week. Two weeks later, I figured I missed my chance and they went with someone else." Sound familiar?

Effective salespeople don't guess themselves into a sale. To ensure you're operating with the facts, ask yourself this, "Do I have evidence to support my assumption or how I'm feeling?"

Enjoy the peace of mind that comes from gaining clarity by relying solely on the facts rather than drowning in the stories that you believe are true.

## The Least You Need to Know

◆ Sell and present in the manner in which your prospects like to buy, not the way you like to buy.

◆ Listen for what is not said. What is implied is often more important than what is spoken.

◆ Listen with an open mind, without preconceived notions, judgments, or beliefs you created or perceived.

◆ Recognize the hidden cues when a prospect is no longer listening to you.

◆ If you sell the way you buy, you are creating the very objections that you are hoping to avoid.

◆ When you listen through a filter, you are allowing either past experiences or future expectations to cloud your thinking and ability to listen for new selling opportunities.

# Chapter 6

# Advanced Listening Strategies

## In This Chapter

- ◆ Listen for the sale and for the right time to ask for it
- ◆ Encourage silence to close more sales
- ◆ Make people feel heard
- ◆ Eliminate communication breakdowns that destroy sales
- ◆ Develop critical listening skills

"You've got to be kidding me! Another chapter on listening? Keith, I get how important it is, but another whole chapter? C'mon let's get to the closing stuff!"

My dear reader, we are deep in the closing stuff. Maybe we should do a review. Now, have I ever, in all of my books, blogs, forums, articles, and coaching, ever steered you wrong? We both know the answer, so just trust your coach on this one—again.

What, you need an incentive? Fine, if you don't get at least one big gem from this chapter, call me and I'll take the money out of my wallet and refund you personally.

In this chapter, we discuss the additional barriers to effective listening, as well as proven techniques that will enable you to become the Zen master of listening.

# You're Prejudging, Not Prequalifying

To eliminate any confusion, let's draw a distinction between what it means to prequalify and prejudge someone such as a prospect. As you know if you read my book *The Complete Idiot's Guide to Cold Calling*, I'm a strong advocate of prequalifying anyone before you invest your very limited and precious time in them. Conversely, prejudging someone is something you do that shows up in the filter you have in your listening.

Here's another way to distinguish between the two. When you are prequalifying someone, you are arriving at a conclusion that determines whether there's a fit worth pursuing based on a defined set of criteria that you uncover through the use of well-crafted questions. Prejudging, said simply, is all about you. Here you are relying on your faulty and costly assumptions, thoughts, and beliefs to determine prospects' needs and whether they will potentially buy from you.

---

### Closer's Corner

When you prejudge someone, you're making assumptions before you ask any questions or uncover any facts.

When you prequalify someone, you're asking questions to uncover the prospect's unique and specific needs without making any assumptions so that you can determine very quickly whether there is, in fact, an authentic fit worth pursuing.

---

# Encouraging Silence Closes More Sales

Many of us wait only a split-second to respond to a person's comments, questions, or objections. And when we actually know the answer, it expedites our reaction even more. Sorry, you don't get any extra points for going faster. You actually lose more sales this way than you'd care to realize. But enough about dwelling in the past. We've got an awesome future filled with sales to create just for you!

Now, many of us are uncomfortable with silence; we feel the need to fill it with superficial talk. But imagine if you can get comfortable with silence. Look at the opportunity you are going to create.

If you are comfortable encouraging silence and most of your prospects are not, then what do you think will happen? They're going to talk more. Chances are, if they talk more, they are going to tell you more—more about what is important to them,

> **Closer's Corner**
>
> Look at the two words *silent* and *listen*. Notice that these words share the exact same letters.

how they want to be treated during this process, how they like to be sold and how they make decisions, and their fears or concerns.

As natural as the sun rising each day, you are going to learn more about them effortlessly, giving you an edge over your competition—who, by the way, is also uncomfortable with silence.

Ironically, one of the easiest gauges to recognize whether you are listening to the prospect is the most obvious. It is simply this: become aware of how long you actually wait before responding to a prospect's comments or questions. Most salespeople do not wait longer than a split-second before their lips are moving and they begin to sputter something that is generic, shallow, insincere, and meaningless—you know, the stuff you say to someone that you wind up regretting that you said later.

Here's how to combat this. Get in the habit of waiting a minimum of *3 to 5 seconds* before responding to a prospect. You must consciously count to yourself to ensure that enough time has elapsed before replying. This conscious pause accomplishes five essential objectives and establishes you as a sales champion, leading to more sales with less effort.

1. Encouraging silence creates a safe environment for that person to explore their feelings and ideas with you. Although many people find it challenging to stay quiet, since it takes a conscious effort

(5 seconds can feel like a lifetime during a closing situation), silence creates the space that will motivate the other person to say more.

2. Encouraging silence provides you with additional time to effectively process the information you have received. It gives you the opportunity to truly weigh what the prospect is saying or trying to say. This gives you enough time to respond thoughtfully and intelligently to the prospect's specific comments, needs, and questions.

3. Encouraging silence builds trust and credibility. It shows the prospect that you are not just regurgitating the first thing that comes to mind or shooting from the hip. This adds more credibility to you and to what you are saying. By contemplating thoughtfully, it shows that you care about and have a genuine interest in and concern for the other person, and that you understand that person's specific needs and have a way to fill each one.

4. Encouraging silence motivates the prospect to share more information. Encouraging silence motivates the prospect to talk. As we've painfully established, no one likes uncomfortable silence. It is an insecurity of most people. Most people feel they would rather fill silence with superficial conversation. For a prospect, this silence will create a safe place to talk more. The real issue is making sure that the salesperson keeps his mouth shut. This is not an easy task. Doing this will take time as well as a conscious effort. It is human nature to fill silence with noise. Learn to keep silent—free from unnecessary static and interference that you may produce during the conversation.

5. Encouraging silence enables you to resist the rebuttal. Here's an interesting statistic. People can listen to between 400 and 500 words per minute, yet we speak only about 150 words per minute. As you can see, there's a clear gap between our speaking speed and our listening speed. The problem? We usually fill it with daydreaming, arguing, and thinking what we will be saying next.

And to add to this challenge, people have a natural tendency to resist any new information that conflicts with what they believe. Often enough, when we hear someone saying something with which we might disagree, we immediately begin formulating a rebuttal in our minds that can obscure the message we are receiving. And if we are focused on creating a rebuttal, we can't be listening.

Remember, you can always rebut later, after you have heard the whole message and had time to think about it.

## Focus More on the Message Than on the Messenger

Another simple yet powerful technique to improve your listening is this: focus on the content or message the person is delivering, not solely on the messenger.

This will prevent you from passing judgment or listening through a filter or from a past experience. Realize that the message is what should take precedence in normal conversation.

To compound this challenge, we have a tendency to group together all of our prospects and clients, and listen to them as if they are all one person with the same goals, needs, objections, and challenges.

This is, in fact, another filter in our listening, and it gets us in trouble because it's where the assumptions usually start growing. As such, this creates a barrier to learning and listening to the authentic needs and the type of person each prospect truly is, as an individual.

Now, you may be thinking, "Well, Keith, sure. I can do my best to change how I listen, but what about how everyone else—especially my prospect—listens to me?"

Great question; I'm thrilled you asked. Here's my response, in the form of another question back to you.

"Whose listening do you think needs to change first? Yours or your prospect's?"

> **Closing Bell**
> Have you ever gone to a doctor's office for an appointment and felt that you were part of an assembly line? We've all been there. How do you feel if you were treated like a commodity rather than a person? So while you are going to focus on the message, do so while honoring each client's individuality.

Yours, of course. So the benefit here is this. When you successfully remove the filters in your listening, you'll miraculously notice that the way in which your prospects listen and communicate with you has changed as well. (If you still don't see a change, please give me a call.)

Finally, to increase your spider senses and listen the sale out of a client, let's draw a distinction that will further impact your ability to listen. I call it listening to versus listening for.

# Listening "to" Someone or Listening "for" Something

Consider that most of the time we spend *listening to* information in the course of a conversation with our clients. Simply, this is when we hear the words they've used, often the noise coming out of the person's mouth that many have referred to as words. As you may have rightfully surmised, this is more of a passive and desperately ineffective listening approach.

However, when you are *listening for* information, you are looking under the words to explore the implied meaning behind them. This prevents you from listening through a filter and wrongly prejudging or misinterpreting the message that the person is really communicating to you.

There are five main things we listen for when speaking with a prospect. Although we can spend a good portion of time on each one, for now I want you to be aware of them so that you can begin practicing and building on each one. Moreover, you'll be developing questions to ask every prospect that will enable you to identify these five essential areas that we need to be sensitive to and listen for.

1. Listen for people's needs. What are their desired results, goals, or expectations? It's often obvious what they may want, but what do they really need?

**Closing Thoughts**

Decide that people are worth listening to.

2. Listen for the truth. While you certainly want to collect the indisputable evidence and facts to support your selling efforts, you also want to consider what is not being said—people's

emotions, reactions, body language, and so on. Rather than base the truth solely on the obvious facts that the prospect is sharing with you, or worse, on a combination of facts and expectations/ filters, listen for the additional nonverbal messages to uncover any inconsistencies and ensure that the prospect's spoken truth is aligned with what they are not saying.

3. Listen for pain, concerns, and fears. What aren't prospects saying that they are concerned about? What are their worries, their problems, and their fears that are going to delay or stall the sale?

4. Listen for buying signs. How do your prospects buy? What are their values, their decision-making process, and so on? What criteria have you developed that enables you to recognize the buying signs of your prospects?

5. Listen for what is missing, or for what I call The Gap. Listen for The Gap. After all, this is what you are ultimately presenting to your prospects—that is, your solution, which, in turn, fills their void, gap, or problem. So sell the gap! Your solution, product, or service becomes the bridge that takes prospects from where they are today (present state) to where they want to be (desired state).

Keep in mind that this can be different from what they want or need. This is something that the prospects themselves may not even be aware of. If you can identify this gap, you can then bridge it with the right solution.

For example, a client of mine hired me to train their sales team. As I explored deeper, I discovered that the company was experiencing a large amount of turnover. There were many inconsistencies and breakdowns during their recruiting and hiring process. Nothing was documented as it relates to a process that people could follow consistently to attract the best talent, especially when it came to screening candidates and developing a strong retention plan to retain their new hires.

I found that they were experiencing a 35 percent attrition rate. I proposed not only providing a sales training program, but also creating a more in-depth solution to developing and strengthening their recruiting and retention strategy to reduce the amount of attrition, which would complement the training.

The result was a comprehensive recruitment and retention strategy that ultimately reduced turnover within the company dramatically. That was the gap I was able to fill. Simply by listening deeper, I was able to uncover what their true needs were, where the breakdown was beginning, and what their core challenges were—the challenges that they did not articulate on the surface. I listened for what they weren't saying, their needs and greatest point of pain.

There's a symbiotic relationship between the way we listen and the questions we ask. For example, if you're already listening from a certain place or through a filter, chances are you are not going to ask certain questions that can create new selling opportunities.

**Closing Thoughts**

Start listening to what you are listening to—not only to what other people are telling you, but to what you are telling other people and, most important, what you are telling yourself.

After all, if you keep listening from the past and reacting based on a past experience or a future expectation, you will continue to create the same results as before.

## Make People Feel They Are Truly Being Heard

Finally, to become the Zen master of listening, this little treasure will, quite frankly, blow your mind when you start noticing and creating more selling opportunities than you ever knew existed. To become a masterful listener, make the person feel heard.

How do you know when you are heard? How does it feel?

Feeling heard is a level beyond just being listened to, and few of us ever cause other people to feel as if they are truly heard. Sure, we may be able to become effective listeners, but it is crucial to relay to your prospects that they are being listened to and understood.

To make someone feel heard, respond to what the person says during the conversation by using *clarifiers*. Rephrase in your own words what the person said, to show that you not only heard, but also understood him.

Here are some examples:

- For my own understanding …

- What you are truly saying is …

- What I am hearing you say is …

- Help me understand …

- Can you say a little more about that?

- Tell me more about that.

- It sounds like the criteria you're using to make your decision is …

- What do you see as the next step?

- Here's what I'm hearing.

- How do you mean?

- Can you say that in a different way? (Can you ask me that question in a different way?)

**def•i•ni•tion**

Use a **clarifier** when responding to what you've heard during the conversation. Rephrase in your own words what the other person said, to show that you not only heard, but also understood the person. Then confirm the next course of action.

**Closing Thoughts**

Clarifiers are also known as the "You'd better confirm the accuracy of what you're hearing from the prospect, or you are running an unnecessary risk of destroying this sale as well as completely wasting the time, money, and energy you invested in getting in front of this prospect" response.

# Reflective Listening

Reflective listening is another strategy that enables you to connect with your prospects on a deeper level. Reflective listening is simply repeating some words and phrases the prospect uses. As you listen to the person speak, you then respond in a similar fashion. For example, a prospect says, "I purchased a computer system only a couple of years ago, and it is already outdated. I need something more powerful that will grow with my organization." Respond by saying, "Something more powerful? What would a more powerful system do for you that you are unable to do with your current system?" Another prospect might say, "I have heard of your company. You have a great reputation in this area." You would reply, "Oh, you have heard of our company? Great! What have you heard about us?" At this point, you allow the prospect to continue speaking.

This technique allows you to build a stronger rapport by …

◆ Showing the prospect that you are paying attention to what he is saying.

◆ Demonstrating your understanding of what the prospect is saying.

◆ Implying that you care about what is being said.

## Paraphrasing

Paraphrase listening works on a similar principal. Instead of repeating the same verbiage the prospect used, paraphrase what was said. A client might say, "I am spending too much time recruiting and training. Unfortunately, I have to do this every few weeks." You can reply with a comment that supports and confirms what was said: "Yes, trying to find the right employees to help the long-term growth of your business is probably one of the biggest challenges management is faced with."

Another client might state, "I do not want to spend any money that won't help grow my company." You can reply, "I totally agree. I only want you to invest your money so that it will result in a measurable increase in your production."

These techniques are effective in establishing mindshare, stimulating the prospect's thinking and, thus, encouraging the prospect to continue talking. Sharing your understanding of the specific situation motivates the prospect to reveal more information concerning what is important to him and what his concerns are when making a purchasing decision.

**Closing Thoughts**

The top salesperson will listen to more than simply the spoken words of the prospect.

Using these techniques will accomplish two core objectives:

1. Clarifiers ensure that you received the message that was intended. If you did not receive the accurate message that was intended, the other person now has the opportunity to clarify their intended message, which prevents misunderstandings or putting the wrong meaning behind what's being heard. Clarifiers ensure that we have accurately received the message the other person intended to send.

2. The other person feels as if he is truly being heard and listened to.

Poor, ineffective listening can cause communication breakdowns, damage relationships, blow sales opportunities, and deteriorate the level of trust between you and your prospects, customers, family, and co-workers; however, listening actively and deeply accomplishes the following:

♦ Active listening enhances relationships and improves your credibility. Listening creates a safe environment for that person to share and explore his or her feelings on a deeper level.

♦ The fact that someone knows you are really listening produces trust and makes the other people you are communicating with more willing to listen to you.

♦ Listening prevents prejudging or trying to fix the other person.

♦ It shifts you away from listening through your filters and giving out unsolicited advice so that you can listen with an open mind and an open heart.

Listening is a learned and practiced skill that will open up new selling opportunities you may have never noticed before. It allows you to receive and process valuable information that you might have missed or neglected otherwise.

Remember, when speaking with someone, you certainly don't learn anything about them from listening to yourself talk.

Invest the time needed to sharpen your listening skills. When you actively and intentionally listen, not only will you know what you know, but you will know what the other person knows.

Besides, all people ever want in a conversation is to be listened to and acknowledged. Notice what happens when you give someone the gift of your attention and the gift of your listening. It stimulates the principal of reciprocity: if you listen to me, I'll listen to you. This is a great time to begin giving this gift of listening to others, and it costs nothing to give.

I hope that at this point you have a deeper understanding of how critical it is to your selling and closing efforts to become a master at listening. Take the time to fine-tune your listening skills so that you can hear more about what your customers want most. Soon, you'll be listening the sale right out of them.

Think of it this way: if you are taking the time to do so and your competition is not, you've just developed another competitive advantage and a way to create new and innovative solutions for your prospects, while your competition is doing the same thing it did yesterday.

> **Closer's Corner**
>
> It is easy to talk yourself out of a sale. However, no salesperson ever listened himself out of a sale.

The fact that someone knows you are really listening produces trust. Do not be afraid to let go of your need to "sell" or pitch your prospects by constantly talking. Pay attention to what is being said. You will be surprised how much easier the closing process becomes.

## The Least You Need to Know

♦ Encourage silence to develop a competitive edge by motivating prospects to share information with you that they would not share otherwise.

♦ Sell The Gap. Your solution, product, or service becomes the bridge that takes prospects from where they are today (present state) to where they want to be (desired state).

♦ Adjust your listening skills so that you catch anything that doesn't make sense. If a prospect is saying something that you sense is hiding the real truth or objection, ask follow-up questions until you are satisfied that you know and comprehend what the real story is.

♦ The more you listen, the more you're learning and the more you're moving the process toward the natural conclusion: the sale.

♦ If you're not listening for the sale, then you're simply listening to the words people are using to sell you on why or why not they're going to buy, thus limiting your chance to recognize selling opportunities that exist in the deeper layers of your listening.

♦ Take the time to authentically make people feel heard, and they'll want to do business with you.

# Chapter 7

# The Myths of Presenting to Your Prospects

## In This Chapter

♦ Stop pitching and start having a conversation

♦ Ask permission to move the sales process forward

♦ Craft questions that prevent and defuse objections

♦ Avoid the presentation paradox

♦ Eliminate the barriers to the sale that your presentation actually creates

You didn't think this book could escape having a chapter on how to deliver an effective presentation, did you? Well, as much as I may have tried, it was a mathematical impossibility. In fact, it's essential that we discuss the deep impact your presentation plays on your closing efforts.

Besides, I just couldn't leave my loyal readers sitting in the dark, wondering why, after using all of the highly effective closing strategies outlined in this book, they aren't working as well as they had thought (and as well as I guaranteed they would).

That's why we have to take the time to ensure that you are not leaving any holes unplugged during your conversations with prospects that would prevent you from uncovering, addressing, and defusing all of their concerns and objections before you even arrive at the closing table—that is, when you are finally ready to ask for the sale.

By the end of this chapter, you will realize why the more time you invest in crafting a permission-based presentation (not the traditional type of presentation you may be thinking of), the fewer objections you are going to hear when you finally ask for their business.

# Dangerous Knowledge

As I mentioned earlier, if you want to make your job easier when it comes to closing the sale, then invest your time up front and throughout each presentation and interaction you have with a prospect, to ensure that you are defusing the prospect's concerns along the way. Doing so enables you to address the prospect's key objections or barriers to making a purchase early on, when they are manageable, rather than giving these initially minor concerns the environment to fester and grow bigger until they finally become the very obstacle that prevents the prospect from buying from you.

This reminds me of an experience I had one afternoon with an advertising salesperson. I had recently purchased some advertising space in a national magazine. I have been a subscriber for years and knew everything I needed to know to select this magazine as an advertising vehicle. I called with one intention: to place an additional order.

When I called the office, the salesperson began doing what she felt was appropriate: to start *selling* me. She began with the history of the magazine, then moved into a discussion about her subscriber base and how effective an advertising campaign can be, and ended with information about her ad design team. She was unaware that I already knew all the information that she decided to share with me.

**Closing Thoughts** _____

Think about the number of presentations you've given over the course of your sales career. Now ask yourself, "How many times did I ask permission to even deliver a presentation and ask whether they even wanted to hear one?"

I'm always amazed when salespeople continue to deliver presentation after presentation to prospects who will not buy from them because of the very same presentation that the salesperson felt he needed to deliver. If the prospect didn't ask for or acknowledge the need for a presentation, or if the prospect did not make it explicitly clear what he wanted to hear or learn from your presentation, then why are you giving one? (Hint: It's now your agenda rather than the prospect's agenda.)

She never took the time to ask what my intention or expectations were in running the ad, or what information I might be interested in hearing more about. While she was speaking at me, I could only think about how many selling opportunities this must have cost her when dealing with prospective clients who didn't have the time or patience to listen to information that didn't fit for them.

This is not an unusual problem. Many salespeople spend much of their time during a sales call attempting to educate the prospect about their product, service, and industry. They think it will stimulate interest and increase the odds of earning the business of a new client. In many cases, this is the same strategy that compromises their opportunity to create a relationship with that prospect.

Unfortunately, this is the easiest way to lose someone's attention. When people hear something they aren't interested in, or if they feel you are providing information that doesn't apply to them, their interest is lost and they stop listening.

To continue to build upon the work we've done, it's time to uncover the paradox of presentations. You will learn how to properly present to the prospect and, more important, how to ask better questions and incorporate the responses you hear

**Closing Bell** _____

Another paradox: the act of delivering a presentation to a prospect without uncovering that person's agenda often creates the very objections you're hoping that your presentation would eliminate.

into a custom solution that will successfully drive your selling efforts toward more sales.

# The Paradox of Presentations

For most of us, delivering a presentation is defined as sharing information with someone else verbally, visually, or through a combination of communication platforms in some type of one-way dialogue or lecture format.

There's a new model available that turns this traditional and widely used approach to presenting upside down, one that actually defuses your prospect's concerns and objections throughout your conversation or meeting with them. Conversely, most of the time salespeople are waiting until the end of the conversation or presentation to handle objections, in the hopes that their presentation actually "worked" and defused any potential ones that may arise which would prevent the prospect from buying from them.

Additionally, this new, radically different process is one that salespeople embrace 10 to 1 over the traditional style of presenting, claiming that it's more comfortable, more dynamic, more interactive, more natural, and more of a conversation than a pitch. The result? Breakthrough performance.

That's why the most effective presentation is made up of questions rather than content to determine the direction in which the conversation will flow, including the information you share with them. Yup, I know this is counterintuitive. That is, a masterful presentation is now less about presenting information and more about extracting information through better questioning. (You just have to realize that you're better off behind the counter serving your prospects than dancing on top of it in the spotlight.)

A sales call or presentation is not the time to prove how much you know. It's the time to find out more of what you don't know about the prospect and what the prospect doesn't know about you. It is not your knowledge that sells, but how effectively you customize your knowledge to meet each prospect's specific needs.

> **Closing Bell**
>
> Your presentation can be interrupted at any time. You can be sitting there with a prospect and suddenly the person's mobile phone rings. Before you know it, you're hearing, "You know what? I've gotta go. Thanks for your time, and we'll call you if we're interested or want more information."
>
> If you're not monitoring your presentation and adjusting it around the information that is important to each prospect, then you are running the risk of delivering information that may not be important to that prospect. If this happens, you may not have shared the right information to grab the person's interest and be a conduit to a return visit or a return call that would enable you to finish the remainder of your presentation. The person instead left and is gone.

The most effective presentation is going to be judged by the outcome that you produce, not how much information you provide. This begins with finding the right balance of information that your prospects want to hear.

Now, before we jump into your step-by-step solution to delivering dynamic presentations, let's take a look at some tools you can start using immediately that will enhance your performance on stage.

# Questions That Gracefully Correct and Create a New Selling Opportunity

There may be times when a client holds certain inaccurate perceptions or beliefs about your product, service, or industry, thus limiting your chance to earn that client's business.

When this occurs, a salesperson may react by telling prospects they're wrong. Now, making someone wrong can come in a variety of shapes and sizes other than the obvious "No, that's not correct" or "You are wrong about that." Let's face it, when someone is told they're wrong, it puts them on the defensive. Consequently, prospects either shut down and stop listening or come out fighting in an attempt to defend their belief or statement. When this happens, a confrontational atmosphere is created between you and the client. (And guess who always wins?)

Rather than reacting to their remark, demonstrate your interest in understanding what they are truly saying, what motivated their comment, or the source of their information. Use this as an opportunity to validate and empathize with some aspect of their feelings. Saying things like, "I appreciate how you feel" or "I understand your feelings on that" lets the other person know that you are sincerely trying to understand what they said and where they are coming from. Respecting someone's point of view, whether you agree with it or not, demonstrates a willingness to continue with the dialogue.

To avoid confrontation with your prospect, respond to the prospect's statements with a question that directs the conversation toward creating a new possibility, belief, or solution. Questions allow you to correct someone without having an emotional reaction or telling them they're wrong. Using the following questions will enable you to create a new selling opportunity that would otherwise be left unexplored.

1. What else do you feel might be possible?

2. Can you please share with me your thinking on that?

3. May I share my view on that?

4. Is it possible that there may be another approach/solution here?

5. Is it possible that there may be more/other facts to consider?

6. How can I best assist you now?

7. When did you decide that was true?

8. That's interesting. Can you share with me why you feel/see it that way?

9. What else is true about that?

10. I'm not too sure what you mean. Can you say more about that?

11. Hmm. I'm not familiar with that. Can you please tell me a little more about it?

12. May I ask where you heard/learned that?

Most important, learn to put your ego aside and let go of your need to "sell," prove your point, or be right.

> **Closing Bell**
>
> When listening to what your prospects already know, some of the information you receive about your product or industry may be inaccurate. Address this carefully. Instead of correcting them, simply add another truth to their statement by asking another question or adding more to what they said. Otherwise, while making yourself look right, you run the risk of making the prospect wrong, thus putting them on the defensive.

# Telling Isn't Selling—Asking Questions Is

If "What are your strengths in sales?" is the question, here are some responses that suggest a misunderstanding of what professional selling is really all about. "I present well. I am a good closer. I can sell anything." Needless to say, this person is the victim of faulty thinking that could have stemmed from experience or training, thus creating the misconception of what selling truly is.

Many people in the sales profession simply regurgitate information. These are the same people who may possess certain essential characteristics that salespeople need (being an extrovert, feeling comfortable approaching and talking with people, and so on) but who can't figure out why they are not able to enter into a higher income bracket.

How are you ever going to be able to sell anything without getting the proper feedback from the prospect who is making the purchase? If you keep talking, at what point do you find out what the prospect's needs are? When do you ask questions in order to get a response? If you are trying to sell reading glasses to a blind man, how successful do you think you will be?

Learn to take the information that you would typically share with the prospect in the form of a *statement*, and instead turn it into a *question* to get feedback or a response from the prospect. I know, it may not be your natural tendency to ask questions. Salespeople would much rather tell or give information, advice, opinions, or solutions. That's why learning this new approach is a challenge for many salespeople, since it is something that they don't instinctively do. Their first reaction is to regurgitate information or tell.

**Closing Thoughts**

Turn what you "tell" into a question so that you can "sell."

You must learn to consciously phrase your statements into questions. Once again, it will take a focused effort to change this habit and replace it with a more effective one. After all, if I asked you to change the dominant hand you use for everything you do, it would take you a little while to adapt (for example, changing from being a lefty to a righty). Every time that you are ready to "tell" the prospect something, stop yourself and turn it into a question so that you can "sell." Here are some examples.

**Tell:** "We have a great company. You will love to do business with us."

**Sell:** "What is important to you when choosing a company to handle a project like this?" "What would make us your first choice?"

**Tell:** "Our product is perfect for you."

**Sell:** "If you could eliminate three of your biggest problems and headaches, what would they be?" "Based on what I've shared with you, what about our service most interests you?" "At this point, what are the features of our product that you like the most?"

**Tell:** "This is the best quality."

**Sell:** "What type of quality are you looking for? What features are a 'must have' for you, regardless of price?" "How do you typically determine whether the quality of the product meets your expectations?" "How important is quality to you when purchasing something like this?" "How familiar are you with the different products available?"

**Tell:** "Don't worry, I'll give you a great price."

**Sell:** "Was there a range that you wanted to stay within?" "Are you familiar with how much a project like this would cost?" "Is there a certain budget that we should keep in mind?" "How much were you expecting to pay for something like this?"

**Tell:** "There is no other company that will offer you this level of service."

**Sell:** "To ensure that I meet your expectations, can you share with me the level of service you have come to expect from your other venders?" "Based on what I've shared with you, does our service cover or exceed all of the requirements that are important to you?" "If there were three things that you would like to see improved upon regarding the level of service you've gotten from your current vender, what would they be?" "What service issues would you want a new vender to finally resolve for you?"

Instead of you continually talking, asking prospects questions will keep them talking. Besides, what are prospects more likely to believe, what comes out of your mouth or what comes out of their mouth?

**Closing Thoughts**

The prospect should be doing most of the talking during your meeting with them.

Think about it. Do you learn anything about the prospect by listening to yourself talk? Of course not. If you continually have the prospect answer and respond to your questions that reinforce their need, their desire for your product, and the benefits you offer, then they are conditioning themselves to buy.

When asking questions, be sure that your questions succeed in achieving the following objectives:

- Be direct and candid with your questioning and communication. Do not be vague or tiptoe around the subject or question. Make the question clear, focused, direct, and concise.

- Make sure that your questions open up new possibilities, ideas, and opportunities in the minds of the prospects that they never considered. Do they enable the prospect to see a new and better solution and envision more measurable worthwhile results, based on the information that you have provided?

- Have the prospects draw from previous purchasing experiences to determine their buying habits, wants, priorities, pains, concerns, and needs.

- Learn to question what is said and what is not said. Never prejudge a prospect until you have the evidence to support your assumptions. Utilize questions until you are satisfied with the response.

- Use questions to achieve mindshare and agreement, as well as to gracefully uncover and correct the inaccuracies and misconceptions they may have about your product or service.

**Closing Thoughts**

You will never learn what the prospect wants or needs by listening to yourself talk.

**Closing Bell**

You do not want to sound as if you are firing a list of questions at prospects, as if they're being interrogated under a hot lamp. Doing so may put a prospect on the defensive. Instead, weave them into the natural flow of your conversation.

Questions will help you determine the style and content of your presentation. After the prospect answers these questions, you will be able to determine your course of action regarding the context of your presentation. You will find out the buying habits of this particular individual and how this person perceives salespeople. You will uncover what obstacles need to be defused. You will find out what type of salesperson the prospect likes to purchase from. And you will uncover the hot button that motivates the prospect to buy from you.

# How to Create More Obstacles to the Sale

As you craft and practice the questions you ask during each meeting or presentation with a prospect, you will see how easy it really is to work these questions into the flow of every conversation. Your questioning sequence will then come across naturally, especially since you know how to adjust the questions so they fit the prospect's style of communication (see Chapter 4).

Now, I realize that there may be some people who still believe, "Keith, my presentation sells. Why should I stop doing something that I know already works?" As I've alluded to before, the pendulum can swing to both extremes. We're looking to strike a healthy balance between asking questions and delivering information. That is, first you ask the question, then you deliver the information that is important to them. For those salespeople who are still reluctant to ask more questions, consider what it will cost you by not doing so.

What type of results can you expect if you decide to skip asking these questions during your meeting with a prospect? Just ask Scott.

Scott truly believed that every time he walked into an appointment and delivered his presentation, he was walking out with a work order. His confidence was high, along with his energy level. These were certainly healthy characteristics that were common among most top producers.

Eventually, the true effectiveness of Scott's sales approach got challenged. Luckily, it happened early enough in his sales career that he was able to quickly learn and adjust his approach accordingly. Here's what transpired.

Scott cordially greeted Mr. and Mrs. Mullaney and, without going through his questioning sequence, began his presentation. Mr. and Mrs. Mullaney were very receptive to what Scott was showing them.

By the time Scott introduced the investment amount to the Mullaneys, he thought he had earned their business. At that point, Mrs. Mullaney replied, "We really like what you have shown us, Scott. There are, however, just a couple of things that are holding us back from doing anything right now:

- ◆ We are not looking to make this investment right now because we have other projects that take precedence over this one.

- ◆ We need to speak to our partners before we make any final decision.

- ◆ We have a scheduled appointment tomorrow with another company.

- ◆ I know someone in the business who is also going to discuss this project with us.

- ◆ I need to research your company.

- ◆ I need to find a way to pay for it now that I don't have a job.

- ◆ I don't think I need it now."

Scott never skipped over asking his questions again. If you fail to utilize the right questions, it is like playing Russian Roulette with the prospect; you are gambling with the potential of each sale every time you do so. If Scott had uncovered this information before moving into his presentation rather than cutting corners in his selling strategy, he could have adjusted his presentation around these particular concerns in order to defuse them before they became obstacles that could not be easily overcome.

# Process-Driven Selling—the Question Is the Answer

Without writing a whole book on the subject, I've managed to make your life even easier by condensing a very concise, step-by-step, permission-based approach to presenting practically anything you sell.

First, let's establish some baseline gauges that you can incorporate into your sales approach both in what you do and in how you think—that is, your tactical as well as psychological presentation strategy.

# The Objective of Delivering a Presentation

Take a moment and think about how the typical conversation or meeting flows with a prospect. What does your typical presentation consist of? What do you talk about?

The basics: you may begin by giving some background on your company and who you are. You would probably talk about what you sell. You may even discuss what your product or service is, or what it does and how it could benefit the prospect. And if you have some time, you might share some technical data, a PowerPoint presentation, or some marketing materials.

With all of these various topics to address, only one stands out as your core objective and the primary goal of delivering a presentation. Here are the most common responses I hear:

- To educate my prospect on who we are, the industry, and the product I sell

- To get the sale

- To create a rapport and build trust

- To develop a competitive edge and a reason for becoming the prospect's vender of choice

- To give each prospect a good reason for buying from me

Now, we're looking for the *primary* goal of delivering a presentation. Although these objectives that I just listed are critical to achieve during a well-organized sales effort, none of these resembles the primary objective.

To illustrate this point, let me ask you a few questions. Based on these five objectives I just listed and your approach when presenting during a meeting or conversation with a prospect, are you able to answer these nine questions by the time you finish your presentation?

1. What are their core objectives?

2. What are their immediate needs?

3. Who is responsible for making this purchasing decision?

4. What information do they want to hear from you?

5. What are their expectations of the meeting/conversation with you?

6. What is their biggest concern that would prevent them from buying from you?

7. How do they make a purchasing decision? What's their process?

8. What criteria do they need to evaluate in order to make a decision?

9. Are they "sold" on using you, your company, and your product?

Unless you did a stellar job prequalifying a prospect during your initial contact (use my permission-based prospecting system I discuss in my book *The Complete Idiot's Guide to Cold Calling*) and this meeting or conversation is actually your second contact with the prospect, then the chance of you being able to accurately answer these questions simply by delivering your content-rich presentation is pretty slim.

That's why the primary goal when delivering a presentation is different from what you might have imagined. The core objective of a presentation is to uncover the information you need (through questions) to determine whether there's a fit, and then refine your approach so that the solution you present is now customized to reflect the unique and specific needs of each prospect. Now, you can laser in on what is most important to each prospect and what they want to hear. As a result, the prospect is now in the best position to make an educated (or impulsive) buying decision based on the selling atmosphere that you created or to take action regarding the next step in your selling cycle (proposal, demo, vender review, and so on).

> **Closer's Corner**
>
> The information prospects want to hear is not necessarily dependant upon the questions they ask, but more on the questions that you ask. The only questions you can control and ensure get addressed are the ones you ask.

If you're asking better questions up front, you may have noticed a change in the flow and direction of your meetings and, more specifically, in the information you are hearing as well as presenting. You may have also noticed that many of the prospects you met with in the past were the same prospects that you now realize were not a fit, ones that would never be a fit, and ones you had no business ever meeting with or spending the time following up on in the first place.

## The Least You Need to Know

- Purposely pitching prospects puts you in a precarious position. Phew.

- The only thing more valuable than your time is your prospects' time when meeting with them. Leverage this time wisely with well-crafted questions.

- Identify the knowledge gap to uncover what the prospects don't know, as well as what they do.

- The primary objective of delivering a presentation is to see if there's a fit, while stimulating enough of an interest in and desire for your product by uncovering the prospects' core need and then demonstrating how you can fill that need; this will then get the prospect engaged in taking the next step in your selling cycle.

- If you cut corners in your presentation, you're making yourself vulnerable to objections that you could have avoided in the first place.

- There's a distinct difference between delivering a presentation with a healthy balance of solicited information that was uncovered by well-crafted questions and using the same canned pitch for everyone.

# Chapter 8

# Make Your Sales Presentations Objection-Proof

## In This Chapter

- Close with your ears—conversational selling
- Become a powerful communicator
- Identify the Knowledge Gap
- Customers don't want a relationship with you
- Learn the five steps to a permission-based presentation that pops

I'm so excited to share this chapter with you that we're going to jump right into what I know will create breakthroughs in your performance—that is, the five key steps to delivering highly effective presentations, which I refer to as Permission Based Presentation. It's an innovative, conversation-based model that you'll hear more about in my upcoming book.

This process that I've developed and coached thousands of salespeople on is the same process they give credit to for propelling them into top producer status. These same salespeople also reported that this approach has dramatically shortened their selling cycle, reducing the time they need to spend with each prospect before they become a happy customer.

As you might imagine, what you're going to find here may challenge your current assumptions about what it means to deliver effective presentations and the way that you are currently doing so. But hey, if we don't challenge your thinking and what you are currently doing, then what's the point of reading this book and making positive change?

# The Five Steps to Delivering a Permission Based Presentation

Now, throughout the rest of the book, I refer to the topic we discuss in this chapter as your *presentation*. However, I am not suggesting that you continue to present in the traditional way that many of us have been taught or have been doing historically. You know, the old "Show up and throw up" presentation model, delivering preformatted content or having a one-way conversation with your audience as if you were an actor standing on a stage. Instead, I use the words *present* and *presentation* to suggest the new, more effective model that I introduce to you in this book.

### Closing Bell

You don't get paid for delivering presentations or proposals—unless, of course, you're a public speaker, trainer, or coach, or have a job description that very closely resembles that of a professional speaker or trainer whose sole job is to present or write proposals, and you get compensated for the act of doing it.

Companies spend thousands and thousands of dollars on crafting presentations and leveraging technology such as PowerPoint and the Internet to ensure that they are coming across to the prospect as professional and polished as possible, hoping to engage prospects and grab their interest and attention.

However, this same strategy often creates the very problems they are looking to avoid.

Think about your presentation. How many questions do you have woven into your presentation to keep the prospect engaged and your finger on the pulse of the meeting?

Here's a key point regarding how you can change your thinking about what it means to deliver a presentation:

Stop presenting and start having a conversation.

What do I mean by this? I mean, have a conversation with them, a two-way, interactive dialogue. Talk with them, ask questions, have them share how they feel and what they are looking for so that you can better determine whether your product is a good fit for them.

**Closing Thoughts**

Get off your soapbox and stop preaching to your prospects. They really don't want to hear it.

In order to accomplish this in a natural and very comfortable way, here are the five steps to a Permission Based Presentation that will act as your guiding light during every presentation or conversation you have with a potential customer. These five steps will direct you where you need to begin and where you need to end each meeting with a prospect:

1. Introduction

2. Discovery

3. Clarify

4. Solution

5. Close (a.k.a. Reconfirmation and Opening)

The remainder of this chapter breaks down and defines the objectives of each step. As a bonus, I provide you with specific, well-crafted questions you can use immediately to boost the impact of your presentation that will act as a strong foundation for you as you begin to reinvent your presentation.

## Step One: The Introduction

You may have heard about how important it is to develop a rapport, some immediate connection or bond, with the prospect before you can even begin to sell anything. On the other hand, some prospects are not the least bit interested in developing any type of relationship with you other than what needs to happen to complete this transaction. (If you've never heard of this, then now you have, so take it as gospel).

So a bit of a conundrum you have, yes? How do you know when a prospect wants to invest some time developing a business relationship (because this is the type of person who doesn't buy from anyone he does not like) and when the prospect just wants to get to the bottom line?

As you may have guessed, being as keen and insightful as you are (after all, you did buy this book, which automatically scores you high), your friendly and highly evolved coach has a solution for you. Here it is.

**Set the expectation of your meeting.** Rather than taking it upon yourself to assume or determine your selling approach and decide on what information to share with each prospect, ask the prospects what their expectations are to ensure that you deliver only solicited information, while honoring their agenda rather than yours.

Before you present or deliver any information about your product, service or company, what do you need to do first?

Do you know what their interest level is? Do you know what their hot buttons are or what is important to them? No, you do not.

Start your conversation (before your presentation) by asking certain questions.

Questions will enable you to uncover the relevant information to provide and identify the prospects' objective and expectation of the meeting, while eliminating communication breakdowns that result from faulty assumptions of what you think they want to hear or what you perceive is important to them. What is important information to one prospect may not be important to another.

Ask questions to determine the prospects' agenda for the meeting and what information is important to them. Here are a few questions to uncover and manage the expectations of every conversation or meeting you have.

1. Mr. Prospect, I'd like to be sensitive to your time and make the most of our meeting. In order for me to do so, what are your expectations of our appointment/meeting/time today?

2. To ensure that I'm providing you with the right information, what is most important to you when making a decision like this?

3. What do you need to know about us and our solution/product/service that will give you the confidence/comfort/peace of mind in knowing that you've made the best decision?

4. What are your objectives/expectations of our meeting today?

5. I know that I'm the one who initiated this meeting, Mrs. Prospect. That said, with the limited time we have today, what would you need to hear about regarding what I can do for you that would key in on/be a perfect complement to what's most important and timely to you?

6. In the spirit of using the time we have together wisely, I want to ensure that I'm not offering you features and benefits that aren't aligned with your goals and what is currently going on within your company. May I ask, what are some of the current or ongoing initiatives you can share with me so that I can make the data/information I have most interesting and relevant to you?

7. Based on your current objectives, if there was one topic or solution that would grab your interest immediately, what would it be?

8. What information can I provide that would assist you in making the right decision when choosing a (new vender, service provider, contractor, etc.)?

9. I realize that each person has his or her own criteria for making a decision regarding the purchase of (state service/product). What information can I share that is most important to you when making a decision like this?

10. What would we need to offer you that would make us your first choice when choosing a new vendor?

11. What information can I share that is most important to you?

12. What would you like to see as an outcome of our meeting together?

13. How can I make the most of our time together?

14. Mr./Ms. ..., I want to be respectful of your time and make sure you enjoy your visit with us. How can I help you make the most of your visit today?

---

**Closer's Corner**

Every presentation should begin with managing the expectations of your prospect. In other words, let them tell you what you'll be telling them.

---

What have these questions accomplished? You have determined what information to provide that's important to your prospects.

These questions uncover what you need to know regarding what they need and want to learn.

# Customers Don't Want a Relationship with You

To become a great salesperson, you need to foster and build strong relationships with your prospects and clients. The stronger the relationships you build, the easier it will be to sell them, serve them, and support them. Although this is certainly true, essential, and indisputable, in some cases and professions (with doctors, coaches, therapists, and certain transactions with long selling cycles, to name a few), it is not an absolute principle that I endorse.

Here's why. Some people are just not interested in a relationship. Some people want to get in, make a purchase, and get out, keeping it purely transactional. After all, when was the last time you went out to lunch with the person who fills your gas tank, your pharmacist, your local cable provider, or the rep you speak with when calling your phone company?

There's a big difference between developing a relationship and being pleasant, friendly, and service-driven. One requires no extra time on your part; one can potentially become all time-consuming (research, reports, diligence, follow-up, and so on). Just to be clear, if you are truly looking to build a relationship with your prospects and customers beyond the scope of what is considered common business practice, then you have a few of your personal needs and agenda wrapped up in the sale. No good.

Look at this from a different angle for a moment. Let's say you sell insurance. Before you sold insurance, did you ever go out to lunch or meet on a social level with your insurance agent? How about the person who sold you your home, copier, or car?

> **Closing Bell**
>
> All customers do not define or look at relationships the same way that you do. Find out what their definition of "building strong relationships" actually means and how important it is to them.

So what is ultimately my point? Here it is. Rather than you assuming that your prospects want a relationship, ask them. Ask a question to uncover what their expectations are regarding the type of relationship they want with the salesperson, such as "What are your expectations of the person you are going to buy from?" "What quality of service or level of interaction are you used to receiving?" "If you were in my shoes, what would I want to know about you that would help earn your business?"

While these questions assist you in crafting the perfect relationship and presentation every time (since the prospect is telling you how they want to be sold), other questions are essential and must always be asked in order to further reduce any faulty assumptions on your part. That is, identify the Knowledge Gap.

## Identify the Knowledge Gap

The Knowledge Gap is the space between what people know and what they don't know. Instead of assuming what they know, start determining what they need and want to learn in order to ensure clear communication and fill in this gap so they can make an educated buying decision. Keep in mind that what may seem old or common knowledge to you as it relates to your product or industry is new to them. Use questions up front to uncover what's needed to fill in the gap.

Before you can uncover a prospect's individual needs and educate the person on how your product will meet those needs, you must first uncover what your prospect already knows.

> **Closing Thoughts**
>
> While your content may change, your questions don't.

Your company's presentation materials are designed to assist you in educating your prospects. However, it's your job to determine and provide the appropriate information that will fit their specific situation through the use of well-crafted questions.

For example, if you sell real estate, it doesn't help you if you're discussing the school districts to a couple who either doesn't have children or whose children are all grown. It doesn't help you to discuss a dog walk if they don't have a pet, and it doesn't help you to discuss the gym amenities if they're not interested in using that to stay in shape. Doing so can actually create other objections, especially when prospects feel that you're sharing information with them that they don't care about; to them, this demonstrates either that you're not listening or that you simply don't care about their personal needs.

To identify the Knowledge Gap and best manage your presentation and the expectations of each prospect, use the following questions:

1. "Just so I don't sound repetitive, how familiar are you with (for example, this area [location] and our development)?"

2. "Just so I don't sound repetitive, what do you already know about ...?" Then, based on the information you receive, you can craft your presentation around what they do and don't know.

**Closing Bell**

Determine what is important to your prospects. Otherwise, you run the risk of providing information that they just don't care about or are not ready to hear. And if this occurs, what happens to their listening?

Based on how the prospect responds, you can fill in the blanks or what they don't know with the information they need to know without sounding redundant.

## Step Two: The Discovery

This step is also known as your qualifying step, needs analysis, evaluation, diagnostic, and so on. Bottom line: here's when you ask questions rather than deliver information to uncover what your prospects need and whether you can fill it.

For the sake of keeping it simple, there are two types of questions we discuss. First, there are *fact-finding questions* that relate specifically to your industry and your deliverables, providing you with the information you need to see if someone even minimally qualifies as a prospect. In other words, you probably have an ideal client type or at least some criteria of the people who purchase your product.

Do prospects have to be in a specific industry, profession, income class, age, geographic location, or community? Do they need to have already purchased from you or from one of your competitors? Do they need to be using a certain product, service, or technology? Are they bound by certain governmental regulations in terms of how they procure and purchase from venders? Do the companies you call on need to have a certain number of employees, computers, buildings, or salespeople for you to even be able to offer your product or service?

For example, if you sell a specific software for CPAs and accountants, you are not going to get far calling on a list of dentists.

If you sell an industrial solution, then you have to ask the questions up front that relate to whether they even use your product and whether they could, regarding compliance laws and regulations.

And finally, if the way in which your prospects choose a vender dictates how you would approach that sale and present to this prospect, then it wouldn't make sense to deliver blindly to anyone who would listen.

Let's say you sell a web-based product to small businesses that helps them get in front of more qualified prospects. In order to determine what information to share with each prospect and whether it even makes sense to do so, here are a few examples of fact-finding questions this salesperson would use:

1. How are you currently going about bringing in new business/ customers? How are you promoting your business now? (Do you advertise in other magazines, websites, newspapers, etc.?) What have you tried?

2. Is this generating the results you're looking for? How is it working for you? Are you happy with results?

3. Are you currently using the Internet to generate more sales/ business? Do you feel that you are effectively leveraging the power of the Internet to bring in more business? What have you tried?

4. Is one of your goals for advertising to generate more business? Do you have any other expectations? What else are you looking to accomplish by advertising (branding, membership, database, more traffic, and so on)?

5. How do you go about choosing what marketing to invest in? How is that budget typically allocated?

6. Do you typically outsource your (state service), or is this something that the company does in-house?

7. Who is your target/ideal customer?

---

### Closing Thoughts

I got an e-mail one morning from one of my clients who calls on catering halls and reception places, and connects them with the large population of brides, newlyweds, and other segments of this demographic. It was in response to a discussion we had about making sure you have a qualified list of people (they are suspects before they become prospects) to call on. She shared with me what happened when this one person answered her sales call. Although she knew better, she began pitching her services rather than qualify this prospect. Finally, the prospect said, "You know, what you have sounds really interesting. However, do you know what type of reception hall we are?"

"Why, yes, you're a reception site that hosts wedding receptions."

"Correct, but it's a nudist resort."

"Aaahh … aaahhh."

We both burst out laughing and ended the call with some humor. "I'd understand having a nudist resort in the Caribbean where it's warm all year round, but in Canada?"

The lesson? Know your audience.

---

Once you have determined that the prospect is, in fact, a candidate for your services, the second type of question is the *emotional trigger question* that uncovers the psychological needs and barriers each prospect has. These questions focus less on data, evidence, and measurables, and more on our experiences, including the ones in our past, those in our present, and the ones we want to have in the future.

These questions target how prospects feel at the time, what their desired state would be, their discomfort or pain by not changing—these all trigger an emotional reaction within the prospect. The good news, as we've already learned, is that emotions motivate people to act. These questions move the sales process forward and closer to the point where your prospect is ready to buy from you. Here are a few examples of these types of questions you can use:

1. If you could magically eliminate three of your biggest problems, headaches, or stresses as they relate to attracting and retaining new customers/generating new business, what would they be? (If there were three problems that you would want to see resolved with your current advertising efforts/vender what would they be?) (Time, money, ineffective programs, frustration, stress, etc.)

2. How do these challenges affect your business (bottom line)?

3. How does this (current problem, headache) affect you and your job? (Tie in the challenges to their position they are experiencing. What's their personal cost as a result of these challenges? Bigger workload, longer hours, higher stress, looking bad on their evaluation, job security, and so on.)

4. If you don't make any changes, then what do you think it's going to cost you over time? (What is it going to cost you by not changing? What additional opportunities do you think you're letting pass by? Do you think there is business you may miss out on by not changing? What cost do you incur by keeping things the way they are?)

After gathering the information from the discovery questions you've created, you still have a few more steps to go before asking for the sale. However, you will be able to use this information to conclude your sales process and ask for the prospect's business. If done effectively, all you are really doing in step five is reconfirming the information that the prospect previously shared with you

### Closer's Corner

A question has to be worth asking. If the information you get isn't worth asking for, or if it doesn't support the prospect's goals or solve the problem and move your sales process forward, don't waste your time asking the question. Wrong questions equate to getting the wrong answers or answers that don't do anything to move you closer to the sale.

as to why he wants to use your company—because, at this point, you've satisfied all of his needs.

## Use Segue Questions When Presenting

Before we move on to Step Three, I want to bring something else to your attention that will make your communication flow smoother, especially when you're looking to conclude a discussion on one topic and want to begin discussing something else. A *segue* is the verbal bridge you build to smoothly transition from one thought, topic, or conversation to another.

**def•i•ni•tion** _____

Using **segues** in your communication and especially when delivering any kind of presentation immediately boosts the impact of your delivery, your confidence, and your results. Segues can come in the form of a question or a statement that seamlessly brings one topic to its apparent conclusion while simultaneously opening up the possibility to explore another topic.

Think about the different areas or topics you discuss with a prospect that at some point would typically be woven into your presentation. Here's a short list:

1. Company

2. Product or service

3. Process (how it all works)

4. Team

5. Customer service

6. Pricing

7. Client list

8. Territory

9. History and founders

10. Warranty or guarantee

11. Most valuable proposition or unique offerings

12. Measurable benefits and end results

For example, if you sell real estate, there's going to be a point during your conversation with a prospect where you would discuss the community and the neighborhood. Now, if you can anticipate these questions or concerns from the prospect and actually draw out this information, what type of questions can you ask to uncover the prospect's hot points or core values that you can then adjust your presentation around? What aspects of the community would make sense to discuss and highlight? Here are some segue questions you could use before you do an information dump on the prospect, to uncover what that person wants to hear.

◆ Mr. Prospect, putting the type of home you want aside, each person has different expectations and needs as they relate to their neighborhood. What are the unconditional deciding factors that are going to determine where you live?

◆ What is going to most influence your decision on where you are going to buy your home?

◆ What are some of the important features you are looking for in a home that are must-have's?

Before discussing your company, product, or service, you must determine what your prospects want to hear that's important to them. Here are some additional examples of segue questions you can use:

1. What information can I provide that would give you the peace of mind of knowing that we are the right company for you?

2. How do you go about choosing a company for a project like this?

3. What do you look for in a company?

4. What do you want most (to happen) as a result of using our product and service?

5. What results would you need to experience that will increase your desire for this type of product?

Let's go back to the example I shared earlier about discussing the community. So you ask the question and then the prospects share with you what's important to them.

> ### Closer's Corner
>
> Every new topic or component of your presentation that you introduce should begin with a question that uncovers the prospect's areas of interest. Every component of your presentation should end with a question that confirms agreement and seals any opportunity for an objection to grow or fester.

You then craft the information in your presentation around what they are interested in. But that's just part of the equation.

You now need to confirm that the information you share has satisfied their need, in order to close any loose ends and prevent potential objections that could later surface.

Achieving this objective can be done using the following questions:

- Mrs. Prospect, based on what you've seen about the neighborhood, does it meet your expectations?

- So putting the home itself aside for a moment, can you envision yourself living here (in this area)?

- Does the home I've shown you meet the needs of your family and provide you with the features that are most important to you?

Here are some additional questions you can use:

- Based on what you know about my company and me, do we meet or exceed your standards for choosing a new vender?

- What would be some of the advantages that you can envision realizing once this software is integrated into your system?

- Are there any other features or functionality that you would like to see in our product that we have not demonstrated to you?

- Based on the timeline we've discussed as it relates to fully integrating this solution into your company, do you see any potential obstacles at this point as they relate to meeting your current deadlines?

- While I know you mentioned this product isn't something you have tried before, now that you've seen what it can do for you firsthand, has it made a believer out of you, or are you still a bit reluctant to make a change like this?

The discovery process will help determine the information you share, the direction you will take your presentation, and how the meeting will unfold, but keep in mind that you will still be discovering more and more about your prospects throughout your entire courtship and conversation with them. The point here is, your discovery process continues indefinitely as you continue to ask questions up until the time the prospect becomes a customer.

As you will see, your discovery or questioning will overflow into every step of this five-step Permission Based Presenting process. Segue questions will allow you to confirm that your company, your product, your process, your people, and the other criteria we mentioned earlier will be satisfied by the time you ask for the sale. Remember, if you get objections after you ask for the sale, there were some additional questions that needed to be asked to confirm mindshare and that the prospects' criteria for making a purchasing decision had been met.

Now you're ready to segue into the third step of your presentation: clarifying.

## Step Three: Clarifying

Clarifying goes beyond making sure that you heard the words the prospects uttered by parroting back to them what they said. Clarifying ensures that you have not only heard them, but confirmed that you received the accurate message they intended to send, whether through spoken words, physical gestures, or body language.

In addition, this step enables you to confirm with the prospect that your message was accurately received and understood. Finally, the clarifying step ensures that you still have your finger on the pulse of the prospect, their level of interest and desire, where they are in terms of making a purchase, and the degree to which they are in agreement with what you are proposing.

You can use three different tools when clarifying. Depending upon what stage you are in during your selling cycle or during a conversation with a prospect, you may use any one of these three clarifiers accordingly and throughout your interaction with a prospect.

**1. Recap, summarize, and confirm what you've learned.** At this point, you have asked some well-crafted questions. You have learned about what your prospect's wants and needs are. You have learned what their current challenges and objectives are. You have uncovered what their primary concerns are as they relate to making any change (or purchase).

Before you go any further in your conversation with a prospect, it's critical to ensure that you are both singing from the same sheet of music. These clarifiers confirm that you accurately heard what the prospect shared with you.

When this is accomplished, you are in a much better position to deliver a custom solution that will specifically address this prospect's pain, needs, and goals.

To effectively summarize and confirm what the prospect has said, use this type of clarifier. Here are several clarifiers that resemble the ones we discussed in Chapter 6:

◆ For my own understanding, what you are saying is …. Is that correct?

◆ If I understand you correctly, you are currently experiencing a situation (challenge) where …. Is that accurate?

◆ So if I'm hearing you right, it sounds like the real pressing issue for you now is …. Have I missed anything?

◆ So if there's one thing that we can accomplish for you that would make this investment worthwhile it would be …. Is that correct?

◆ Okay, reducing or eliminating the problem of (restate problem and pain they experience) that would enable you to (restate the goals they shared with you) is your number-one priority right now, is that right?

**2. Take the prospect's pulse.** If recapping and summarizing what you've learned confirm the realistic landscape of the prospect's situation, then taking the prospect's pulse identifies what he has accurately heard from you, further qualifying his level of interest and desire in taking the next course of action.

These clarifiers reconfirm that the prospect heard and understood the information and advantages to making the purchase that you intended him to hear. Here are several examples of questions that take a prospect's pulse:

◆ How are you feeling about what we've discussed so far?

◆ With what we've discussed so far, what stands out most for you?

- What do you see as the next step?

- What features are you most excited about using?

- Based on the different advantages and benefits I have shared with you, which ones are most important to you?

- With any new purchase, there's always a chance for a concern to arise in the back of your mind. What might be a concern of yours at this point that may cause some hesitancy in making your decision?

- While I know it still may be too early to tell, do you think at this point you would want to initially roll this out for just one department or company-wide?

- At this point, what differences (advantages) do you see in using our service compared to the one you're currently using?

- Based on the results that our other clients have experienced, what result do you want to achieve that will carry the most weight in your decision?

- With everything I've mentioned, what features or results are not as important to you right now?

- How does this fit with your style, goals, and objectives?

**3. Preclose.** You've done a fabulous job confirming clear communication, eliminating communication breakdowns and misunderstandings, and taking the pulse regarding your prospect's level of interest and desire for ownership of your product. Now you are ready to confirm the prospect's current level of commitment to buying and eliminate any concerns or objections that may get in the way of the sale. Said another way, now is a great time to preclose the sale, to ensure that this person is, in fact, a highly qualified and interested prospect. This way, you can determine whether it makes sense for you to continue investing your time moving this prospect to the next step or if there is some collateral damage that needs to be addressed, such as a concern or objection that needs to be handled.

Besides, if your next step is to deliver a proposal, schedule another meeting, or deliver a prototype or demonstration, it only makes sense to get confirmation that, as long as your solution fits with what the prospect is looking for and what you have already discussed, this person is in a position to buy from you.

Otherwise, you are running the risk of wasting your precious time doing proposals and follow-up work for a prospect who, in the end, will not buy from you.

If you think a proposal or a demonstration is going to change anything at this point, then you'd better re-evaluate your thinking around this. At this point, all objections and concerns need to be uncovered and defused. Your proposal and demo will not do this for you! (Unless, of course, the only thing left in the way of the sale is the need for the prospect to experience your product or service firsthand before making a commitment.)

Remember, with the new permission-based selling model I've introduced to you, if prospects are not "sold" or committed to moving forward with you at this point with a purchase or with the next step (if you have a longer selling cycle), barring any unforeseen changes in your solution or in their situation, then you missed something during your communications with them.

That's why it's called the preclose. It is the close or reconfirming questions you use before the close to gain solid mindshare of where this relationship is ultimately heading. This way, in the end, you don't really have to close them at all! (Chapter 1, remember?) The preclose ensures that, all things considered and as long as you can deliver on what you promised and what was discussed, then there should be no surprises that will get in the way of them making a purchase or keep the sale from happening.

What follows are several different questions and approaches you can use to preclose the prospect and reconfirm what the next steps are going to be (rather than making assumptions, ignoring the signs, or hoping that when you deliver the proposal or demo, everything will miraculously work out).

♦ If the next step in your sales process is developing and delivering a proposal to a prospect, you can use this preclosing question:

"Based on what I'm hearing you say, if the proposal meets the needs and objectives that you've shared with me, is it safe to say that we can take the next step in working together?"

◆ "So if I can provide a solution/service/product that enables you to (state three of the benefits/end results you provide that you discussed with the prospect):

1. _____

2. _____

3. _____

Is it safe to say that we can we take the next step in earning your business?"

> 3a. "Mr./Mrs. Prospect, on a scale of 1 to 10, where 10 means that it's safe to say that we will be taking the next step in working together and 1 means there's not a chance of that happening, where do you stand?"
>
> Then follow up with: "So what do I need to do to make this a perfect 10?"
>
> 3b. If you are on an appointment, using humor could also help to get a prospect talking more.
>
> "Mr./Mrs. Prospect, on a scale of 1 to 10, where 10 means that it's safe to say that we will be taking the next step in working together and 1 means you are looking forward to shutting the door behind me, where do you stand?"
>
> Then follow up with: "So what do I need to do to make this a perfect 10?"

4. "Based on what I've shared with you, as long as we can honor your budget and your timeline, is there anything else you can think of that may get in the way of us working together?"

5. "One final question before we wrap up here and I start working on this proposal for you: to ensure that I'm respecting your process and where you stand, as long as we can (state conditions for the sale to occur—for example, work within your budget, turn this project around within your tight deadline, generate the results we spoke of, such as ..., and so on), is it safe to say that we can take the next step after reviewing the proposal and work up an agreement?"

6. "What would you need to see in my proposal that would make us your first choice for this project?"

7. "Do you have any preferences regarding how you would like me to format the proposal, both in length and what exactly to include, that will make it easier for you to decide to work with us/purchase from us?"

---

**Closing Bell**

Get all of the prospect's concerns and objections out of the way. You certainly don't want to get blindsided by an ever-growing objection simply because you missed asking the right question.

---

Take a look at your presentation. How many questions are currently woven into it? Here's an opportunity for you to adjust your presentation accordingly. Keep in mind that the number of questions you ask depends upon the information gained in preliminary conversations you have had with each prospect. That's your foundation. From there, the degree of questions you ask to further qualify the prospect is dependent upon the amount of additional information and confirmation you need from the prospect in order to confirm the prospect's buy-in and offer a solution the prospect wants and needs.

## Step Four: Discuss Solutions

Here's where you finally get to turn the spotlight back on you so that you can enjoy your time to shine (the old definition of presenting). Whether that means delivering your PowerPoint presentation, webcast, or product or service demonstration (such as a free coaching or training call, consultation, software trial, and so on), here's your chance to demonstrate firsthand to your prospect that you have something they can't live without.

However you have it formatted, you're now prepared to discuss solutions, how your product or service performs, and what prospects can expect as an end result in a way that will be a perfect fit for them. The solutions and information that you now share have been modified and crafted to fit them as a result of the questions you've asked during your discovery step and throughout your meeting with the prospect.

> ### Closer's Corner
>
> Here's a great idea for you to try. If you sell retail or real estate, or if you spend a majority of your time on-site with prospects coming to you requesting similar information, this may be a great time-saver for you. If you feel like you're saying the same thing to different prospects all day long, develop a client questionnaire or a "Help Us Find What You're Looking For" card. Some of my clients have had great success developing an overview or a frequently asked questions page that they hand out to interested prospects. This can also cut down the time it takes you to complete your discovery step. And yes, this can act as fabulous qualifying tools as well!

## Step Five: The Close

Chapters 10 and 11 cover the closing step in much greater detail in terms of asking for the sale and defusing any objections you hear. So as far as this chapter goes, I simply point out the only two general action steps that you can take at this point in your meeting, conversation, or presentation with a prospect.

**1. Ask for the sale.** Many products and services can be sold during the first visit with a prospect. Whether the prospect has come to you or to your store or office, or you are at the prospect's home or place of business, several factors will determine whether you can successfully and rightfully ask for the sale during your first meeting.

These are clearly identified and mapped out in the sales funnel. (Go back to Chapter 3 and review the sales funnel.) This is the best formula for you to determine whether you can achieve all of these objectives and meet all of the criteria a prospect requires to make a decision during your first meeting. If your sales process requires several meetings, decision heads from various departments, and proposals and product demonstrations that need to be scheduled, chances are you are not a candidate for the one-call close.

Notice that I did not mention that if the price is too high, then you can't ask for their business. Who determines how high is too high, you or the prospect? That's another friendly reminder of the dangers when selling like you buy. Realize that it's not the price of your product or service that determines whether you're able to ask for their business during the first visit with them, but how effectively you are able to deliver the relevant information (based on the sales funnel) they use to make an educated purchasing decision.

Here are several examples of the language to use when presenting your price or solution to a prospect and finally asking for the sale. Keep in mind, when presenting the price to a prospect, before you "lay off" the price, make sure that you've recapped exactly what you will be doing for them; the solution they are investing in; the product or service they are buying to ensure you've built the value of your product in their mind as well as the justification of their purchase. Once you have done so, continue with one of the following statements or questions to close the sale and earn their business.

1. Would you like this service to start now or later in the week?

2. So, would this be a good time to discuss installation dates?

3. All I need from you is a check or a credit card number and we can and get you on the installation calendar.

4. Would you like our company to be the company who handles this project for you?

5. How do you want to move ahead with this?

6. Were you interested in our financing options or will you be paying by check or credit card?

7. When should we discuss installation dates?

8. How would you like to proceed?

9. What do you see as the next step in moving ahead?

**2. Determine the next step.** Well, if you can't ask for the sale based on meeting the defined set of criteria we just discussed, you can determine what the next step would be in your sales cycle that would move the sale along.

This typically translates into setting up the next appointment to review the project, proposal, product, or service demonstration, or to meet with the main decision maker or additional decision makers who will play a part in this buying decision.

If the next step in your selling cycle is to put together a proposal, here is an example of the language you can use to keep the sales process moving forward.

You: "I can probably get you a proposal by next Monday. If I can get this proposal to you by then, when do you feel you would have some time to review it?

Prospect: "Probably by Thursday or Friday."

You: "Great! So, let's get something on the calendar to go over it together the following week. Mr./Mrs. Prospect, do you have your calendar handy? What day would be good for you, toward the beginning or the end of the week?"

Prospect: "How about we shoot for Tuesday?"

You: "And do mornings or afternoons work better for you?"

Prospect: "Let me take a look. How about, say, at 10:00 in the morning?"

You: "That sounds perfect. I look forward to meeting with you then."

 **Closing Bell**

When you are confirming the next steps with prospects, make sure you not only confirm the time you will meet with them, but ensure that this time will be after they actually have a chance to review the necessary information to make an informed decision or move your sales process forward. Otherwise, you're running the risk of playing the follow-up game that sounds like, "Hi, did you have a chance to review my proposal yet? Not yet? Okay, I'll call you next week." This gets old and annoying fast, to both you and your prospect. While we're on the subject of making costly assumptions, make certain that you have also confirmed who the decision makers are and, most important, exactly what they want to see in your proposal. Review the preclosing questions that I shared with you earlier in this chapter to get a better idea of how to get this information from them. Take a look at *The Complete Idiot's Guide to Cold Calling* for a very robust and detailed chapter on developing a powerful follow-up system that you can put on autopilot.

**Closing Thoughts**

Presentations don't sell prospects. Prospects sell prospects. (They sell themselves!)

I hope that at this point you have a deeper understanding of what it means to deliver an effective, permission-based presentation and become a master at presenting a well-crafted customized approach for each of your prospects with ease, in order to uncover the ones who are a perfect fit for you.

Oh, and did I mention without the fear or reluctance often associated when doing so?

## The Least You Need to Know

♦ Use segues to conclude one topic, open up another, customize the information you deliver, and reconfirm the prospect's interest in and desire for your product.

♦ During a conversation, if the majority of the talking should be dominated by the prospect, then the majority of the well-crafted questions asked need to be dominated by you.

♦ If you truly value your time like your money, then realize that the investment in qualifying your prospects is well worth avoiding the costly activity of calling on, meeting with, and following up with prospects who you had no business calling on and following up with in the first place.

♦ Clarify and preclose throughout your meetings with every prospect, or you run the risk of uncovering the wrong need and delivering the wrong solution.

♦ If you don't take the pulse of the prospect on every point throughout your presentation in hopes you'll talk through their concerns, you may wind up with a DOA by the time you're done presenting.

♦ Stop presenting and start having a conversation with your prospects.

Part 3

# Permission Based Closing: Get the Prospect to "Yes!"

Your style of selling and communicating needs to manifest itself from your heart and who you are, not from your head or from a book telling you what to say. Well, almost. Prepare for the most powerful step-by-step system to uncover and defuse any objection. It's all about getting permission to close the sale by opening up another possibility or solution. That's what makes the difference between coming across as sterile, generic, and robotic and coming across authentically. Here's a process that's aligned with your natural talents, values, integrity, and who you are, while still incorporating the baseline strategies, behaviors, and proven techniques that get to "Yes!"

# Chapter 9

# The Top Ten Types of Closers

## In This Chapter

- ◆ Learn about the most common types of closers
- ◆ Identify what type of closer you are
- ◆ Recognize the pitfalls in each closing and communication style
- ◆ Avoid the most common obstacles that will destroy a selling opportunity
- ◆ Develop and refine your closing style to best fit you

I absolutely love coaching people to achieve their fullest potential and watch as they achieve what is most important to them in every area of their life and career (if you haven't figured that out yet). And for several reasons. First, it is the most rewarding part of my job—that is, as my clients experience measurable breakthrough results in their performance and in how they feel within 30 days. I'm talking more sales, more qualified prospects in the pipeline, and a level of confidence and positive attitude that cannot be swayed. Second, what makes coaching such a rewarding and enjoyable experience is the opportunity to work with such a wide range of companies and individuals, along with the varying styles and personalities of each person I coach.

Although there are certain core competencies that must be developed and refined within each person in order to build a strong foundation, one of my core beliefs is that all salespeople need to develop an individual style of selling so that it's aligned with who they are and their values, strengths, and personality.

Unfortunately, some salespeople take the concept of incorporating their own style of selling to the extreme, fully exploiting their personality and infusing it into their selling and closing approach without realizing there are some baseline strategies, behaviors, and techniques that still need to be honored (and abandoned!), while at the same time, aligning them with their communication style.

Let's take a peek at the various types of closers that are disguising themselves as professional salespeople so that we can learn what attributes make sense for us to adopt, while also uncovering the ones that we need to let go of and keep at bay. While doing so, you will soon see that our personal strengths and positive attributes are also, paradoxically, our greatest weaknesses.

# Hopeful Harry

Harry remembers when he first started going out on sales appointments. He spent hours studying up on product knowledge, the presentation, and any closing techniques that he could get his hands on. However, with all of the knowledge that Harry had obtained and absorbed, he still was not selling up to his potential.

It took Harry a solid month of delivering presentation after presentation, and a heavy amount of frustration to determine what was preventing him from performing up to his desired level.

Harry knew that when you enter a home or an office for a sales call, you need to adapt to each selling climate or environment by first assessing the situation. He knew that in order to find out the needs of the prospect, you need to probe and ask questions. It was ingrained in his head that it was essential to uncover the wants, needs, and desires of the prospect. Yet with all of the knowledge that Harry had acquired during his training and recent experience, he was still not performing.

The bottom line was that Harry was not implementing what he knew because he was scared—scared of rejection, of saying or doing the wrong thing, of controlling his presentation and information, and, worse, of turning off the prospect. Harry felt as if he was walking on eggshells while giving a presentation, careful not to upset the almighty prospect. He was like a jellyfish during a presentation, floating in the direction where the prospect decided to push or pull him.

Harry's closing strategy? "I hope that with all of the information I provide, they decide to buy from me."

The bottom line was, Harry never even bothered to ask for the order!

> **Closing Bell**
>
> If you are relying on hope to do the selling for you, or prospects to tell you when they are ready to buy, then you are already giving sales away to your competition. These are not selling strategies, but wishful thinking, a pipe dream. However, if you firmly believe this is a strategy you employ, then maybe if you hope hard enough, the sales fairy will come and leave a sale under your pillow while you're sleeping.

Well, anxiety set in (or maybe it was desperation). It's incredible what a person is capable of doing in times of struggle. Since Harry had nothing to lose, it was time for a change. After all, you have to fail first in order to succeed later. How else are you going to learn what works for you and what does not?

Harry then began on a quest to overcome his fears and implement what he knew. Something very strange began to happen. He started closing sales. "You mean this stuff actually works, Keith?" I love when clients have that first breakthrough. How truly simple it was once he had his fear behind him. Harry's eyes opened up to a new and insightful world! It was a revelation!

Once the possibility existed for Harry to implement what he knew, he experienced a greater clarity. Harry was a new man—or, at least, a new salesman. This inspired him to implement his knowledge in all areas of his life. Once Harry became conscious of his fear, he was able to overcome it. He also began crushing every eggshell he could get his feet on.

# Pontificating Peter

About a year or so after we moved into our newly constructed home, we soon realized that living close to the water and having a basement had its disadvantages.

By the second flood in the first year, we knew we had to do something. So we started investigating what it would take to waterproof our basement.

After conducting my own research and speaking with three companies at this point, I was fairly educated on what my options were. I narrowed down the companies I would consider and had one more company scheduled for an estimate.

At about 4:30 in the afternoon, my doorbell rang. "Hi, Peter from Mid-Island Waterproofing," he announced. I invited him in and showed him to our basement. I had some questions about their process and the results I could expect. But I guess Peter had his own agenda: to talk my ear off until I couldn't listen to him anymore.

Pontificating Peter did not ask me one single question regarding what was important to me, when I wanted to do the work, what factors I was considering when choosing a company, what my biggest problem was, or even where I felt the water was coming in! Nope, Peter just talked and talked, and then when he was done talking, he managed to talk some more. I knew at that moment that Peter would find his way into my next book about selling.

Pontificating Peter may be the Guru of Gab. He may even know his product and service better than anyone else. However, since he never took the time to ask me what information was important to me, what I wanted to hear, and what I expected from our meeting, he continued to share his opinion and the information that he felt was important rather than what was important to me.

Now here's the best part. Peter and I were standing in the basement. I wouldn't call it assessing, since Peter never even examined anything, nor took out a tape measure or even a calculator to come up with his price. (I guess that really is the true meaning of the word *estimate*.)

So Peter finally gave me his price. I didn't say a word. Not 5 seconds later, Peter was already telling me a story about how he can justify his price drop! Peter proceeded to take off another $1,000, and I never uttered a word. Talk about creating your own worst objections (which we actually discuss in Chapters 5 and 12).

# Friendly Freddie

Everyone loved Freddie. Freddie was the kind of guy you enjoyed being with. He was an all-around nice person. Freddie was funny, extroverted, and sensitive to other people's needs. It was clear to the prospects Freddie spoke with that he actually cared about them. Freddie took his time asking the right questions, uncovering their problem, identifying their needs, and then ensuring that his solution was a perfect fit.

Freddie spent as much time as prospects needed, educating them about their available options. Out of the entire sales team, Freddie was invited by his clients and prospects to more outings, barbeques, and social events than the other salespeople in the company combined!

If there was one thing Freddie did accomplish on practically every sales call, it was making a new friend. Freddie was so well liked by his prospects that it started to become a problem to schedule all of his appointments due to the constant invitations he received for dinner or lunch!

Yet with all of these personal successes Freddie experienced, it was not resulting in new business. Freddie's wonderful characteristics and traits actually became his greatest weaknesses.

You see, by the time Freddie was actually ready and able to ask for the sale, the relationship he had fostered with the prospect was so strong that it actually became a detriment. After all, these prospects, in Freddie's mind, were now his "friends." And when these new friends gave Freddie a reason why they couldn't buy, Freddie was quick to accept their reasoning without probing further to see what concerns they truly had that he could then defuse and overcome, creating an atmosphere for the sale to occur.

As you may imagine, Freddie also had more callbacks than any other salesperson in the company—that is, the list of prospects he met with who told Freddie, "Give me a call in a couple of days/weeks/months. That's when I'll be ready to do this." And each day, it seemed that Freddie's follow-up list grew and grew.

Because of Freddie's caring disposition, he was more concerned about insulting someone and "losing a friend," which got in the way of him asking for the sale and being pleasantly persistent.

Well, Freddie finally was able to find the right balance of business and pleasure.

He changed his belief about what it meant to build a relationship with each prospect. After all, Freddie wasn't getting paid to make friends, nor was he being compensated for making follow-up calls to his new-found buddies.

Freddie learned what it meant to set boundaries and realign his priorities when on a sales call or during a meeting, more clearly separating his business from his personal life. Although Freddie never changed his disposition, the one thing that he did change was his expectations when meeting each new prospect: to give value first, to get the sale, and, if there is time and a fit, to make a friend later.

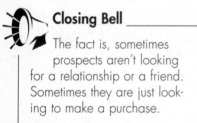

**Closing Bell**

The fact is, sometimes prospects aren't looking for a relationship or a friend. Sometimes they are just looking to make a purchase.

# Hank the Hammer

"It's pretty bad, Keith," was how the VP of sales put it, describing a situation he was having with one of his senior salespeople.

"I'm getting call after call from potential customers about Hank's inappropriate and offensive behavior. Whatever he's doing, it's preventing us from even getting back in the door with them. The prospects that Hank meets with won't even give us an opportunity to send another salesperson out to meet with them, even though they realize that our product is the leading product in the market. Can you believe that these prospects are actually telling me they are going with the number-two company in the market simply because they refuse to deal with us?"

Can I believe it? Of course I can. Especially when it comes to someone like Hank the Hammer, the old-school closer who thinks that pressure, coercion, and manipulation are synonymous with professional selling.

The landscape has evolved over the years in terms of what consumers expect and tolerate from a salesperson, and Hank was still living in the days of "Hey, if a customer doesn't kick you out of their home or office, then you didn't push or try hard enough to close them."

This approach accomplishes nothing but leaving a bad taste in the prospect's mouth about you and about your company, shutting the door on any future opportunity to earn their business.

If your product is that good and you have effectively defused all objections up front through the use of well-crafted questions, then this type of behavior is better left to reflect the days of the caveman.

# Not-to-Blame Zane

Zane was recently recruited to become a salesperson for a pharmaceutical company. He was excited, energetic, and eager to learn about this industry. After completing 3 weeks of training, he was sent out into the field. He was supplied with approximately 10 to 15 company-generated appointments within his first 3 weeks. At the end of his first 3 weeks in the field, and 15 appointments later, Zane still had not closed his first sale.

Although it is common in many industries not to perform effectively during the first few weeks or so, Zane was beginning to lose his interest and enthusiasm. He became discouraged. Instead of going to his supervisor for assistance and support, he began blaming the company for his lack of performance. After another week or so, Zane quit his position, convinced that the reason he did not perform was the company's lack of training, lack of managing, and poor product line.

Zane repeated this same process with three other companies within the same industry over the course of six months, only to arrive at the same

**Closing Thoughts**

"It certainly isn't me, is it?" Excuses do not build wealth and success. Only the right actions will.

conclusion as before. His failure was everyone else's fault but his own.

Did Zane have what it took to be a successful salesperson? He might have. Did he believe that it would be different somewhere else? Was he scared of accepting failure? Possibly.

That's when he called me one afternoon, inquiring about my career-coaching services.

After a lengthy conversation, it seemed that Zane was more of a rabbit, jumping from one sales job to another. His resumé listed about 10 different sales positions he had held, but Zane's tenure at every position had never lasted longer than one year! "If I do not succeed at one company, I will go to another company that offers better training, products, and leads so that I can succeed" was Zane's resounding philosophy when it came to his strategy for success in his career.

Reality check! Do you think that it is different somewhere else?

The truth is, much of the time, it has nothing to do with the company, but the individual. Many salespeople fall into the mode of thinking that if they blame their failures on everything else besides themselves, then in their minds, they have not truly failed. When this occurs, you have to ask yourself, "Where does this get me? How does this benefit me? What role am I playing in all of this?"

**Closing Thoughts**

A true professional takes full responsibility for and ownership of his or her performance and actions, and the results of those actions and behaviors.

Unless you surrender it to someone or something else, only you hold the power to create what you want most or to destroy your dreams. It is your choice whether to be a failure or a success. You are fully responsible for creating the life you want to live, for no one else will make this choice for you. If a salesperson starts blaming his performance on anything other than himself, this is the first sign that this person has either given up on himself, lost hope, or simply does not want to be fully responsible for his performance.

- "The leads that I am getting aren't any good."

- "The product isn't the best out there, and it's overpriced."

- "The people I meet with really aren't interested in buying this product."

- "The market is becoming way too saturated and competitive."

- "The technical aspects of this product make it almost impossible to shorten my sales cycle. People just can't make a decision on this so quickly."

- "How do you expect for me to go out and sell this with the limited training that you gave me? I'm not getting the support I really need to excel in this position."

- "There's just too much to learn and too many other administrative responsibilities I have to handle aside from just going out and selling, which is keeping me from actually selling anything."

These are common excuses salespeople use for justifying their performance.

### Closing Thoughts

If you are looking for a new career in sales, then choose to work for the best company in that industry based on what you define as your criteria. This way, if you fail, it is no one else's fault but your own. You do not have to fool yourself into believing that if you work for another company, things will be different. Depending on the industry you are in, this may be challenging yet possible. You may need to do more due diligence and research in order to acquire the experience and knowledge before securing a position with one of the top companies.

How do you avoid falling into this trap? Does this mean that if you are not performing up to your expectations in one company, it is always within your control to change it? Not exactly. After all, some obstacles a salesperson cannot control.

For example, you may not perform because …

- The company is not established, and name recognition is important within this industry.

- The company has a poor reputation.

- The product or service is not competitive in the industry (poor value, overpriced).

- The company requires you to go out and generate your own business leads after informing you that leads were generated by the company.

- There is no formal training that will help you better your performance.

- No sales tools (presentation book, product samples, marketing and collateral materials) are available for your type of sale.

- You do not enjoy working with the people in the company (personality clash, unethical behavior, no unity or team collaboration, no office support, and so on).

 **Closing Bell**

If you continue to play the helpless victim role, you are continuing to surrender all of your personal power and your ability to think as well as act by choice. When all is said and done, you'll have a lifetime of excuses compiled rather than a lifetime of achievements.

These are some reasons that could certainly inhibit your selling performance and may be outside of your control. However, keep in mind what you can control. That is, you can always control the choices you make, the position you decide to accept, and the way in which you respond to the obstacles that are presented.

# Methodological Mike

The master of metaphor, the wizard of words, the emperor of expertise, the president of process. Methodological Mike is the guy you call who knows it all.

Enough with the puns. As you probably have guessed, Mike is as linear as they get. He would have become an accountant but felt that he wasn't cut out for that type of work. Instead, Mike has exhaustedly spent countless hours refining his sales process and presentation. He's up on the latest trends and solutions available in the market.

Prospects were always very happy with Mike. After all, he was able to answer every question that they threw at him about his product. Prospects always commented, "Mike, you really know your stuff. Thanks so much for such an in-depth and comprehensive meeting. You've certainly given me all of the information I need to make a decision."

"So, what gives?" you may be wondering. The prospects said straight up that they have everything they need to make an informed decision. So why weren't they, or were they?

As we discussed in Chapters 3 and 4, it takes more than being an expert to turn a prospect into a client. Knowledge and expertise will take you only so far. There needs to be a healthy balance of both logic and emotion to create the perfect environment for a sale to occur.

Mike felt that he was definitely leaving business on the table, but he couldn't figure out why. Maybe you have already figured it out.

Yes, Mike was relying on his vast amount of knowledge to close the sale. While Mike did a stellar job educating his prospects, he fell short on getting them emotionally involved in the purchase to the point they had ownership of it.

Mike finally learned to loosen up and become more excited about what he could do for his prospects. He saw the results when he was able to transfer his feelings and enthusiasm into the prospects' hearts, not just their minds.

# Paul the Perfectionist

Paul, one of my clients, was involved in a terrible car accident that almost left him paralyzed. Being an eternal optimist and a student of possibility, Paul persevered. He didn't listen to the naysayers and to the doctors when they told him he may never be able to walk. He tapped into his internal strength and refused to surrender.

After several lengthy surgeries, the addition of a titanium rod in his leg, and countless months in rehab, Paul regained his ability to walk.

Paul turned what could have been a tragedy into a new career for himself, as a motivational speaker. Now, for those of you who are wondering how one goes about becoming a motivational speaker, it's pretty much the same as developing any other business. You need to develop your product and brand, presentation, sales strategy, business plan, and marketing campaign.

It was about the fourth month we were working together that Paul was ready to start marketing his services. He had his first presentation or seminar developed. We worked together on finalizing his sales and marketing strategy. Paul was ready to hit the streets and start bringing in new clients.

At least, I thought he was. Wait, that's not accurate. He *was* ready—I knew he was ready, and Paul verbally admitted that he was ready from an organizational standpoint. However, there was a disconnect between the things Paul developed that were ready for launching his business and actually *feeling* ready to go out and close his first sale.

Here were some of the red flags that indicated there was something else going on in Paul's mind that prevented him from putting himself out there in the marketplace.

"Keith, I'm almost ready. I'm just not ready yet. You see, I still have to get my business cards done."

One week later, here's what I heard from Paul: "Keith, I'm still not ready yet. I also need to complete my website. And then there's my presentation that I need to tweak a little bit. Once that's done, I'll be ready. Oh, I mean after I finish the PowerPoint presentation. And I still have to get that professional photo taken and …."

Just when I thought Paul had exhausted all the possible excuses that were preventing him from taking action, he came up with one last one. (Actually, it was the last one I allowed him to come up with before calling him out on all of these diversionary tactics he created for himself that justified his avoidance of taking action and selling.)

It was during a coaching call when Paul would typically inform me about his achievements throughout the previous week.

Paul was telling me about how much progress he had made with identifying his initial round of companies to target they would be a perfect fit for his services.

"That's wonderful," I exclaimed, happy to hear that he had identified the companies to begin calling on. "So what day this week do you want to commit to calling on these companies?" I asked.

"Well," Paul began reluctantly, "Here's the thing. I need to do a little more research on these companies before I start calling on them."

Paul was clearly wearing his perfectionism on his sleeve. I inquired, "Okay, Paul, so tell me, exactly when *will* you be ready?"

"Well," Paul began. I sensed he was about to come up with a laundry list. Yup, I was right. I stopped him before he got on a roll.

**Closing Bell**

Believing that you are "almost ready" is the same as saying, "I almost made that sale." Neither pays the bills.

"Paul, let's look at this through a different set of lenses for a second, okay? What if you were ready right now, today? After all, you shared with me that you have essentially everything you need to launch your company and start selling, and most important, you have your heart, your passion, and your drive to share your story and inspire others."

"Yes, but, well, it's still not completely finished."

"So when you say, 'completely finished,' is it possible that what you really mean is 'completely perfect'?"

Silence. A few minutes later, Paul reluctantly agreed with me.

Paul suffered from a clear case of perfectionism. And although this is a very elusive diversion we often use to keep us from taking action, Paul felt that in order for him to be ready, he had to have everything perfect, including himself.

When researching the companies he wanted to call on, it only made sense that Paul became a knowledge junkie, believing that if he could get everything perfect and learn everything he needed to know about public speaking and about his prospects (which, of course, could never actually be achieved), he would then be ready to go out and sell. (Thankfully, we caught this early enough, before he even tackled the thought of developing the "perfect close.")

After discussing the consequences of his actions (or lack thereof), Paul soon realized that who he is, his experience, and his story are the greatest gifts he could share with his audience.

Besides, if you strive for perfectionism, and there's truly no such thing as being perfect, then what kind of disconnect do you think you would create between you and every prospect you speak with (you being perfect and everyone else being, well, a mere mortal)?

> ### Closer's Corner
>
> Perfection is paralysis. It keeps you stuck in one place, continually justifying your actions and inactions. The root of perfection is often fear. So ask yourself, "What am I really afraid of?"

Paul welcomed himself back to the human race and soon found out that it was the vulnerability he had experienced from the accident that people connected with and made him human. Paul continues to inspire people around the world to this day.

# Stu the Yesaholic

"Yes! Of course! Absolutely. Sure, we can do that. Yup! No worries! Not a problem. No problemo. I can definitely deliver on that."

How quickly do these words roll off your tongue? Hopefully not as fast as Stu the Yesaholic.

"Just tell the prospects what they want to hear and worry about it later. Just get the sale."

Stu can't remember exactly where he learned this gem of wisdom. He feels it probably came from one of his earlier sales managers. Regardless, it was a limiting belief that created a great deal of trouble for him.

The thing about Stu was, he actually posted some sales. His heart really was in the right place. Stu was just, well, a bit misguided. (Not uncommon, considering the state of affairs among management today. But I'll save that topic for my next book. And feel free to e-mail me if you want to learn more about it.)

The downside of Stu's masterful selling strategy? About 40 percent of all his sales were cancelled within a week. In this day and age, it doesn't take much for prospects to figure out that what they thought they were getting isn't going to be everything they are actually getting. Not that Stu was a liar. His natural inclination when a prospect asked for something was to react with a resounding "Yes!"

Of course, this was a job for Super Coach.

Funny, I remember someone like Stu I was forced to deal with. It was the contractor who built my home. (Yes, another home story. What can I say? When something consumes your time as much as this, you're bound to get some really good content out of the experience.)

My wife and I were in the final stages of building our new home. We were in the twelfth month of a four-month project, so we believed the job was almost done.

Although my contractor did good work, he didn't honor any of his timelines. At least he's the only one who accrues expenses for every additional day the job takes to complete, right? Not exactly.

In truth, this project was always a twelve-month project. But he didn't want to tell me that. Instead, he wanted to keep me "happy." My contractor thought that telling me what I wanted to hear would make me happy. Happy that I had to extend my stay in temporary housing. Happy that I was billed every additional month for storage. Happy that I was paying my mortgage and utilities without living in my home. Happy that my wife and I had planned our lives (school for three children) around a four-month timeline. No, I was the farthest thing from being "happy."

You will make more money, have happier customers, generate more referrals, and deal with fewer headaches if you simply are honest. I'm not suggesting that my contractor was lying by doing something illegal or immoral. (That's a whole other book.) The fact is, I trusted him. I'm suggesting being honest about what you know to be true and sharing it with your customers, even if the customer may not like what you're saying.

For example, have you ever said "Yes" when you're better off saying "No"? Have you made promises that you can't keep or have to struggle to honor? Do you have a hard time telling the customer the truth about how long a project may actually take or what it may cost? Do you withhold information from your customers that you know they want or need to hear, in fear of a confrontation or losing a sale? Do you believe you need to please people for them to like you? Is your schedule frequently overbooked? If so, you may be a "Yesaholic."

When you instinctually say "Yes" without first thinking whether you can realistically deliver on that timeline or expectation, you always have the best intentions in mind. You believe you can "do it all." Yet think about what happens when you promise to deliver on something (completing a project, meeting with a customer) and you're not able to honor that promise? How does that make you and the other person feel?

Saying "No" is often perceived as a bad thing. After all, you don't want to say "No" and fear letting someone down, looking bad, or losing a sale. The irony is, if you inevitably say "Yes" all the time to keep everyone happy and don't follow through with your commitments, you wind up creating what you wanted to avoid from the start. That is, you let others down and create stressful situations that cost time, money, and problems by continually overcommitting and not delivering!

Being honest and honoring your boundaries (saying "No") is a very attractive trait. You'll find that more people will hire you, since people respect those who have strong boundaries.

The next time someone asks you to do something (including promises you make to yourself), give yourself the time to process their request by saying, "Let me check my schedule and I will get back to you," or, "Thanks for the opportunity. I will consider it." Then ask yourself these five important questions before you respond. (How important are these questions? In terms of a measurable cost, these questions would have saved my contractor $32,200.)

1. Is this something I really want to be doing?

2. Is this something I have to do? (It supports your goals, responsibilities, lifestyle, priorities, and so on.)

3. Can I meet this person's expectations?

4. Do I really have time for this? (Are there other activities you have committed to that take priority?)

5. What is a reasonable deadline/expectation I can commit to in the absolute worst-case scenario?" (If you plan for the worst, you wind up building buffers into your schedule that would enable you to handle unforeseen problems while still honoring your commitments. The result? You'll look like a hero!)

After practicing this a few times, you'll quickly see the benefits, since your life will became easier and more simplified once you eliminate the problems that result from over-committing. Remember, either you run your life or other people and circumstances do.

> **Closing Bell**
>
> Just tell prospects what they want to hear, and you can sell them anything. Then you can watch as they call and cancel or return their orders the next day.

# Adrenalized Angie

By the time Angie and I had our second coaching call, I saw the adrenaline on the wall.

As a coach, part of my role is to hold up that mirror so that my clients can see the real truth of what's preventing them from achieving greater success in their lives.

"Angie, this may sound a bit strange, but you may have a drug problem."

"What? I don't do drugs, Keith. What are you talking about?"

Not that type of illegal drug. But more of a natural drug that becomes our source of fuel and gets us through each day.

Many people today are hooked on a commonly abused yet elusive drug whose widespread use seems to be flying under our radar. That drug of choice is adrenaline.

The classic symptoms? Saying "Yes" when you mean "No." Over-committing or overbooking your schedule, and then finding it difficult to deliver on deadlines or complete tasks. Procrastinating until the last moment. Believing you "work best under pressure." Being easily distracted.

Consider that an adrenaline addiction may be creating many of the problems, employee challenges, and obstacles to a sale that you want to avoid. Tolerating stress, chaos, disorganization, poor planning, lackluster team performance, or undesirable customers creates situations that provide the adrenaline rush associated when working in overdrive.

Like any drug, adrenaline has its rewards. On the surface, it may appear that this legal, seductive drug provides a burst of energy to get something done, tackle a project, or meet a deadline. Being superhuman enables you to accomplish more than what a mere mortal is capable of producing.

However, it's more dangerous than we realize. The body produces adrenaline when stressed, when in pain, or to protect us from imminent danger. While used to handle a crisis, you don't want the drug to control you and dominate your lifestyle. After a day of riding the adrenaline roller coaster, you crash.

Too much adrenaline from other sources (nicotine, chocolate, caffeine, etc.) can also lead to stomach and heart problems, high blood pressure, and anxiety. Aside from feeling drained, burnt out, and exhausted, adrenaline lowers your productivity level and sets you up for failure. If you thrive on chaos, it's difficult to maintain your focus, concentration, peace of mind, or mental clarity. If you're a salesperson, a congested mind does not allow for the space to create the best solutions for your customers during a sales call.

If you're overwhelmed with a pile of tasks, then you can't be "present" with or listening to your customers. This affects your ability to follow a sales process, ask the right questions, uncover your customer's needs, and even create or recognize a selling opportunity, creating holes in your selling approach that many promising sales fall through.

How can you possibly turn an objection into a "Yes" if you are hyped up on adrenaline? Without a clear mind, you cannot create a new possibility or solution for the prospect.

### Closing Thoughts

To kick the habit and prevent sporadic results, shift away from using adrenaline and start creating the momentum that produces consistent, long-lasting results. Momentum is a healthier, more sustainable energy source than adrenaline.

Adrenalized Angie runs on raw emotion and enthusiasm when she sells. She's highly reactionary, making it virtually impossible for her to recognize the prospect's nonverbal cues or body language. Adrenalized Angie reacts pretty much the same way to each prospect, as if she's been living in a vacuum.

Here are a few ways that you can start your journey to get off the adrenaline train:

1. **Just say "No."** What a coincidence! Yesaholics are also fueled by adrenaline! Do you instinctively say "Yes" without first considering whether you can realistically deliver? The irony is, saying "Yes" and not following through creates what we wanted to avoid. You let others down by overcommitting and not delivering, costing you frustration, happy employees, new or future business, a satisfied customer, even referrals.

   Before you respond with a start/delivery date on a project or proposal, ask yourself, "Is this something I want to be doing?" "Do I have the time for it, and, if so, when?" In other words, "Are there activities that I've already committed to that take priority?" I'm sure your family would appreciate (be shocked?) if you made it home for dinner.

2. **Develop a healthy relationship with time—underpromise.** Adrenaline junkies often force the end result into an unrealistic time frame. Instead, increase (even double) the timeline you've allocated for each task by considering the worst-case scenario. This provides a buffer of time when completing tasks even if you experience some bumps along the way. One client said, "If I add 50 percent to each activity timeline, my day would end at midnight rather than 5 P.M.!" Herein lies the greatest lesson. You're overcommiting!

3. **Do complete work.** "I've always been a great self-starter but not a good finisher." Sound familiar? Keeping incomplete projects alive becomes another source of adrenaline. It provides us with a sense of purpose. After all, combing through the details in order to get something finished is boring, but starting something new is exciting! Instead of continually stopping and starting something new, commit to seeing each task through to completion before taking on the next one. When you've cleared out some space as a result of completing one task, you can add another in its place.

Like kicking any drug habit, you'll experience withdrawals, so take the time to get ahead of the curve and catch up on all of the overcommitments you've already made. You'll reduce your stress level, experience more peace and calmness, create more time, become incredibly productive, and enjoy a healthier energy source. You'll then be able to choose to redesign your life and career the way you really want. Take it from a recovered adrenaline junkie.

### Closing Thoughts

Even a deaf and blind squirrel will trip over a nut every once in a while. The point is, if you pull someone off the street and put them in a sales position that doesn't require much training, education, or mental acuity, they'll bump into a sale every once in a while. This certainly is not any true measurement of skill, competency, or sales acumen and expertise.

## Accountable Alice

Alice recently began working for an Internet marketing and search engine–optimization company that was in need of some changes. Within this company, however, there were several representatives who were generating the income she needed in order to live the lifestyle she was accustomed to. Although Alice did not generate enough business her first few weeks to substantiate any acceptable income, she persevered. Alice knew that there was a learning curve involved in any new position, especially one in which all of the selling took place over the phone.

### Closing Bell

There's a big difference between being accountable and beating yourself up for not doing something. Accountability doesn't mean that you're getting "everything" done, but that you're taking ownership of your life, career, and situations that are showing up in your life, learning from them and moving on to a more productive path or solution. If you're being too hard on yourself, consider that you are getting something out of doing so. Do you like making yourself wrong and taking a stand for your smallness rather than your greatness? I don't think there's any cheese down this tunnel, eh?

She listened in on sales calls the top salespeople made and took notes on the way they conducted their presentation. She constantly asked her sales manager for additional training and advice. She spent a few hours every day reviewing her notes from training class and picked up a few sales books from the bookstore. She made sure to invest time searching the Internet for more useful resources to support her in achieving her goals. Alice even hired a sales coach.

She continued her learning, studying, and practicing, doing her best
to incorporate and implement the
knowledge and experience she
had been acquiring. When Alice
entered her second month with this
company, things seemed to click.

**Closing Thoughts**

It is not the company that makes the person; it is the person that makes the company.

She finally developed and integrated her own style of selling that she was comfortable with. She even helped create a new presentation and submitted several ideas that resulted in generating more appointments for the entire sales team.

Although Alice is continuing her lifelong education, she is now utiliz-ing her time bringing in work orders and adding satisfied clients to her database. When the company recruits new salespeople, it is Alice that they look to for advice. Alice has become the model salesperson that the company uses as the gauge for acceptable and expected performance.

**Closing Thoughts**

Get clear with the expectations you have of yourself. Isn't it time you raise your level of activity, now that you've raised the bar on what you expect to produce? If you are not performing at an acceptable level after the first 30 days or an acceptable period of time it takes for the top salespeople to perform in your industry, you must determine what's getting in the way or what additional tools, skills, and strategies you need to ensure your success. Bottom line: hire a master sales coach so you don't have to waste your time practicing on your prospects and then attempting to figure it out on your own.

Although we have identified several *external* factors that may contribute to the reason a salesperson does not perform, there also exist *internal* factors that will psychologically undermine your efforts and abilities. Often the circumstances we cannot overtly see—the limiting beliefs and fears—create the barriers to performance. What follows is a list of certain beliefs, habits, or characteristics to look out for and eliminate.

# Why Salespeople Fail

There are dozens of reasons why salespeople fail. In one company I owned, I even went so far as to develop an "excuse board" when I inherited a team of salespeople who were notorious for their laziness and keen ability to waste their time. I thought it would be a great way to sift through their excuses quickly and build some accountability within a culture where it was desperately lacking, in a fun and light way, of course.

This sales team (did I mention that I did not hire them?) spent more time coming up with creative reasons as to why they weren't selling or why they couldn't go out on an appointment than they did in taking the actions that would generate immediate income for them.

Here's how the excuse board worked. Every time a salesperson came up with a new excuse, I wrote it on the board. Once the excuse was written on the board and visible for everyone to see, that particular excuse could not be used again by anyone. Now that we were tracking their excuses (talk about another useful field in our CRM software or sales reports!), this prevented every salesperson from using their excuses more than once. It also prevented them from coming up with excuses that someone else had used!

Unfortunately, I had to end this little experiment after the third 6-foot dry-erase board got completely filled up within two weeks. At that point, I had bigger problems to deal with and some housekeeping (and top grading) to contend with.

To laser in on some of the most common excuses, I've made a checklist for you to review, to see if any of these behaviors sound familiar.

Salespeople will fail because they ...

◆ Blame others for their mistakes or inability to perform.

◆ Lack the necessary level of persistence.

◆ Do not believe in the product they are selling.

◆ Do not commit to lifelong learning.

◆ Fail to listen and learn from those around them.

◆ Lack understanding of the industry or product knowledge.

- ◆ Fail to develop the essential attributes or skills required to become a masterful salesperson.

- ◆ Allow their ego to get in the way of change. (They try to do it their way and play by their rules.)

- ◆ Are out of their comfort zone and fail to adjust.

- ◆ Cannot cope with change.

- ◆ Are not committed to creating a better possibility for themselves.

- ◆ Forget that the objective of selling is to deliver value to each client.

- ◆ Care only about what's in it for them and how much money they can make.

- ◆ Do not demonstrate the level of patience required for meeting the demands of some clients.

- ◆ Choose to fail and simply give up.

- ◆ Do not ask for the prospect's business because they feel they shouldn't have to.

- ◆ Do not ask for help.

- ◆ Do not invest the adequate amount of time in their own training, coaching, and development.

- ◆ Are driven by fear rather than developing their personal vision and measurable goals that honor their priorities and keep them in their integrity.

Instead of tapping into this list in search of additional excuses that justify performance (I'm sure we can come up with several more pages of reasons why salespeople fail), Alice used this as a checklist to uncover the areas she could continually improve upon.

Although each one of these types of closers possesses certain qualities worth imitating, relying solely on your dominant characteristic will create the very barrier to the sale that you are looking to avoid. Just ask any of our friends that we introduced to you in this chapter.

Instead, do what Alice did. Become fully accountable for your success. Be honest with yourself about what you are great at doing, as well as what you know you need to improve upon. Putting more emphasis on your dominant trait does nothing more than overcompensate for a weakness.

Once you align your sales process with your strengths and values, you can start developing the additional skills, strategies, and processes that will result in a well-organized and balanced selling and closing approach that works for you consistently.

---

### Closer's Corner

If you can take full accountability for your life and work with a coach to raise your awareness about the things that you cannot see on your own, you will be at the most powerful place you can be in your life. You will have the ability to fully tap into the power of choice. To recap, you first need to take full accountability and then amplify your awareness; then once you have awareness, you have choice. (You can't make a choice around the things you cannot see on your own!)

---

## The Least You Need to Know

♦ Recognize when you're about to create your own objections and talk yourself out of the sale.

♦ Being friendly, approachable, and well presented is one thing; being Freddie is another.

♦ To tap into your fullest power and potential, become fully accountable for your life, your success and mistakes, and the experiences you have.

♦ To best connect with anyone you meet, be human and who you are. This is all the perfection you need.

♦ In order to continually meet your clients' expectations and reduce the stress and overwhelm when you don't, learn to say "No" and underpromise.

♦ Get off the adrenaline train and visit www.profitbuilders.com/adrenaline-assessment.htm to take your free online assessment to see how *adrenalized* your life has become.

# Chapter 10

# Planned or Canned? The Hybrid Closing System

## In This Chapter

- ◆ Sharpen your verbal acuity to enroll a prospect in changing a "No" into a "Yes"
- ◆ When to use a precrafted response to defuse objections
- ◆ Blend the canned and creative approaches to closing
- ◆ Use compelling stories to motivate a prospect to buy
- ◆ Stop stumbling, freezing, or getting tongue-tied when you hear an objection

In my own defense, I fought gallantly and made costly sacrifices, yet the man in the ivory tower persevered. "It fits the format," is what I heard. Just don't, for one second, think that I conformed in any way. So to make this clear, here's what the hype is about: me telling you, my entrusted reader, that it's okay to use a scripted or canned pitch to overcome objections. Yup, you heard me right.

Now, I hope you know me well enough by now that my approach to coaching sales champions may sound a bit incongruous to this. After all, I believe that your style of selling and communicating needs to manifest itself from your heart and who you are, not from your head or from a book telling you what to say. That's what makes the difference between coming across as sterile, generic, and robotic and coming across authentically by using your natural talents and strengths, and being who you are.

With this in mind, I came up with a unique approach to what is traditionally known as the canned or cookie-cutter response to objections. I did it with integrity, with class, with passion, and with panache. Of course, I came up with something even better. Imagine how much more effective you would be if you could use a predefined, well-languaged response to turn a hostile objection into a new selling opportunity while still being able to ask questions and honor your integrity and authenticity. Dream on? You don't have to.

Combining the best of both closing techniques (pitching a canned response to defuse an objection, and asking an artful question to gather more clarity and insight) has resulted in an eclectic approach to defusing objections—what I now refer to as Permission Based Closing, a.k.a. the Hybrid Closing System.

# The Hybrid Closing System

Let me introduce to you the Hybrid Closing System. An eclectic blend, a perfect symbiotic and evolutionary balance of art, self-expression, functionality, and proper form. Gee, I sound like my architect.

What follows are the golden notes on how to defuse some very specific and common objections. Remember, if it doesn't fit for you, then fine-tune these responses to fit your style. (But trust me when I say, don't change them too much.)

Most important, practice each response a minimum of 30—that's right, 30—times out loud (not just reading it) before using each preformatted response not only so that it flows better because you are now more comfortable using it, but so that it comes across as a natural conversation.

So prepare yourself for the most effective cookie-cutter closes ever!

# The "Exclusivity" Close

This little gem is designed with price in mind. Currently, this floor model is available only for salespeople who sell some sort of marketing, advertising, and business-consulting service. This close is available today for defusing the following objections.

- ◆ We're going to another (cheaper) option.

- ◆ You're too expensive.

You: "Mr. Prospect, aside from the price, which I know is one of your most important considerations, what else is important to you when choosing where to advertise and how to market and build your business?"

Prospect: "Credibility of the magazine, website, or company; their reach; circulation; perception; the target market; reputation—things like that."

**Tip from the Sales Coach:** If they can't think of any, then make suggestions. For example: "What about [circulation, target audience, the price, the reputation, and so on]? Is that important to you?"

You: "Okay, thanks. Do you have a second for me to share something with you that you'll probably find very interesting?"

Prospect: "Sure."

You: "If you go online and visit some of the well-known business websites and portals that are on the Internet and use their online directory, you will find something very unique. Each directory is powered by the same company. I'm talking about companies like (state several examples, such as *Inc.* magazine, *Fast Forward*, *The Wall Street Journal*, even *Business Week*)."

**Closing Bell**

When using statistics, check and recheck your sources. What is factual today can change tomorrow. If there's a specific website you reference, I suggest checking the website and making sure your information is still current. Then while you're on the phone with (or in front of) your prospect, you can even suggest visiting the website you're discussing. Doing so adds credibility to what you are selling, especially if the prospect can experience it firsthand.

"Their advertising model allows only a maximum of five venders in each geographic area to advertise with them. That's it! The reason they are doing this is twofold. Number one, as an added value to the consumer, they are listing only venders who are truly qualified to be there and who offer a great service. Number two, as a value to the vender, there are only five venders. This not only reduces your competition, but it provides you with tremendous exposure, which also creates a sense of exclusivity for the few venders that are listed. This, in turn, adds to your credibility and unique position in your market, especially with such a high-profile position on these websites. After all, how you look in the marketplace is important to you, right?

"Think of it this way. If your competition is going to the least expensive advertising option and you're one of our exclusive clients, you've just increased your exposure dramatically as well as the impact of your ad campaign by removing the competition in your market. "So I guess you have a choice. You can be lumped in with (dozens or hundreds or thousands) of other venders in your area (like a herd of cattle) that all look the same and act the same, and are all trying to make a dime competing against price for the same budget-conscious customer that's sending a ton of inquiries or RFPs to you and dozens of other companies, or you can stand out among them all and create your own competitive and exclusive edge. You are also being seen by potential customers who wouldn't have access to you otherwise or know you exist. May I ask, where you would rather be positioned?"

# The "Going Out of Business" Close

This beauty can roll over practically anything in its path. While great for the suburbs and average sale, this vehicle is best known for its ability to perform well in climates that are very high in price.

You can rely on this close for defusing the following objections:

- ◆ You are so much more than everyone else.

- ◆ We have no budget for you.

- ◆ Your competition is cheaper.

- ◆ You raise your prices while your competition is lowering theirs.

You: "Mrs. Prospect, thanks for being so up front with me. I do very much appreciate it. (Pause.) I'm curious about something. You may have seen these signs in retail stores. Just drive into any major shopping area, and I'm sure you've seen a sign in at least one store that says something like, 'Sale! 50 to 75 Percent Off Everything. We're Going Out of Business,' or 'We're Shutting Our Doors Forever. Everything Must Go.' Have you ever seen a sign like this?"

Prospect: "Yes."

You: "And in your opinion (being a business owner yourself), why are they having a sale like this? Why would a company do this?"

Prospect: "Because they're going out of business and want to get rid of their inventory."

You: "Exactly. Now, Mrs. Prospect, think about how this applies to any other business, such as the media or entertainment industry, Internet advertising, even magazines and newspapers. If companies are continuing to drop (cut) their pricing or even maintain their pricing in such a competitive market like this, what does that tell you?"

"Either they aren't getting the new business they need and they're getting desperate, or their clients aren't getting the results they need and, because of that, the company is losing customers daily. And if they are losing customers daily, they are losing market share and circulation, the very things that minimize the impact of their advertising vehicle/ program. So instead of trying to create more value for their customers and fix the source of the problem, they do the exact opposite by taking the shortcut and doing what many businesses do: that is, cut their pricing.

"And if they are cutting their pricing, they are losing revenue, which leads to finding other ways to lower expenses by cutting more internal overhead and other costs. Can you see how this is dangerous and costly for their customers? (Does this make sense? Would you agree?)

"Then the next thing you know, they, too, are going out of business! Do you know how many media companies, newspapers, and other publications go out of business every year?

---

**Closing Thoughts**

Notice how I reference the number of publications that go out of business each year. You will become a much stronger closer if you have facts and figures to back up any claim you make. Although I'm not sure myself about the number of publications that go out of business each year (it just takes a little more research to uncover and I had to focus on getting this book completed instead), it could certainly be an interesting statistic to use!

---

"Keep in mind that our company is the most well-positioned company that reaches more of our target audience than any other publication. So instead of cutting our prices, we took another approach to weed out the companies that aren't a great fit while giving more value to our priority customers through greater results and market penetration. And yes, with results like these, this does come with an added investment and commitment on the advertiser's side.

"That's why we realize that our [publication/program/campaign/approach] isn't for everyone, nor do we want it to be. That's what makes us unique—and, in turn, it makes our clients unique and stand out to their customers.

"After all, we could always do what everyone else is doing and drop our price. Just like you can always get cheaper advertising somewhere else. But what good is spending even $50 for an ad if it doesn't pull the results you're looking for?

"Sure, the price is great, but it quickly becomes an expense when you don't generate any new business from it.

"So Mrs. Prospect, unless you would rather look like everyone else out there doing the same thing you're doing, if I can continue to position you in front of more qualified prospects for pennies a day while increasing your exposure to (state number and target audience, such as "10,000 stay-at-home moms every month," "more than 1 million home business owners every day," and so on) who are looking for your services and don't even know you exist, would you be open to discussing this in more detail?"

**Tip from the Sales Coach:** Here's another closing question you can use instead of the one I just shared with you.

"So is it the price that's really important to you, or the new customers and credibility you will gain from partnering with us?"

Or ...

"Here's one other thing for you to consider, Mrs. Prospect. When these companies that are selling at the lowest price finally do go out of business, how do you think that affects you if you're the one who's buying from them? (How does that make you look to your customers or venders? What is that going to cost you?)

Conversely, wouldn't you rather be associated with the winner?"

# The "Price Increase" Close

This close goes from zero to the bottom line in less than 3 minutes. Take it for a test drive and you'll see for yourself.

This powerhouse is the perfect gift for the salesperson who is looking for a way to defuse the following objections:

- They are frustrated about your price increases.
- They want to cancel.
- They feel your price is too much compared to other options available to them.

You: "Mrs./Mr. Prospect, I can completely understand how frustrated you can feel about our price increases. Quite frankly, I wish I didn't have to be the bearer of this news, but pricing is something that I have no control over. If we were to look at how the price increase affected you, it looks like $15 a month, is that correct?"

Prospect: "Yes."

You: "Aside from the price increase, were you happy with the results you were generating?"

Prospect: "Yes."

You: "And you were getting some new business as a result, is that right?"

Prospect: "Yes."

You: "So if we look at this from the perspective of whether this was a good investment for you, if your cost per sale is only $15 dollars more and you are still bringing in new business from our website, then doesn't it still make good business sense (for you) to continue advertising with us, rather than pulling the advertising and losing out on that new business altogether?"

You can also use the following closing question:

You: "So, while I can completely understand your frustration, would you agree that the new business you are generating still covers the minimal increase in the cost of every newly acquired customer?"

**Tip from the Sales Coach:** Price increase, take two. What follows is another example of how you can defuse a similar price objection.

You: "Mrs. Prospect, putting the price increase aside for just one moment, let's focus on what is most important to you: the results of your campaign.

"Based on the marketing program we put together for you, are you still getting inquires and leads?"

Prospect: "Yes."

You: "Well that's great to hear. Let me ask you this, what is the average amount of each sale?"

Prospect: "I would say about $3,000 to $5,000."

You: "Thanks. So basically, you need only one sale to have this marketing campaign not only pay for itself for the entire year, but also experience a return on your investment, is that accurate?"

Prospect: "Yes."

You: "Got it. Now Mrs. Prospect, I still haven't run into a client of mine who was happy to hear about a price increase. Personally, I feel like I see one every month when I open up my phone and utility bill.

"However, based on what you are sharing with me, our price increase still doesn't compare to the average price increase that most companies have each year, which, as you know, happen for a variety of reasons, one of them being the cost of fuel and other operational expenses that keep increasing. The fact is, based on the results you are getting from the listing you have with us, it is clearly still a great investment, even with the price increase.

"And just looking at this practically for a moment, even if the monthly fee was $500 a month and you're getting at least one new client from it each month, that is still a great return on your investment, wouldn't you agree?"

**Tip from the Sales Coach:** But what happens if the prospect responds to your earlier questions with "No, I'm not getting any leads from my listing/advertising with you."?

You: "Really, no leads whatsoever? (Hopefully, you have the ability to monitor and track their statistics, which you should have available at your fingertips at this point.) I'm surprised by that. So then really, the main issue is not that we've had a price increase of (state amount), but the fact that you have not gotten the results you expected, is that correct?"

Prospect: "Yes."

You: "Let me ask you this: what is the average amount of each sale?"

Prospect: "I would say about $500 to $1,000."

You: "Thanks. So basically (do the math!), you need about two sales a month to have this marketing campaign not only pay for itself each month, but also experience a return on your investment, is that accurate?"

Prospect: "Yes."

You: "After all, if you were getting the results you expected, then even with a minimal price increase, you would still be generating a very healthy return on your advertising investment, is that correct?"

Prospect: "Yes."

You: "So let's talk about what we can do to improve the response that you are currently getting from your listing. If we can come up with a few ways that would bring in some more leads for you, would you be open to giving it a try and continuing with us?"

# The Risk Reward Close

This close is for the high-flying adventurous type who loves the adrenaline rush. Fast cars, fast business, fast—well, you get the point. This one is simply a work of art.

If you need to defuse objections that are more elusive and have to do with a sense of reluctance, apprehension, or fear on the prospect's side regarding making this decision (you know, the emotional stuff), allow this one to offer a smoother perspective and feel as you drive the sale forward—with the top down, of course.

You: "Mrs. Prospect, would you agree that, in life, the bigger the risk, the bigger the reward can be?"

Prospect: "Sure."

You: "Let's look at this from a practical perspective for a second. There are essentially two outcomes as a result of using our service.

"One, you generate more new business and we would not be having this conversation.

---

### Closer's Corner

You may have noticed how I've sprinkled some humor (or my attempt at humor—oh, there it is again!) throughout this book and within some of these responses. Many people believe that humor is the source of more sales than any other sales technique you can use. That is, if you can get someone to laugh, you can definitely sell them something. A little humor goes a long way.

---

"Two, you do not, or you don't get enough new business to the point that justifies the investment.

"Is that a fair statement?"

Prospect: "Yes."

You: "So Mrs. Prospect, now let's look at the worst-case scenario. For you personally, what's the worst-case scenario if you were to do this? I want you to put all the possibilities on the table so we can talk about any concerns. What's the worst thing that can happen?"

Prospect: "No business."

You: "So if you get no leads or inquiries at all, and this campaign is a flat bust, the worst thing that's going to happen is that you won't generate any new business. (However, you did get your name out there a bit more in the marketplace.) And what did this mistake cost you?"

Prospect: "Well, based on what you've quoted me, this campaign is going to cost me about $2,500 each year. So the worst thing that would happen would be the few headaches I would get from this not working and losing $2,500."

You: "Okay. So a few aspirin later, you're out $2,500, which, as you know, is a tax-deductible expense.

"Now what's the best-case scenario?"

Prospect: "Obviously, I'm getting more business than I know what to do with. I get to pick the customers I want to work with."

You: "Okay, so let's say you, like most of our customers, do get healthy, new business through us. What's your average sale?"

Prospect: "I'd say $75,000 to $125,000"

You: "What is the average cost of that sale, should you generate business through us? That is, the amount of money it costs you to bring in that customer to your doorstep?"

Prospect: "Gee, I'm not exactly sure. But I'll bet it's probably between $500 and $1,000 for every qualified prospect we generate that turns into a sale."

You: "So let's simply look at your ROI here. Now, you're a numbers person, right? We're going to let the numbers speak for themselves.

"If you get only one sale over the next 12 months, and if your average sale is $75,000 and the cost of that sale is $1,000, then your return on your advertising investment is $74,000. And that's being ridiculously conservative. Most clients are generating at least 20 to 30 qualified, interested prospects per month.

"So it sounds like you need, what, only/less than [one sale, two, etc.] to generate not only a breakeven, but a return on your investment. Is that accurate?"

Prospect: "Yup."

You: "And that return on investment covers the entire amount of your advertising campaign for an entire year! You get it back after one sale. So now that we broke it down in a way that the numbers make sense, would you agree that the reward is clearly greater than the risk?"

Prospect: "Yes. I guess you're right."

You: "The campaign we put together for you will pay for itself over and over again. And you have more business that's coming through consistently year after year. What kind of stress would this take off your shoulders? At this point, enjoying these benefits would certainly be worth the cost of this campaign each month, which would be about $200. Would you agree?"

Prospect: "I guess you're right."

You: "So the only thing we need to do at this point is discuss which options you would like to start with and when you would like to launch this, okay?"

> **Closing Bell**
>
> Don't assume that everyone has the same definition and understanding of words or concepts such as "marketing" or "promoting your site online to bring in more click-throughs," "market penetration," or "market share." If a prospect doesn't understand something and you fail to create a safe place for the prospect to ask questions, the prospect will begin to back away from you, and you won't even know why you lost that sale.

# No Budget, No Worries

I love budget objections because, boy, do I have the perfect set of budget busters for you. These twin turbo closes pump out 11 questions that are going to blow away your competition as well as the budget objection.

Here's why. Most of the time, "no money, no budget" is not the real objection. (We talk more about this in Chapter 12.) The following questions will enable you to go a few layers deeper to uncover exactly what the real objection is.

Here are just a few objections that these questions can defuse.

- We don't have any money now.

- Let's wait until next year.

- I don't see the value/return.

- I don't have the money for this.

- We don't have any budget for this.

When you hear any of the objections I just mentioned, use the following questions to gain further clarity on exactly what regarding the budget or the money is getting in the way of the sale. Then you can uncover what the actual objection really is—which, I assure you, is several more questions deep.

1. Then has this money been allocated in the budget for next year?

2. So if you did have the money for this, we would be moving forward?

3. I understand you would like to wait. However, can you really afford to wait and miss out on new business opportunities and new clients that are buying from your competition rather than buying from you for an entire year?

4. May I ask, are you looking at this an expense or as an investment? If you're looking at it as an expense, why is that?

5. Is it really about the money or the fear/concern of it not working and, as a result, you look like you have egg on your face?

6. May I ask, is it that you have no budget now, or no budget ever?

7. May I ask, is it that you don't have a budget at all, or is it more about the hesitation to try something new and different that has not yet been proven to work for you?

8. Has the budget been cut altogether, or has it just been reduced?

9. Is it a budgetary concern, or are you more concerned about the value you will receive?

10. So then, is it more a function of not having the money to invest, or is it more about making sure that your limited budget is being invested in the right place to ensure a measurable return on your (marketing, sales, IT, staffing, advertising, investment, and so on) dollars?

11. So if you don't have the money right now, who in your company does?

# The Fear of Change Close

Darrin was well into the closing—or, as I refer to it, the reconfirmation sequence—of his presentation. Darrin felt as if he had defused all of the possible obstacles the prospect had expressed. Although Darrin had satisfied the prospect's concerns, the prospect still did not make the decision to buy.

Darrin felt that some type of fear may exist to prevent him from buying. Darrin realized this must move this prospect out of his comfort zone. Darrin knew that he had to remove this prospect from his current state to his desired state—fast. Darrin had to guide this prospect to uncover the cost of not taking action in order to then take the right action that would change his present condition (pain). Here's how Darrin handled it.

"Sir, did I do a decent job identifying and explaining all of the benefits you'll experience from going ahead with this investment?" Darrin asked.

"Yes," the prospect replied.

"Are you confident you'll experience the results we discussed?" Darrin inquired.

The prospect once again replied with a "Yes."

When Darrin asked the prospect what the biggest reasons were for making this investment, the prospect offered several substantial reasons. Darrin continued in probing the prospect for additional information. The prospect responded positively to the following questions that Darrin asked:

- Are you comfortable with my company and myself?

- Have I fit this investment into your budget so that it is affordable to you? (Are you comfortable with the affordability of this investment?)

- Can you envision how this will increase the performance within your organization?

The prospect then replied, "I really can't make a decision right now."

Darrin responded, "Well, sir, I can relate to how you are feeling right now. So can the majority of my customers. After all, you have successfully operated your business this long without me coming along and demonstrating what we can do for you that's different from how you're currently doing it today, right?"

"That is true," the prospect agreed.

"Sir," Darrin began, "I know that this is a big change for you. I know that there is never a really good time for a change. What happens is that people, just like you and me, wind up postponing change until it is absolutely necessary. By that time, unfortunately, it is usually too late because then we are forced to make a change, giving up all the power and control to make a better decision on our own terms. Can you think of a change that you have made in your life that if you had not made, you would be worse off for?"

Darrin continued, "Everyone is always a little reluctant to change. Is that what's really holding you back from moving ahead?"

"Yes," the prospect replied, "It is."

"Okay, and thank you for being so up front with me." Darrin began, "What could I do for you to alleviate any apprehension about moving ahead?" ("What will give you the added confidence and peace of mind that this is the right decision to make?")

"Well, let me see your guarantees and, maybe, can I talk with a couple of your current clients?"

"Absolutely," Darrin happily confirmed. "To start, let's review the added functionality and results you will experience by making this change and the guarantee that supports them."

After reviewing the information, Darrin replied, "There never is a good time for change. Let's make a positive change this afternoon so you can become even more effective in [state benefit the prospect will experience] this week. Fair enough?"

**Closing Thoughts**

How about the "Control Freak Close"? It would sound something like this. Let's say you work in a car dealership or repair shop. You have a prospect who needs to get some work done on a car, but he keeps putting it off. Here's how you can respond. "Mr. Prospect, I know you are someone who likes to make definitive decisions and control the choices you make. I was just wondering how you would feel if you had to give up all of your control and power as it relates to making this decision. In other words, if you wait any longer and your engine fails, you no longer have a choice regarding when, where, or what you would like fixed. In addition, it's going to cost you more to replace your engine than to make the repair you need to avoid having to do so. If you go ahead and make the changes you need now, you can control the situation as opposed to the situation controlling you. Fair enough?"

# The Why Close

One simple question has the power to investigate what a prospect is truly saying, get clarity, open up a conversation, and gather more information and feedback to close more sales. That question is, "Why?"

"Why do you feel that way?" This one-question close should be used at least 10 times over the course of your presentation. Why? Because it will assist in getting the truth out of the prospect. Why? Because once you have the truth, you can diffuse the obstacle or resistance the prospect is giving you. Why? Because the more you ask, and the more the prospect shares with you, the deeper you are traveling through to the very core of what makes a prospect buy from you. Why? Because the truth shall set you, and your sale, free—free to post on your sales numbers this month! Yeah, baby!

# The Shopping List Close

Mr. Prospect, when you go out shopping, do you usually have a list with you? Now, whether the list is in your head or written down, you know before you go into the store what you're shopping for and then you can cross those items off the list, right? Well, why don't we make a shopping list for you now? The main things you will be shopping for in order to make a smart purchasing decision are …

♦ A reputable company.

♦ Qualified installers or technicians (if applicable). Ease of installation, the process, and so on.

♦ A product that will perform up to your expectations.

♦ A product or service whose advantages will outweigh the initial investment.

♦ Something that will enhance productivity or your lifestyle.

♦ A method of payment that is affordable.

♦ An affordable price.

♦ A strong warranty and service policy.

**Tip from the Sales Coach:** Write these things down.

Is there anything else that you would be shopping for that we can add to our list? Great.

**Tip from the Sales Coach:** With the list in front of you and the prospect, go through each item, asking a reconfirming question and then checking off each item that is satisfied. Here are some examples of the questions you can ask:

♦ Now, have I demonstrated to you that (your company, you) is the company that you would like to handle this?

- Why?

- Are you comfortable in knowing that our company employs only people who have undergone a rigorous training program?

- Can you see how this product or service will benefit you and your organization (family)?

- What was the biggest reason for you to invest in something like this?

- Have I offered you an installment program that fits into your budget?

- Is this affordable for you?

- Is this the best time for you to go ahead with this? Would there be a better time?

- Does the turnaround time/deadline work in your schedule?

You would then end with: "Okay. Now that we have checked off all of the things that you are looking for, what is the correct spelling of your last name?" (If it is a financial transaction that requires getting some credit information from the customer, you can close with this question: "Who will be the one filling out the credit application?")

This close either can begin a presentation or can be utilized at the end of one to substantiate all the facts the prospect committed to during the presentation. If you use this close to begin a presentation, then as you hit each point on your shopping list that the prospect shops for when making a purchasing decision, cross it off the shopping list. When you have filled every need that the prospect had expressed, simply say:

You: "Well, it seems that we have gotten everything on your list. Is there anything that we have missed?"

Prospect: "Nothing that I can think of."

You: "Great! Now that we have checked off all of the things you are looking for, which option that I have shared with you is the one you would like to move ahead with today?"

# Sentence Completion

"And your name is ...?"

Allow the prospect to finish completing the statement you are making. When the prospect is the one who is finishing the statement, whose belief is it now? And the prospect is certainly going to believe what comes out of his mouth, right?

Since he is the one who interacted and completed the sentence, the prospect has taken ownership of that statement. As such, he is the one who created and strengthened the belief and sold himself. The following examples illustrate this point.

1. You want to invest in/purchase this product because ...?

2. The biggest advantage you have seen in my service was ...?

3. You said something to me before about not liking your (state their current product or service) because ...?

4. I'm sorry. The biggest reason you don't want to go ahead with this is ...?

5. I'm sorry, you said you wanted to make this change because ...?

6. You usually make a purchasing decision by ...?

7. The most important thing for you when deciding what company to use is ...?

8. The person's name involved in making this decision is ...?

9. I think by this time you have gotten the ...? (Sorry, another attempt at some ....)

# Negative Reversal

Here's an example I have used to enroll people in developing an internal coaching program for their management and sales team.

"Mr. Smith, the three biggest reasons people decide to make developing an in-house coaching initiative a priority are:

◆ To eliminate the large amount of money spent on unnecessary overhead

◆ To reduce the high rate of turnover within their sales team

◆ To increase personal production from each salesperson by as much as 85 percent

"Do you currently have any initiatives that are targeting/focused on achieving these results?" or "Would attaining these results happen to be a current priority for you?" or "Would achieving these results be important enough to you to discuss this in more detail?"

This opens up the conversation and allows the prospect to admit and expose the pains he is experiencing. The prospect can relax and not feel pressured, opening the door for him to be more comfortable, open, and honest.

# Pride of Work Close

Prospect: "The person who gave me the last proposal said they would charge me only for materials, not for installation."

You: "It sounds like a great deal. May I ask you a question?"

Prospect: "Certainly."

You: "Mr. Prospect, your time is very valuable to you, isn't it?"

Prospect: "Yes."

You: "Time is the one thing we can never make more of. If you put a value on your time, would you consider it to be your most precious commodity?"

Prospect: "Sure."

You: "Now, let's say that one person is charging you $1,000 to install the (state product) correctly. In this situation, do you agree that this person considers the value of his time to be worth $1,000?"

Prospect: "Yes."

You: "He probably feels that his time is worth what he is charging. If another person is charging only a fraction of what a reputable organization would, then what value do you think his time is worth?"

Prospect: "It might possibly be worth less."

You: "Exactly. And isn't it possible that the value he places on his time could be reflected in the quality of his work?"

Prospect: "I'm sure it is."

You: "Mr. Prospect, if a person's time is free, then what is it worth?"

Prospect: "Nothing, I guess."

You: "So is this the type of person you want on your job site doing the work for you?"

# With Your Permission ...

These statements allow you to gain permission from the prospect to continue questioning him during the closing sequence.

- ◆ May I offer a suggestion?
- ◆ Can we further explore ...?
- ◆ Would it be all right if ...?
- ◆ With your permission, can we ...?

When you have permission to do something, you are then better equipped and able to continue providing another solution without resistance from the prospect, a solution that may be a better fit if the first solution you propose did not.

Let me explain. If I was at the proverbial closing table with a potential client, either on the phone, face-to-face in the office, on the golf course, or wherever we were conducting business, and the prospect was reluctant to go ahead and make a decision, here's what I might say to offer a friendly reminder as to why we were talking in the first place.

### Closing Thoughts

If you feel that you've lost your way during a meeting and are losing a sale, go back to the initial objective that the prospect shared with you—you know, the pain they wanted to eliminate or the pleasure they wanted to gain. This happens to be the same reason that prospect is meeting with you in the first place. You can say, "So tell me again what your main objective was," or "Tell me again what you hoped to accomplish," or "If we could just accomplish one thing as a result of working together that would make it worthwhile, what would that be?" What are your expectations of working together?" "Why did you hire me?"

Me: "Sarah, you've shared with me on several occasions that you wanted me to design an internal sales-coaching program for your company's sales team. I know this was a huge initiative to get off the ground, and I realize how much time and effort you've invested keeping it alive and moving. Now we're down to deciding which of the two options you have been authorized to proceed with, and I'm sensing some hesitation. Do you remember the numbers we came up with?"

Sarah: "Which ones? There were a few."

Me: "Of course. The numbers that we came up with regarding the return on investment that you would expect from this program. You know, the ones that showed that with a minor investment in each salesperson, the investment would pay for itself within 90 days."

Sarah: "Oh, those numbers! Yes, I remember."

Me: "And Sarah, do you remember what you told me it would mean if you were able to increase sales by a minimum of just 2 percent across the board per month? Forget the 10 percent number we were working with."

Sarah: "Yes, I do, Keith. The numbers were a bit staggering."

Me: "Sarah, with your permission, can we discuss the terms of the agreement for this engagement that I can then draft for you, or do you have a template that your legal department would prefer we use?"

Well, that's about as templated as you're going to get out of me in this book. Please let me know how these responses have worked out for you. Remember, you won't know until you take them out for a test drive.

Once around the block doesn't qualify, so try them several times each to get a good barometer of what works and what doesn't. If you can measure it, you can then manage and refine it.

Remember, closing is presenting the opportunity for the prospect to make an educated purchasing decision while moving toward a positive result. Although memorizing closes takes away from the sincerity and creativity of the salesperson, these closes can be easily adapted and tailored to fit your personality and get results.

Oh, one more thing before I forget: they will bring in more sales for you. You just have to use them consistently. Will they work every time? Nothing works every time when it comes to selling. But what would a 25 percent increase in sales mean to you this month?

## The Least You Need to Know

- The goal of a permission-based close is to enroll the prospect in first discussing another possibility that would be a better fit and then share your story, concluding with you asking for the sale.

- Logic, measurable facts, and statistics often allow for the reduction of doubt in your closing statements as seen through the eyes of your prospects.

- If you break down the final price into the ridiculous and they still don't buy from you, there's something else going on.

- Lead into every prescribed close with a question that allows you to continue having a dialogue with that prospect.

- Although there's a time and a place for a prescribed response, you must first open up the prospect's listening so they are able and willing to even hear it.

- If you regurgitate a one-way pitch on a prospect in a desperate attempt to overcome an objection, you'll be the one left to clean up the mess.

# 11

# Closing the Sale—with Permission

## In This Chapter

◆ Permission is power

◆ Three steps to defusing any objection

◆ Why most closing techniques need to retire

◆ Respond with questions rather than reacting with statements

◆ Let prospects defuse their objections

You're at a crossroad. One way is well traveled. You've been down that road before. You know the landscape, you know the obstacles, you are aware of the results. The other road is hard to see beyond just a few steps, as it's less traveled.

Right here and now is going to be your defining moment as it relates to how you close a sale. This chapter is a culmination of everything that we have discussed up to this point and will support the final chapters as well.

Here is when you decide how you are going to respond when you hear an objection. The response you choose is what will make the difference between leaving the sale on the table for your competition to take or realizing your fullest potential. It's time to stop reacting to objections. It's time you stop developing an adversarial climate every time you attempt to defend yourself or overcome an objection. It's time to stop being intimidated by them; they're just words anyway. It's time to use them as a tool to help you sell more.

Maybe some of the more canned or templated closes don't fit for you as much. You may feel the need to express yourself fully without any limitations or inhibitions. Here's a friendly little model to uncover and defuse any objection that you can use anywhere, any time.

# The Secret to Overcoming Objections— Don't

Here's a little-known secret that the top salespeople are aware of. They never have to "close" again. You will never have to worry about sounding like you are "selling" (as in, pushing) a prospect again. The alternative action that I'm suggesting results in more profitable sales with less effort.

Many salespeople believe that their product or service should speak for itself. Once they encounter any resistance, they are quick to ask for a time best suited for a follow-up call. Unfortunately, this "dead time" is when many selling opportunities are lost.

The word *closing* has certainly gotten a bad rap because of the negative connotation associated with it. After all, look at the root of the word, *close*, which is synonymous with "shutting," "locking," "finishing," "final," and "end."

Instead of closing, create a new opening without having to close. You can accomplish this in a simple conversation that does not threaten your integrity by sounding too "pushy."

The word *closing* is really the wrong title for this phase in the selling process. This phase should be considered the "reconfirmation phase," "agreement phase," or "opening phase." As opposed to closing the opportunity for a sale to occur, you are opening up the possibility to work with that particular prospect by agreeing to move the sales process further along and explore other solutions.

At this time, you are suggesting an alternative option in the form of a question for your prospect to consider that might better suit his or her needs.

Here are the most generic and common obstacles or objections to closing the sale:

1. "I need to think about it."
2. "The price is too high."
3. "I want to shop around."
4. "I need more information."
5. "The monthly installment is too much."
6. "I'm already working with another vender."
7. "I'm not the only decision maker."
8. "We have no budget/money."
9. "I'm not interested."
10. "This is a bad time."
11. "We're going to stick with what we currently have."

How can you create a new opening or possibility that can overcome these concerns?

Here's a friendly reminder of the definition of an *objection*.

## def•i•ni•tion

An **objection** is simply a concern, a question, or a feeling that the prospect either shares, implies, or is not saying that needs to be acknowledged, discussed, and satisfied so that the natural conclusion of your selling process, the sale, can occur. Objections suggest that the prospect is interested in what you have; otherwise, this person would not invest the time in deciding whether to purchase something from you. Conversely, failure to address an objection properly will continually result in lost sales.

It's a sign of interest: a request for more information or a prospect's concern or fear that needs to be satisfied in order to continue guiding the prospect through your sales process to its natural conclusion. Therefore, what the prospect is not saying in the previous list of common objections is "No, I don't want to and never will use your product or service." What the prospect is really saying is, "I'm saying 'No' or a form of 'No' because you haven't given me enough of a compelling reason to explore what you have in more detail."

In other words, instead of fearing objections, embrace them. Every objection provides you with a new opportunity to uncover the right information you need to share with a prospect that can move that prospect to the next step in your sales process. In addition, you'll learn where the holes are in your approach so that you can fill in those holes and refine your presentation before meeting with your next prospect.

# Defusing Objections Head-On

The most common mistake salespeople make is reacting to an objection rather than responding to one. When you hear an objection or run into an obstacle that is preventing the prospect from moving forward with you, rather than reacting with a statement to defend your position, learn to respond to what the prospect says or does with a question to uncover the real reason that is stalling the sales process, in order to create or explore a new solution. Bottom line: respond to an objection with a question rather than a statement.

**Closing Thoughts**

Rather than reacting to an objection with a statement that creates an adversarial posture between you and the prospect (for example, defending your position, service, or product), respond to the objections you hear with questions.

Here are several examples of how you can respond to the objection "We don't have a budget for this. (We can't afford this.)"

The intention behind the following responses is to first ensure that you are, in fact, dealing with an actual objection rather than a smokescreen. Therefore, isolate the objection down to its core to see if the initial objection the prospect shared with you is really the truth or if it's something else.

The "something else" could be that the prospect doesn't like you, doesn't trust you yet, doesn't believe you or your product can help, isn't the decision maker, has been burned before, is having a bad day and is using you as the new target, is not the best prospect for you, and so on.

Rather than react to an objection with a statement that, for the most part, forces you and the prospect into an adversarial posture that builds more resistance between the two of you while actually fueling and strengthening the prospect's objection, respond to the objections you hear with a question. Here's how.

**Closing Thoughts**

Here's another tip from your executive sales coach. The art of closing and defusing objections is the ability to continually create new and better possibilities for your clients.

# Three Steps to the Sale–I.G.O.! Right to the Close

When all else fails, when you've tried every predefined or templated response in hopes that it would destroy the objection, here are the three simple steps you can always take to get the truth out of a prospect as well as a sale.

Step 1: I. Isolate the objection.

Step 2: G. Gain permission to have a dialogue.

Step 3: O. Offer solutions or new possibilities.

## Step 1: Isolate the Objection

Chances are, there have been many times you have attempted to or thought you had overcome an objection, only to find that another two obstacles grew in its place. Why? Because you didn't uncover the objection—the real objection that's stalling the sale.

Ensure that you are actually dealing with a valid objection rather than an excuse, also known as a smokescreen. You don't want to overcome smokescreens, because you can't. That's the inherent quality of a smoke-screen; if you overcome one, the prospect will just create another one.

Therefore, isolate the objection down to its core to see if the initial objection the prospect shared with you is really the truth or if it's something else.

> **Closing Thoughts** _____
>
> If a prospect says, "We're not ready now. Call back in a few months," here's a great question to respond with. "May I ask what might be changing within the next few months that would then make it a better time to discuss this?" This question enables you to smoke out the real objection, just in case "We're not ready now" is not. Moreover, you may uncover some additional information you can use that will allow you to reposition or tie in your product with those timely concerns or problems that were initially causing the prospect to delay conversation with you for a few months.

Here's how you can uncover and isolate the core objection.

Prospect: "We don't have a budget for this."

You: "Mr. Prospect, I certainly understand that. It seems as if everyone today is more sensitive about operating within their limited budget, making investments into only proven (products, services, strategies, processes) that they know are going to work."

What follows are some responsive questions you can ask in this situation to isolate the objection.

- ◆ May I ask, is it that you have no budget now, or no budget ever?

- ◆ May I ask, is it that you don't have a budget at all or is it more about the hesitation to try something new and different that has not yet been proven to work for you?

- ◆ How much do you think my product would cost that would cause you to feel that there's no budget available for this?

- ◆ Has the budget been cut altogether, or has it been dramatically reduced?

◆ Is it a budgetary concern, or are you more concerned about the value you will receive?

◆ May I ask what factors you consider when choosing where to invest your (printing, travel, marketing, training) budget? (How do you make that decision?)

◆ So if you don't have the money right now, who in your company does?

After using these types of questions, you should be able to confirm whether the objection the prospect shared is the core objection or whether the real objection is actually something else underneath. These questions will enable you to go deeper and expose what the primary concern actually is.

### Closing Thoughts

What about those prospects that come right out and say, "No, I'm not interested"? Here's a quick question that you can use to salvage any opportunity to convert this person into a viable prospect. "Is that 'no' for now or 'no' forever?" In many instances, you will get a response that would keep the selling opportunity alive and classify this person as a prospect. Here is the response you would love to hear: "I'm working on some other projects right now. Call me back in a couple of weeks (months)." Notice in this example that "no" was not the actual objection. By asking this responsive question, you have uncovered something under the "no"—the real objection. As you can see, the objection was actually more of a timing objection ("Now is not the best time"), which you can wrap your hands around and overcome.

## Step 2: Get Permission

Once you've isolated the real reason that's getting in the way of the purchase, you need to get permission to discuss new solutions and have an open dialogue with the prospect—not pitch them.

Now that you've smoked out the real objection, it's time to offer a solution. However, the key for this conversation to work without you sounding like a high-pressure or "cheesy" salesperson is to first get permission. You can create a new opening to overcome a prospect's concern by asking for permission to do so.

Before offering a response, a solution, or a new possibility that would defuse a prospect's objection, now is the time for you to get permission to discuss a solution to the concern. This way, you will quickly learn whether this person is truly a qualified prospect who is looking for a better solution, someone who you are better off without, or whether the objection stated is, in fact, the only true obstacle to the sale. Here are some examples.

1. "Mr. Prospect, at this point, I'm not sure if we can provide you with the return on investment that my other customers have experienced. However, imagine what would be possible if you could start profiting from (realizing the advantages of) our service within one month. At the very least, wouldn't that be something worth looking into?"

2. "Mr. Prospect, if budget was no longer an issue for you, would you be open to exploring this in more detail?"

   I love using "if" questions. All I did here was reverse or take away the objection to determine whether "not having a budget" is the only thing that's truly getting in the way.

### Closing Thoughts

Use "if" questions. "If, just suppose, imagine for a moment, consider this for a second" hypothetically removes any objection ("If the timing was right, if your partner were here, if you had the money, if you could make the final decision today, if you accepted our proposal," and so on). And if this strategy does remove the objection which is, in fact, the core objection, the prospect's response should be a "Yes," which would then give you the permission to continue your conversation and focus on a solution, such as uncovering a measurable budget, a time they would have a budget, or the results the prospect really wants, rather than dwelling on the objection or the problem. Once again, keep in mind that if the prospect responds with a "No," then there's still something else going on; you haven't uncovered the core objection, or there's another objection or roadblock that the prospect hasn't shared with you yet. So you'll then need to keep digging to uncover the real reason for not buying from you.

3. "Mrs. Prospect, if there was a way to make this slide comfortably into your budget, would you be open to discussing the marketing campaign our team can create for you in more detail?"

4. "Mrs. Prospect, if I can demonstrate to you in just 3 minutes why every one of your competitors is switching over to us, would you be open to hearing more about this?"

Notice how I include a timeline of 3 minutes, to let the prospect know that this will not take up all of their precious time. Just make sure that you can accomplish what you are proposing in the timeline you stipulate.

5. "Mr. Prospect, if I can share with you three solutions to eliminate the current problem you're experiencing that would encourage you to consider us as a possible vender, would you be open to discussing this?"

6. "Mrs. Prospect, just suppose that we could shorten your turnaround time and help you deliver a better product. Wouldn't this be worth discussing in more detail?"

## Step 3: Offer a Solution

Finally, if the prospect responds with a "Yes" to any of these questions, you now have a prospect who is interested in hearing more about the solutions you can offer. So go for the appointment (close, demo, or whatever the next step is in your sales process)!

Since you have gained permission to explore other options, the prospect is now willing to listen to your suggestions. If you fail to ask permission and instead dump alternative solutions or more information on them even before you have a true understanding of what the primary objection is, you are running the risk of sounding too pushy, which causes a prospect to put up a defensive wall that prevents you from making a sale.

The next time you run into an objection, defuse it by getting permission to continue with the conversation. The result will be more sales with less resistance.

Remember, like all selling strategies, there are no absolutes. When some prospects say "No," they actually mean it! However, if you can convert even 35 percent of the "No" responses you hear into selling opportunities, then this process would be considered wildly successful.

The key point here is this: salespeople don't overcome objections; prospects do. The only person who can truly overcome an objection is the prospect. Salespeople create the opportunity and the environment for this to occur through their effective use of questions.

Selling is therefore the art of asking questions, listening openly and intentionally, and gathering information—not giving it.

# Stretch Out Before the Close

The simple truth is, none of the techniques you've read about in this book is going to work for you unless you take the time to practice them, over and over again. Just like when you go to the gym. It would be wonderfully time-efficient if we could go to the gym once and say, "That's it. I'm done. I'm in perfect physical shape." I know it would save me some time.

> **Closing Bell**
>
> Let's defuse this costly myth. Salespeople do not overcome objections; prospects do. The only person who can truly overcome an objection is the owner, the person who created it in the first place. Salespeople create the opportunity for this to occur through their effective use of questions. Selling is therefore the art of asking questions, listening openly and intently, and gaining information—not giving it.

The point is, just as you exercise and train your body, you need to invest the same amount of time developing and refining the skills you need to excel in your career—your selling muscles. After all, think about what happens when you spend more time in the gym or being physically active. Imagine how you feel and how you look. Now consider how much more effective you are going to be when you take the time each day, every day, to invest in your own professional development.

> **Closing Thoughts**
>
> Carve out 30 minutes (even 10 minutes, if you can't do 30) each day to devote to building your selling muscles to become the stellar sales athlete you can be. If you don't, just think about what would happen if you replace your gym time with fast food.

It's no wonder that most sales are lost at the beginning of the selling cycle, at the very start of your relationship with each prospect, rather than at the end. The more effective you are at defusing any objections up front, the easier it will be to close the sale.

So here's what I strongly suggest you do. List all of the objections you typically hear when prospecting. Then craft a response to each objection using the I.G.O. model I showed you.

| Objection | Response |
|-----------|----------|
| _____ | _____ |
| _____ | _____ |
| _____ | _____ |
| _____ | _____ |
| _____ | _____ |
| _____ | _____ |
| _____ | _____ |
| _____ | _____ |

Now, the responses you hear as a result of using these questions will enable you to create a new opportunity for a sale to occur by exploring at a deeper level what the prospect is truly concerned about or what matters most. The prospect will either convince herself that she should hear more about what you have to offer or share with you the reasons why she does not want to continue with this conversation (or if you are at the end of delivering your presentation, the reason why she will not buy from you).

Either way, you now know exactly what the prospect is feeling and where she stands, as opposed to walking away scratching your head and wondering why she did not buy.

# Turn Objections into New Opportunities

Questions motivate people to think and create solutions on their own. Besides, what do you think a prospect is going to believe more, what you say or what she says? After all, your prospects are going to support the solution they create rather than being told what to do.

Being responsive by asking questions rather than being reactive and spitting out statements creates more space within a conversation to explore a topic in more detail, providing a buffer to handle certain obstacles that may prevent the sale. This space will provide you with the room to develop new selling opportunities with your prospects that you may never have noticed before.

Responding to an objection with a question reinforces your commitment to understanding the unique needs of each prospect and becoming their trusted adviser. By uncovering their true concerns, you can then provide a solution that's a perfect fit for them.

This strengthens your relationship with your prospects, as you take the time to provide the information or solutions they want, not the ones you think they want. Now you can determine exactly what is needed to best satisfy your prospect's needs in order to earn their business.

The greatest salespeople know how to respond to objections or what the prospects say with a question, rather than a statement, in order to have the prospects support and explain what they stated. These salespeople actually listen the sale out of the prospect by asking the right questions. At this point, you have the opportunity to do the same.

## The Least You Need to Know

◆ Salespeople don't overcome objections; prospects do.

◆ Use your spider senses and tap into your innate sense of curiosity so that you learn to question everything.

◆ Most of the time, objections are not a "No," but a request for more information that can get you to a "Yes" as long as you're using the right questions.

◆ Instead of closing the sale, open up a new selling opportunity by gaining permission from the prospect to explore other possibilities and solutions.

◆ Most objections you hear can be responded to and defused with a question.

# 4

# How Top Producers Maintain Their Edge

If you're using these tools, you're probably smiling with delight. Hearty kudos to you and to the actions you've taken to achieve a breakthrough in your performance. So how do you keep it going? Keep growing! Are you keeping every prospect's eye on your value? Do you know what the heck you're doing when the prospect wants to negotiate your terms or price? Are you mastering the basics? After reading this final section, you'll be able to develop and maintain stronger relationships with your customers and will experience even more repeat sales. Finally, you'll get a clear glimpse of the possible weak links in your selling process and what you can do to schedule an ongoing maintenance program to continually fine-tune your selling engine to maintain peak performance. Remember, the sale is never over. Put a stop to losing sales to your greatest competitor: yourself.

# Chapter 12

# Handle the Money or Lose It

## In This Chapter

- ◆ Drops in your price can lose the sale
- ◆ The real reason behind price objections
- ◆ Justify your price drop
- ◆ When it makes sense to drop your price
- ◆ You're the one creating the objections, not the prospect

You say price, I say value. You say it's your industry, I say it's what you're saying to your prospects. How do I know that price isn't the only reason why your customers buy from you? Here's why, and I'll tee it up with a question. If everything was free, would you take it? That's what I thought. (Besides, where would you put it all?)

The point is, if you don't get a handle on creating your unique and compelling value proposition that gets your prospects interested, you are setting yourself up to spend the rest of your selling days walking the planet haunted by the imminent and elusive price objection. Yes, the price objection—sometimes your ally, yet most of the time, your greatest adversary.

# To Control or Not to Control—Money Issues

Terry sold home improvements and remodeling for a local remodeling company. Because of the way the company structured the salesperson's compensation and the formula for pricing out each project, Terry felt that she had control over the prices she gave. Depending on each selling situation she was in, she would offer different discounts to the prospect by taking money out of her commission. And if she had to drop the price further, after giving up all of her commission in order to get the deal, she would sell a project even when there was hardly any profit in it.

In one instance, Terry gave a fair price of $60,000 for remodeling a fairly large kitchen. James, the homeowner, stated firmly that in order to earn his business, he wanted to save an additional $5,000. James felt he could get the same value somewhere else at a lower price. What did Terry do? What if she immediately dropped the price to get the deal? What could have happened next?

- The prospect rescinded the next day because he felt that the drop in price was too easily acquired. (Did Terry justify the drop in price?)

- The deal stuck, and the salesperson made no commission on the sale.

- The company had to rescind on the prospect because the job could not be done profitably at that price.

What is wrong with this picture?

Many prospects will balk at the price when it is first laid out in front of them, for five reasons.

1. The prospect feels the salesperson has no control over the pricing and knows that it is an objection the salesperson cannot overcome. It is an easy way out for the prospect to avoid making a purchasing decision.

2. The prospect wants to play with the salesperson to get a better deal. Everyone loves getting a "deal" that another customer could not get.

3. The salesperson did not establish enough value or desire in the prospect's mind to justify the price.

4. The prospect is using a price objection to mask the real obstacle.

5. The prospect is not the real decision maker.

While there are a myriad of reasons why they would do so, I've listed a few just to illustrate one thing. Do not let this discourage you. Here's why. Price is rarely the real reason that prevents someone from purchasing something from you.

Here's an extreme example. If you can purchase a beautiful new million-dollar home (no strings attached!) for just $10,000, would you walk away? Of course not. You would go and find the money.

In other words, this deal was so good that you found a way to make it happen. As a result, you profited greatly.

Here's something else that you can profit greatly from. What follows are several situations you are sure to run into regarding how you handle the money issues with a prospect. This way, the next time you run into these objections or concerns with a prospect, you'll be well equipped to handle them.

# Dropping the Price Isn't Always a Good Idea

Terry should have been able to establish enough value in her product or service to justify the price she initially gave to the prospect. If the prospect wanted to save an additional $5,000, Terry should interpret this as having to establish an additional $5,000 worth of value in the prospect's mind.

Let's say you are out shopping for a car. You walk into a Mercedes showroom. You have just finished looking at some Yugos. Do you ask the salesperson at the Mercedes dealership to drop the price in order to match the price of the Yugo? They would laugh you right out of the showroom.

The price of the Mercedes is justified by the value it has to offer. The highest in quality, safety, durability, resale value, luxury, and performance. If you decide to spend an additional $30,000 on a Mercedes, then the price of the Mercedes has been, in your mind, justified by its value.

**Closing Bell**

If you get into a price debate over your product or service, then you are focusing on the wrong thing. Instead, you need to establish the additional amount of value in the prospect's mind that is equivalent to the additional amount of money he or she wants to save.

Terry could have done a few things differently that may have saved her sale. One thing Terry could have done was write on a piece of paper the amount of money the prospect wanted to save: $5,000.

Then she could have responded to the prospect with a question, such as, "Why do you feel that you can save an additional $5,000?"

The prospect may have responded, "I received another bid, and the other company was doing the job for $5,000 less. But I like you better, so if you can match it, I'll go with you."

# How to Literally Build Your Value

Terry did what we discussed in Chapter 10. Here's how it went.

Terry began by asking James a question. "When tackling a project like this, would you agree that there are more things to consider than the price alone?" James agreed.

Terry continued by asking James, "Let's take a quick look at what I call your hidden costs and see if they're worth anything to you."

Terry then asked the following questions, asking James about how much of a value he would assign each criteria when choosing the right contractor.

- ◆ The fact that we can offer flexible financing terms?

- ◆ The idea of not having to pay us until you are completely satisfied with the job?

- ◆ Using only the very best materials as opposed to inferior ones?

- ◆ Having the most inclusive warranty and service policy within the industry?

- ◆ Using our own installers (trainers, professionals, certified consultants, and so on) as opposed to independent subcontractors? (If that's a benefit for you in your industry or location.)

- ◆ Offering a guaranteed completion date with a penalty to the contractor if it goes beyond that date (instead of having the project drag on indefinitely)?

After every question Terry asked, she should write down the dollar value that the prospect feels each benefit is worth.

After asking all of the questions, the total amount of money derived in additional benefits should either be equal to or greater than the amount of money James wanted to save. According to Terry's math, it looked like it was.

When Terry finished this exercise, she concluded, "James, would you agree that it is not only the price that you are buying, but also the peace of mind and confidence you gain from knowing you are working with a contractor who is actually going to meet your expectations that are more important than the price alone?

"As you can see, the additional amount of measurable value and advantages you will gain from utilizing my services will far outweigh the extra $5,000 you want to save. So will you be putting down a deposit at this time, or are we going to finance this for you?" (Give a choice when you ask for the sale!)

# Always Justify Your Price Drop

If you are in a situation in which you need to drop your price in order to get the sale, you must always justify the discount.

At this point, Terry was $5,000 away from earning the prospect's business. Imagine for a moment that, in this example, Terry reacted and conceded, "Okay, James, I will do it for $5,000 less.

Warning: collateral damage! Because Terry so easily agreed to deduct as much as $5,000 in a split second, the prospect may now be thinking something else. "Gee, if she can drop the price so easily, then I guess that she has control over the pricing. Why didn't she just give me her best price right from the beginning? Maybe I can save even more money. Hmmm. Now I don't know if I can trust her anymore."

### Closing Thoughts

Here's a friendly tip from your executive sales coach when getting hit with a price objection. If you hear "Your price is too high" or a variation of that objection, you may react by offering the prospect some type of reduction in price. If a prospect can get a discount by merely making a statement, think about the atmosphere you are creating. Prospects will feel that they shouldn't buy from you before trying something else to get an even better price—like checking out your competition. "Your price is too high" is not a question you need to defend. Instead of answering it, respond with a question, such as, "Before I explain why my price is higher, why do you feel the other price you received was so low?" or "Why do you feel that way?" Now, you have the opportunity to hear from the prospect their reasons for making the statement, providing you with the opening to uncover the real objection that you can work on defusing.

Consider the potential consequences if you let the prospect know you have control over the pricing. If the prospect feels at any point that you have control over pricing, there is a shift in the dynamic of the relationship. Prospects could now feel intimidated; not knowing if they are getting the best deal. Conversely, prospects might feel the need to continually haggle over the price so that they feel they are getting the best deal. Imagine what would happen if all retail stores suddenly had the power to negotiate prices. I'm talking stores like Home Depot, Best Buy, Target, The Gap, K-Mart, Wal-Mart, and so on. Total pandemonium.

If the prospect wants a lower price, take something away or out of the deliverable you would be responsible for in order to bring the price down. Here are some examples.

- Offer lower-quality or different-quality products.

- Offer lower-quality service and installation.

- Suggest a smaller work order, or scale down the size of the project.

- Offer a lesser warranty or service policy.

- Ask for something in return (for example, references, testimonials, referrals, exposure, and so on).

Remember, prospects do not like it when things are taken away from them. Once you take it away, most of the time they want it back.

**Closing Thoughts**

You need to justify in the prospect's mind how you are able to offer your product or service at a lower price (especially if you've invested the time during your presentation building up the value of your product).

# Recognize When Your Prospects Are Testing You

Some prospects do not care how much a product or service costs, but they care about how much they can save.

Let me say this in a different way. If the prospect wants to save an additional $5,000, they may want to save that $5,000 regardless of whether the price of the kitchen was $20,000 or $70,000. They may simply just enjoy the process of negotiating, or it is how they go about making a purchasing decision.

What's the purpose of having a sticker price on a car? In many instances, it winds up being higher than the price you pay. The dealership could have put down their bottom-line price on the sticker price, but they didn't.

If they did, they would give up their only competitive advantage, saving you money if you buy from them. If the sticker price was non-negotiable, like many car dealers are turning to these days, these salespeople would have no room for negotiation with the prospects who want a "deal."

Everyone enjoys the experience and the feeling of saving money. This flexibility over the pricing enables car dealerships to create their perfect closing environment, making a prospect feel he received an extraordinary deal by tapping into the prospect's emotions and how that person feels about saving money. This, of course, often happens after 3 hours of negotiation.

# Think Again Before You Split the Difference

So how should Terry actually handle this negotiation with James and his kitchen project? It was clear that, after all the value Terry attempted to build, James was set on wanting to save $5,000. Luckily, Terry called on her sales coach for help before calling her prospect. She wanted to make sure she could approach this sale with the least amount of profit loss, which might be required to earn this prospect's business.

"Ring!" it was my bat phone. A client must be in need.

"Yes? Hi, Terry! What? You need some quick coaching? You have an immediate issue with a prospect? A deal that needs to be negotiated? Very well. Let's discuss."

Terry filled me in on what had already transpired with James. Here's what I coached her to do.

"Okay, Terry. What was your first visceral reaction to his request?"

"Well, I would hate to lose the sale, and I already cleared it with the owner that it's still worth doing, so I guess it was to just drop the price and get the sale. So now that I know I can, I'll tell him we can do it."

"I see. And you are certain that he committed to you that if you could come down in price, he would then buy from you and move ahead with this project?"

"Well, no, not exactly."

"I'll take that as a 'No' for now, okay? Which means, if you went back to him and dropped the price, since you said you didn't preclose James, he can then hit you with another objection. After all, he never committed to you that he would go with you and that there was nothing else standing in the way of moving ahead.

"Let's put that aside for a moment. You said that James liked you better, is that correct?"

"Absolutely," Terry confirmed. "He liked our cabinet line and our installation process better, and we did hit it off, so I guess he liked me, too."

"So there's clearly an investment of time on both sides. How about this? Do you think there's a chance you could split the difference with him?"

"Well, I can certainly ask. I think he would go for that. Which would be, what, $57,500 if we split the $5,000 difference."

"Before you do, rather than suggesting to James that you should split the difference, encourage him to make the offer to do so."

"I've never done that before. I wouldn't even know how to do that or what to say."

After Terry shared with me how she might approach this prospect, I shared with her a few ideas and the dialogue she could use that would maximize the sale.

Here's what she could say to James:

"James, it's been an absolute pleasure working with you on this project. I want to again thank you for considering us as the company to remodel your kitchen. Unfortunately, we're going to have to pass on doing your project for you at the price you want. We just can't afford to do your job,

> **Closer's Corner**
>
> The intention of negotiating is to elicit a feeling of success within the person on the other side, leaving them with the belief that they, in fact, have won.

so if you got a lower price, while I know you mentioned you liked our product line and process better, well, if price is really that important to you, then you always have that option to go with and I hope it works out for you.

"I'm really sorry about this. As you can imagine, the last thing I want to do is turn away a great customer, as well as a great project. Personally, I feel it's a shame we can't come to terms on this when we're only $5,000 apart. We can come to terms over what initially started as an $85,000 kitchen remodel and both feel comfortable about it, but we can't come to terms over $5000?"

I continued explaining the key points that Terry needed to make. "At this point, you want to keep reinforcing the fact that James really liked your company much better in every aspect. Remind him that there was a considerable amount of time invested by both parties and that it would be a shame for him to have to start all over. And most important, stress the fact that you are only a relatively small amount of money apart from coming together on this."

Terry called James and conducted herself wonderfully. Afterward, Terry couldn't believe it. James actually responded with something like, "Well, Terry, I hear what you're saying. I'll tell you what … what if we, say, maybe we split the difference? What do you think?" (You mean this coaching stuff actually works?)

Terry then confirmed with James what he was proposing. "Let me make sure I'm clear with what you're saying. If we went ahead and simply split the difference, that would look like, what? I'm at $60,000 and you're at $55,000. So you're saying that you would go ahead with this and I can draw up the agreement at $57,500. Is that correct?"

James hesitated for a moment, then squeaked out a "Yes." (Twice for Terry—she asked again to make sure.) "I'll do it for $57,500."

Terry was pumped up! But she wasn't sure exactly what to do now. So she said, "Well, James, thanks for being flexible. Now at least I'll feel a little more confident presenting this to the owner and hoping for a positive response, okay? So let's get something on the calendar to talk tomorrow afternoon. That should give me enough time to present your proposal to him and gauge his response."

What did Terry do next? You guessed it. She called me.

**Closing Bell**

Don't assume that splitting the difference means dividing it down the middle. The difference between the price you want to sell at and the price the prospect wants to purchase at can be split more than once.

"Great work!" I applauded. "So, are you ready for what's next? You did something so remarkable that most salespeople don't even realize is possible. You shifted the balance of power back to you. What price range are you now negotiating? $57,500 to $60,000. And the kicker is, you didn't give up a dollar yet. Where before your negotiating range was $55,000 to $60,000 because he was willing to split the difference and you did not accept or confirm his offer, you narrowed down the range to negotiate by $2,500 in your favor."

The next day, Terry called James. Here's what the conversation sounded like.

"Hi James. Well, here's what happened. Quite frankly, I didn't think it would be an issue going with $57,500, but apparently, it is. The owner took an hour himself and crunched the numbers and felt that this job could easily become an expense for us, especially with all the other profitable business out there now. He's adamant about not doing this project for anything under $60,000. I'm really sorry. I did my best, though. I hope you know that."

Then Terry thought about what we discussed and continued with, "You know, James, after all this, I don't know about you, but to have this fall apart over $2,500 is pretty ridiculous. I mean, we're literally $2,500 away from you getting the kitchen you really want in your home."

Terry continued this line of exploration with James for a little while longer. As you may imagine, James offered to split the difference again with Terry. Once Terry confirmed this with James and went back to the owner, the next time she called

**Closing Thoughts**

Typically, in any negotiation, there's something that each side needs to concede on.

James, it was to ask him where he'd like the contract sent. The sale went through, and Terry managed to make a customer very happy, while also putting an additional $1,250 back into the bottom line, which certainly made the owner happy. All because Terry was patient enough and waited to encourage James to split the difference not once, but twice.

Most important, James left this negotiation feeling good about his purchase and, more so, that he, in fact, had won. After all, he got Terry to split the difference that he asked for. It was, in fact, the prospect's idea to begin with.

The owner felt more motivated, yet still reluctant, to eventually split the difference because it was James who proposed this solution rather than his salesperson.

Besides, what is James more likely to act on? An idea that he came up with or one you suggested?

**Closing Bell**

Instead of offering to split the difference, encourage the other person to make the suggestion to do so. This puts the power in their corner, as well as creates a deeper sense of ownership since they're the one who created the idea.

# Stop Creating the Objections That Kill Your Sales!

Harry thought this was a great time to begin a career in finance. He interviewed with several companies and landed a position with Third Federal Funding. Harry trained to be a loan officer, showing homeowners methods to reduce their debt load through a process called debt consolidation. The benefits that the homeowner would receive from consolidating their debt were as follows:

- Paying off all their debt and putting it under one monthly bill

- Making their credit card bills tax-deductible, which they were not before

- Offering a fixed, lower interest rate than what they currently have

- Offering cash back out of this loan

- Reducing the total amount they pay out each month in bills after consolidating all of them

"How hard could it be to enroll people in the concept of saving money?" Harry thought. Harry did not close his first three prospects. He could not figure out what he was doing wrong. After all, he was saving people money!

That afternoon, a call came in from someone interested in their services. The ad they ran that morning on the radio had pulled in a handful of inquiries. Harry turned to his sales manager for help. He decided to take Paul, his manager, out on the next appointment he went on.

They arrived at Sandra Smulen's home, and almost immediately, Harry began talking about why he was there. After Harry explained the concept of consolidation, Sandra was still unreceptive. After all, people are very cautious about what they do with their money, right?

Before Harry concluded his presentation, Paul jumped in. Paul saved the deal and walked out with the paperwork he needed to begin the consolidation process for Sandra. So what did Paul do that Harry did not?

**Closing Thoughts**

Paint the verbal picture clear enough for the prospect to understand.

# When the Salesperson Creates the Objection

Debt-to-income ratio, 80 percent loan to value, simple-interest loan, compound loan. These are terms that are foreign to most people. As we discovered earlier in this book, when people do not understand where their money is going, they do not buy.

Although Harry explained the concept of consolidation in terms he understood, he failed to explain it in terms that Sandra understood. In Chapters 7 and 8, where we discussed how to deliver effective presentations, Harry never took the time to take the pulse throughout the time he talked at her.

Lay out your information in terms that prospects can comprehend. Rather than confuse Sandra, Paul made a complex loan appear very simple and beneficial to her. Harry portrayed the process of consolidation as confusing, time-consuming and risky.

Ironically, by creating this perception in Sandra's mind, Harry actually created his very own objection! This would have been avoided if he had delivered a message crafted for Sandra to understand.

Here's what Paul did. Paul simply took out a sheet of paper and listed all of Sandra's bills. Then he listed the interest rate she was currently paying on her money.

On the opposite side of the paper, Paul showed Sandra the amount of savings she would realize with a lower interest rate and the tax deduction. He wrote down the new total monthly payment for all her bills that she would now be laying out. Paul even demonstrated exactly how much money Sandra would be putting back into her pocket every month.

Because of the approach Paul used, Sandra was able to visualize and comprehend exactly how this process would truly help.

Be cautious of creating an obstacle that would not have surfaced without your help. If you make these assumptions in your presentation without actually hearing them expressed by the prospect, you are putting thoughts in their mind that they might not have thought of on their own! Or you're selling the way you buy. (Remember Chapter 5.)

Here are some of the statements I've witnessed salespeople mistakenly make that create their own objection.

1. I know this may be a large investment for you right now.

2. It might take a very long time to process your order.

3. You might have to go through all of this paperwork again.

4. Many companies sell what we have.

5. Do you want to shop around?

6. Do you think the price is high?

7. Are you getting other estimates?

8. Have you gotten any other estimates/bids/requests for proposals yet?

9. You can probably borrow the money cheaper at your own bank or lending institution.

10. Well, obviously [state leading company in your space] is the best, but if you're not going to go with them, with us you are …. (You can stop there. Your foot is already well inserted in your mouth.)

11. Okay, you know my price, you know what we can do. So when you finish doing what you need to do, call me when you're ready, okay?

12. What do you think about the price?

13. You'll never be able to …. (Once again, telling a customer what they can or cannot do is not typically well received.)

Address these concerns only if they are stated or implied by the prospect. Otherwise, you will find yourself climbing over the very obstacles you created. Hey, it's challenging enough to stay on top of your game. No need to add self-imposed detours, challenges, and barriers that prevent peak productivity.

---

### Closer's Corner

A quick connection to make here. If you remember what we learned in Chapter 4, Paul clearly laid out Sandra's current financial condition. He showed her how much money she was paying to all of the credit card companies in interest alone. This was Sandra's current condition or present state (pain). Paul then showed Sandra all of the money she could be putting back into her pocket by consolidating her bills. Writing down this information in front of Sandra helped her visualize the desired state (pleasure) where she wanted to be.

---

## The Least You Need to Know

- While I am not a fan of dropping price to close a sale, if it truly is your last-ditch effort to earn the prospect's business, then you'd better make sure you have a really good reason for doing so.

- By selling the way you buy, you are mistakenly setting yourself up to create the objections you're looking to avoid.

- Communicate to every prospect in a way they can understand, or run the risk of communicating yourself out of a sale.

- Before you drop price, ask yourself if you have done everything to justify the value of your product or service to the prospect.

- When some people buy, they are less concerned about how much the product or service costs than they are about how much they might be able to negotiate and save.

- Before you split the difference, encourage the prospect to suggest doing so; this will empower them to move the sales process forward rather than you having to push.

# Chapter 13

# Stop the Cancellations and Improve Client Retention

## In This Chapter

- ◆ How to handle cancellations and save a sale
- ◆ Remove any weak links in the sale
- ◆ Seven steps to reducing cancellations
- ◆ Aspirin for your client's hangover
- ◆ Keep their eye on your value

You have just invested a considerable amount of time in an appointment. The prospect finally convinced himself to make the buying decision. You finish all of the necessary paperwork that you need to solidify the deal. You then close your briefcase, walk out the door, and drive home.

What do you think is waiting for you in the office the following day? I'll give you a hint. It is something all salespeople dread. It makes the value of your time worth nothing. It also makes every salesperson cringe with agony. Give up? Cancellations!

It's time we address why your once happy new customer decides to cancel and what you can do about it. You are going to learn what you can do immediately to handle a cancellation, what you can do to save the sale, and whether it even makes sense to invest the time in saving the sale in the first place!

But it goes beyond simply averting a cancellation. For those who don't care about cancellations but would like stronger relationships with customers and more repeat sales, you'll learn what you can do during every sale that will exponentially contribute to future sales.

# A Buyer's Hangover

"What do you mean Mrs. Smith canceled on me? I was on that appointment for 3½ hours! What a waste of time!" Why do people cancel? Cognitive dissonance or, as most people refer to it, prospect's remorse. We have all experienced this feeling of buyer's remorse at one point or another. We make a purchasing decision, sell ourselves on buying something, and wake up the next day with a buyer's hangover.

- What did I purchase yesterday?
- What was I thinking?
- I can't afford this!
- I can't do this now.
- I can't be bothered with this. I have no time!
- My boss is going to kill me!
- I don't even want or need this!

Why do we feel this way? We knew what we were buying at the time, so why does the desire for what we purchased suddenly change? After all, it couldn't be something that the salesperson did, or could it? Maybe it's more about what the salesperson didn't do that left the door open for the customer to cancel.

# Don't Take Their Eye off the Value

Now, with a cancellation to deal with, what was once a very cordial, friendly relationship has somehow turned into a hostile, adversarial one. As if this happened practically overnight. Now, for many businesses, it actually does happen overnight because, by law, consumers often have the right to cancel their contract within three business days.

After saving or attempting to save countless deals (mine and my sales teams'), here's what I've learned through the process. To effectively prevent customers from canceling while strengthening their reason for making their purchasing decision, you must ensure that, when you are gone and they continue with their day and their life, you have eliminated the chance of them somehow taking their eye off of the value they expect you will deliver.

Why does someone cancel a transaction in the first place? Because that person took their eye off of your value and started focusing on the cost instead. And I'm referring not only to the financial cost, but to the other hidden costs the prospect feels they would incur if they were to continue with this transaction.

 **Closing Thoughts** _____

When it comes to making a larger purchase, there is typically a three-day rescission period for consumers to cancel their transaction, if they decide to. If they wound up exercising this right to do so, it's because the customer took his eye off the value to the point that the cost of continuing with the purchase outweighed the benefits of doing so.

# Recognize a Cry for Help

As we've established, people ultimately cancel because they no longer see the need or the value of what they bought to be greater than their financial investment.

But there's more for you to consider. Much more. You see, quite often when your customer calls you to cancel, there's another message they really want to share with you. That is, they are calling to ask for your help.

That's right, they are actually calling you because they got scared and want the reassurance that they did, in fact, make the right decision. They may just need a reminder of why they made their purchase in the first place. They may actually still want this purchase to go through, but they need to be talked down a bit.

Especially when it comes to a substantial investment in the prospect's eyes, the next day or so, when the initial excitement and the seductive ether begin to die down, and the reality of cost and the results of what they did start coming into play, another emotion begins to take over: their fear, their remorse, their "What if this is the wrong decision and it doesn't work?" feeling.

So what they're often saying is, "While I may be calling to rescind, convince me why I should not cancel and help me make this work."

Now, think about your approach when presented with a situation like this. Is your selling approach and presentation defusing these issues that lead to a cancellation? Chances are, they are not.

Like anything, if you want to produce a specific result, you need to look at the process you are using to do so. The more organized your efforts are, the more masterfully you can manage them. And the more you manage them, the better you can measure and gauge what's working and what's not as it relates to your selling efforts and your strategy to insulate yourself from cancellations.

We are now going to develop a well-organized, systematic process to assist you in saving and preventing more cancellations than ever before.

# Why Do People Cancel?

If you are wondering why your customers don't send you more referral business and why some of your customers are canceling, it's because of two things they have missed.

1. Misperception

2. Misinformation

Whether developed as a result of a feeling, a reaction, or something they read or heard, here are just a handful of reasons why your customers are canceling.

- The prospect might have felt that he or she can no longer afford the purchase.

- The prospect might have gotten caught up in the excitement of what you were offering at the time.

- An emergency came up, and the prospect could not afford to tie up any money.

- The prospect spoke to someone who said, "You could get the same thing cheaper somewhere else." (Where were these "informants" before, when the prospect was in the market for this good or service?)

- The prospect was given inaccurate information by someone else.

- The prospect couldn't remember the reason he or she purchased the product or service, and did not want it anymore because he or she no longer saw the value in it.

- The salesperson did not leave the prospect with anything to remind him or her of the value of the purchase and why he or she had bought.

- The prospect fears making the wrong decision.

- The prospect fears the unknown.

- The prospect fears that the product or service will not work.

- The prospect is not being patient enough to see the results.

- The prospect does not understand how the product works.

- The prospect is not clear on how the results or the effectiveness of the product are even measured.

Ultimately, prospects feel that they have made a buying decision which no longer benefits them. Bottom line: your customer took his or her eye off the value of the purchase.

The positioning and relationship have changed, and with that, so has your attitude, disposition, and approach.

 **Closing Thoughts**

Cancellations are a condition that your presentation can be immunized from. It starts by taking full responsibility for every cancellation you get.

# Take Responsibility for the Breakdown

What did the salesperson do at the end of the meeting after finishing the paperwork needed to consummate the sale? He packed up and left. Not a good thing to do. Remember, these people entrusted you with their buying decision, and they need reinforcement in knowing they made the right decision. Rushing out of the meeting sends a message to the prospect that the only thing you were concerned about was the sale, not the prospect. Big mistake.

The sale is not over after the prospect makes the purchasing decision. A salesperson must conclude every sale with the reconfirmation sequence.

You are hurting no one but yourself (and the prospect) if you feel this is not a necessary step in your presentation. Ignoring the reconfirmation step in your presentation does not make the prospect's fears or apprehensions go away.

 **Closing Bell**

> Realize that some prospects cannot say "No." Instead, they will sign your contact and all of the paperwork just to get you out of their office or home, and will cancel on you the next day.

You must reconfirm with prospects why they made this buying decision. You must have prospects pitch back to you the reasons why they made the purchase to ensure that they had, in fact, sold themselves on making the purchasing decision.

This is also an opportunity to uncover some critical intelligence regarding why your prospects are actually buying from you. You can then use this information as a barometer to determine what you do right during your presentation that motivates people to want to purchase from you. Now that you know what behaviors, steps, and strategies work, you can replicate them when meeting with every prospect.

# Reconfirmation: The Pitch-Back

So here you are. You've just closed a sale. But instead of running out before the ink can dry on the contract, you take a different approach to ensuring that your sale will stick. Here's one example of how you can conduct this reconfirmation of the sale with your new client.

"Mr. Cohen, now that we have gotten all of this paperwork out of the way, may I ask you a question?

"Since each one of my clients has his or her own reasons for making a decision, I was hoping you could just briefly share with me why you decided to move ahead with this today?"

As Mr. Cohen shares all the reasons why he made his decision, you can continue this dialogue using the following questions.

> **Closer's Corner**
>
> If you are in the presence of the prospect and consummating the sale requires the completion of some paperwork, keep this in mind. As you are going through the process of finalizing the sale, make sure that you leave your briefcase open with the paperwork in it. Shutting your briefcase only threatens the prospect.

- Were there any specific considerations when choosing my company?

- Can you remind me of your core objective that initially supported your purchasing decision?

- I'm curious, was there anything I did you can think of that separated me from the other people/companies you were considering?

- Who will be the first person you are going to tell about this?

- Shall we discuss the implementation process and your role in this?

- Are you interested in hearing about the steps we take from here and what you can expect from now until the installation date?

- Now that you've made the decision, what are you most excited about happening?

You can then continue with the following dialogue that is used to expose any concerns the prospect may have as it relates to this purchase. "Thanks so much, Mr. Cohen. I'm very excited about handling this project for you. Now I'm going to ask you something that may sound a little strange. In the next several days, you might be in the office, at home, or with some friends, and the topic of your recent purchase might come up.

"Now, you know how some people are, always thinking that they can get the same thing done better or less expensively. I'm just curious: if someone were to make a comment like that to you, considering what we discussed today, how would you respond?"

**Tip from the Executive Sales Coach:** If Mr. Cohen cannot answer each of these questions effectively, there is a chance that he was not sold completely on you, your company, your product, or the cost for the investment.

If this happens, instead of avoiding the issue, you must go back and close this door of apprehension. Uncover the hesitancy or concern the prospect has. If you do not, instead of looking at a commission check, you will be looking at a cancellation notice.

If you feel there's some reluctance in your prospect's voice when asking this question, then here's one approach to bring it to the surface.

"Sir, the company that I represent frowns heavily on cancellations. They think that it is the fault of the salesperson for not doing his job correctly. I'm sensing that you're not 100 percent comfortable with the decision you just made. And if that's the case, then why don't we just forget doing this now and revisit this maybe some time in the future?"

Mr. Cohen will either respond with "I am fine with my decision" or "Yes, you are right. I am not ready to do this now." If this is the response you hear, there's another objection or concern that hasn't been fully defused or handled. Get back in there, find out the prospect's true concern, and defuse it. (For example, "Mr. Prospect, what is your biggest concern as it relates to moving ahead with this?")

# When It Makes Sense to Save a Sale

With the limited time we all have today and the number of things we have to do and want to do, saving a cancellation can become one time-consuming task—in some instances, so much so that many salespeople are quick to chalk them up as a cost of doing business without attempting to even save them. They'd rather move on to newer, more promising prospects.

Here's what they tell me:

♦ These sales take so long to save.

♦ It's too frustrating to deal with a cancelled sale after all the time I wasted with that person.

♦ If I'm trying to save a cancellation, it takes me away from selling new business.

♦ It's financially not even worth my time.

♦ Why should I go and save someone who shouldn't—or, better yet, doesn't even want to—be saved?

The question is, are all sales worth saving? And if not, then when does it make sense to save a sale? Some salespeople feel it is worth their time and energy to save every sale, whereas others do not.

What do you need to know that would, first, determine whether the sale is worth saving and, second, make saving a cancellation less time-consuming, less stressful, and more productive?

Here are several questions you need to answer and prepare for before you can successfully attempt to approach a cancelled sale.

♦ What is my customer going to lose as a result of canceling?

♦ What does saving this sale mean to me? What factors do I have to consider that would determine how much time I invest in saving this sale? For example, financially, for your career, for your monthly sales quota, and so on.

♦ If the only factor that I need to consider is a financial one, then based on the average time it takes me to save a sale (time, conversations, money, travel, and so on), does it make sense to pursue this or focus on generating new business?

♦ How can I quickly determine whether the client is salvageable in the first place? Does the client even want to be saved?

♦ How much time do I invest in saving one cancellation compared to the time it would take me to generate one new client?

♦ When approaching this person, what should I say?

- How can I prevent cancellations from happening in the first place?

- Who are the customers that are canceling? Is there a pattern/ trend?

### Closing Thoughts

When prospecting, you never want to continue engaging with a prospect if there's not a fit. You move on to the next one. This same strategy holds true with cancellations. What do you need to know about the person who is canceling that would help you determine whether it makes sense to save the sale?

# Seven Steps to Reducing Cancellations

What follows is a seven-step process for saving cancellations and when it makes sense to save a customer.

Step 1: Get neutral

Step 2: Precall preparation

Step 3: Conduct an exit interview—making the call

Step 4: The rediscovery

Step 5: Save your customer! Open up a new possibility

Step 6: Offer another solution

Step 7: Ask for referrals

So let's set the stage. You're in the office. And you get an e-mail from customer service informing you that there's a customer of yours who wants to cancel.

Once you hear someone has cancelled, what is your first reaction? Let's keep it clean. You're shocked. You can't believe it! You react, "Oh my! Are these people kidding me? After all the time I invested in getting this sale?" Or maybe you just surrender, saying, "Well, I can't believe they want to cancel. I guess they're sure they want to do this and there's nothing I can do about it."

Now I have a question for you. Do you know why they want to cancel at this point? No, you do not. (Unless, of course, they implied it or informed you that they would potentially be canceling.)

Before you make the costly assumption of why they cancelled and react accordingly, exercise step 1 in this seven-step process that is guaranteed to close more sales with less collateral damage.

## Step 1: Get Neutral

Remove the charge and emotion by detaching from the outcome. Unhook yourself from the future outcome of your efforts to save this sale. Does the customer truly want to cancel, or is it more that the customer is frustrated about what exactly to expect and wants you to offer a reminder of why this customer bought from you in the first place?

So take a breath. Clear your mind. Remove the assumptions of what this cancellation means and how it's going to go down. Pause.

Now that you've got your head straight, what's the next tactical action step you take? That's right. Prepare for making the call. To do so, you'll first need to get out of the survival mode of saving something and position this differently. The goal is less about saving a sale and more about exploring another solution for this customer.

## Step 2: Precall Preparation

Research and analyze your customer's account and data. The key point here is to have your facts ready to support any claim you make or need to make that will reinforce the level of trust and desire this person initially had when buying from you. Emotion and enthusiasm may have weighed heavily the first time the customer bought. However, at this point it's not the only thing you'll need in your toolbox to save the deal. Besides, if the customer bought emotionally, he or she may be canceling rationally, after the excitement and impulse has died down.

> **Closing Bell**
>
> People buy both logically and emotionally. If the person who just bought from you did so relying more on emotion than facts or logic (a.k.a. impulse buyer), that person may be canceling rationally, after the initial excitement of making the purchase has died down.

If that's the case, you'll need some solid facts and statistics to offer some additional reassurance that the customer made the right decision the first time.

Here's an example of how you can position this with your customer. If you were selling a web-based marketing solution to generate more business through a listing on your site, you can begin with this: "I'm looking here at your account and some other companies in your category. More specifically, I'm looking at four companies that are doing much better than you in terms of results.

"So the good news is, there are people in your category getting great results, which means it's possible for you to experience the same results they are. Let's see what they are doing compared to what you are doing. This way, we can uncover a few measurable changes and adjustments we might be able to try that could make the difference you're looking for."

Here are just some of the areas this salesperson can look at as a comparison to uncover new solutions for this customer. Go to the customer's website:

- How does it initially come across?

- What is the first reaction you have?

- What is the first thing you see?

- Is it what the customer wants to promote most?

- How is the quality of their pictures and artwork?

- How is the layout?

- Do they have a strong call for action?

- Do they offer resources people want to use?

- How easy is it to navigate through the site?

- How professional, unique, or amateur is the site?

- How well written is the copy, story, and history?

- Are there text issues and spelling errors?

- Is the phone number and contact information easily accessible and visible?

- Does your customer's site list links that take visitors away from the site?

- Is the style aligned with the target audience?

- Look at the customer's package and history.

- How long has the customer been advertising?

- Is the company listed in the best categories?

- How much is the customer spending? Do you have an opportunity to up-sell your customer on a better package?

- How do the best, average, and worst results compare to your customer's?

- Was the customer on the fence when they initially bought from you?

- Was the customer truly the best fit for this service?

- Does this customer line up with your ideal client?

Now that you are tactically and mentally prepared for making the call, it's time to do so!

**Closing Thoughts**

Here's another gauge to use when determining whether it makes sense to save a sale. Is this a great core customer of yours, or can you afford to lose this client? Relate this to the number of hours you have to invest to potentially save the deal, as opposed to investing that time to mine for future customers.

# Step 3: Conduct an Exit Interview—Making the Call

Conduct an exit interview. Are you ready to speak to the customer to uncover the real concern? What do you think is the most effective way to approach the customer ? Are you prepared to remind the customer of all the reasons why he or she bought from you? How did this purchase line up with the customer's goals and core objectives?

But before you can start asking any questions, you need to earn the right to do so. Keep in mind that this person wants to cancel. That's

**Closing Bell**

Stay away from sounding like your long-distance service provider: "Is there anything we can do to keep your business? How about a dollar credit on your next 10-year contract with us?" Was that a bit exaggerated?

where the customer's head is at right now. Therefore, you haven't disarmed this person yet; your customer may still be charged up.

While the customer doesn't want to have confrontation either, this person is prepared that you may call to try to change his or her mind.

People don't like that. And they certainly don't like their decisions questioned or challenged.

An exit interview supports what the customer wants while uncovering the information you will need to salvage any possible sale. Here's what it could sound like.

"I understand you want to cancel. I would be glad to help process your request."

However you language it, you're going to continue collecting information about the account, and by processing the cancellation request, you're putting the customer at ease.

After collecting the necessary information, ask permission from the prospect to conduct your exit interview. Here's what that could sound like.

"Mr. Customer, before I go ahead and process this request, can I ask you for a little help? Thanks, your help will enable us to better serve the needs of our customers so that we don't have people wanting to cancel. After all, it's an expense of time and money on both sides, for our customers and us. And for that, I do want to say I am sorry. That's why I know you can help us improve."

Conducting an exit interview is the most effective way to honor the customer's request to cancel while transitioning into the next step, which is the rediscovery process.

## Step 4: The Rediscovery

The rediscovery step is very similar, if not identical, to your discovery step when delivering a presentation. I call it rediscovery because it's your opportunity to rediscover why the prospect bought from you in the first place and to reinforce in this person's mind why he or she bought from you.

And you're smoking out the true objection or concern that led to wanting to cancel.

If your discovery phase in presenting is when you uncover someone's needs and determine whether there's a good fit, your rediscovery phase is when you uncover someone's needs and determine whether there's a fit still worth saving.

This is exactly the same process you use during your probing, discovery, or needs analysis portion when qualifying a prospect for the first time to see if there's a fit. The only thing that has changed are some of the questions you ask.

You now have an opportunity to re-enroll the customer in why he or she bought from you. So you'll need to again uncover the pain and objection, and find a solution the customer wants that he or she has not gotten yet.

### Closing Thoughts

Rediscover why the prospect bought from you in the first place, and reinforce in this person's mind why he or she bought from you.

Uncover the true objection, concern, and reason for wanting to cancel.

Here's when you would ask these questions that would give you better insight into why someone cancelled and if there's any chance of turning that person around. Here are a few questions you can use.

- Where did we fall short in meeting your specific needs?

- Is this purchase something that you would consider at some point in the future?

- May I ask, has your situation changed or is there something else that's stopping you from continuing/moving forward with this?

- What could we have done better to keep your business and make you confident in your decision to use us?

- Have your priorities changed where this is no longer an issue or concern of yours? (Has the problem been handled? If so, by whom?)

At this point, you have disarmed the prospect and can determine whether it makes sense to not have them as a customer or pursue them with the goal of enrolling them to stay with you. If you feel there's an opportunity, then move to step 5. Here's where you have the chance to take the intelligence you've just gained and craft a question around it, to open up a new possibility or solution that hasn't been explored.

## Step 5: Save Your Customer! Open Up a New Possibility

When you prospect and sell like your competitors, you become a clone, an image of your competitors. As such, you wind up in the position of having to price your product or service, similar to, equal to, or less than your competitors'.

When you continue to market and sell the way you've done in the past in a rapidly changing market, what do you think is going to happen? You are going to experience similar results. Soon, worse results and then, well, you get the picture.

Here's where you create a new possibility to explore alternative solutions by getting permission from your customers to do so, rather than force a solution down their throat. If you do so and start telling them why they shouldn't cancel, you are challenging their decision and creating an adversarial position. The following dialogue can assist you in opening up a new possibility.

"Thank you again for what you've shared with me. I have a much better understanding of why you want to cancel. Thanks so much for your help. You know, based on what you've said and the additional research I've done on your business, there may be something else worth exploring that we haven't looked at yet. But before we do, I was wondering, if we were able to (state the solution you can deliver that would defuse their objection and reason for canceling, such as price, timing, final deliverable, and so on), would you be open to discussing this in more detail?

Now you have permission to save your customer, opening the door to step 6.

## Step 6: Offer Another Solution

Now that you have permission, you can propose alternative solutions that would defuse the customer's concern or objection. Here's where you have the opportunity to discuss what needs to happen to earn the customer's confidence, trust, and renewed commitment to buy from you. Use the following question to open up this discussion.

> If you were to decide to continue with this purchase/project, what could we do that would give you the confidence and motivate you to move ahead with this?

By now, you should know the likelihood of re-engaging this customer or parting ways to move on to more promising selling opportunities. However, there's one big difference here. That is, you can look in the mirror and confidently say that you've tried everything in your power to turn this customer back around.

Moreover, you've gained a ton of experience and intelligence from this process that you can incorporate into your selling strategy.

Regardless of the outcome, customer or not, you still want to pursue your final step, as strange as it may seem to you.

> **Closer's Corner**
>
> If you need a strong contingency plan, you can always rely on the old, reliable I.G.O. approach to uncovering and defusing objections that we discussed in Chapter 11.

## Step 7: Ask for Referrals

This may sound strange, but I suggest still asking for referrals. Just because it didn't work for that person doesn't mean that it won't work for someone else.

As such, there still may be an opportunity to prospect them, but not for what you may think.

If you want to ensure that every selling effort provides you with the opportunity to maximize your time and uncover a new prospect, then consider this your last-ditch effort to find new prospects.

You: "Mr. Prospect, thanks again for taking the time to speak with me today. I certainly appreciate your input. Based on your situation, it seems that our product is not a good fit for you. However, I hope our conversation reinforced what a great job your current vender is doing for you.

"While there may not be anything I can provide you that would make a measurable difference in comparison to what you are doing now, maybe there's another way we can work together. In your line of work, I'm sure you run across other people who have shared similar challenges that you had and might be looking for a better solution. If you know someone who is always looking for ways to do things better and who you feel could benefit from our product, would you be comfortable referring them to me?"

Prospect: "Sure."

You: "That sounds great. Then may I ask who you know that would be a good candidate for our product?"

From prospect to customer and now back to prospect!

Talk about evolution. Look at it this way: you've got nothing to lose and only more prospects to gain.

> **Closing Thoughts**
>
> Two final tips to reduce and eliminate the number of cancellations you may be getting (or would be getting if you don't implement this seven-step strategy into your selling process).
>
> 1. Button up each sale better by taking what you sold away and reconfirming in the customer's words why the customer decided to go ahead with the purchase.
> 2. Set up an agreement to talk with the customer if they are not happy down the road; before deciding to cancel.

Now for those of you who may be skeptical to go through such a process, think of it this way: if you do the reconfirmation step after the sale is made, you won't have to spend your time saving sales in the first place.

## The Least You Need to Know

◆ The sale is never over.

◆ To reduce the number of cancellations and strengthen your sales, develop a solid and consistent reconfirmation, or "button-up," strategy.

◆ If your clients can't tell you why they just bought from you today, there's a strong chance they're going to tell you why they no longer want to buy from you tomorrow.

◆ Ultimately, cancellations are the often misguided action by a customer resulting from misperception and misinformation that the salesperson did not recognize or clarify.

◆ Most cancellations could have been prevented by the salesperson if only they took the time to do so. Ouch.

# Chapter 14

# Master the Basics: The Advanced Course

## In This Chapter

- ◆ Tap into your sales mojo
- ◆ The idiots are the smart ones
- ◆ Identify and embrace your one true competitor
- ◆ Determine your relearning strategy
- ◆ Don't blame the game for mediocre results

Congratulations! You are only a handful of pages away from putting the final touches on your newly revised strategy for turning more prospects into clients faster than ever before—or, as the title implies, closing more sales.

Are you ready for more tools, more techniques, and more preformatted closes? If you are, then I'm sorry to disappoint. Actually, this chapter contains quite the opposite. Less is truly more, and you'll soon see why.

When you first began reading this book, you probably noticed that the subject matter and content is certainly not for idiots, nor are you one. This final chapter reinforces the essential building blocks that no well-organized, refined, and highly evolved selling system can afford to do without. I've also sprinkled in several final tips that will ensure your long-term success at selling, along with the traps to avoid that would prevent you from becoming the sales champion you can be. The biggest obstacle in your way? Well, to be specific, you.

# What's Blocking Your Sales Mojo?

I would typically have a sidebar for the definition of *sales mojo*, but it's a word I created that you won't find in the dictionary. Here's what it is. In essence, your sales mojo is the energy or presence you show up with during every meeting with a prospect. It's that allure, charisma, or vibe you radiate that every one of your prospects feels from you.

Your sales mojo encapsulates the inner game of selling, which is who you are and how you come across when speaking with others. Developing your sales mojo goes beyond the basics of learning a presentation, selling strategy, or pitch, which is what superficial sales training is capable of teaching you. Only an experienced sales coach can assist you in uncovering and developing your authentic sales mojo. The consequences of not doing so can be severe. Just take a look at some of these limiting beliefs that prevent the natural flow of your mojo:

- You can't close someone in our business. They have to be ready to buy. And when they're ready, they'll call me.

- I'm not good at closing. I hate putting pressure on people.

- I've tried some closing tools before, and they didn't work for me.

- I had a horrible experience when I attempted to get the prospect to make a decision.

- I hate when people try to close me.

Whatever the reason, whatever the story, every salesperson, manager, and business owner has an opinion on what it means to close a sale and why he or she can or cannot do so successfully.

# The Wrong Lesson Leads to the Wrong Solution

When I interview people who want to hire me as their sales or business coach to assist them in developing or refining their selling strategy, I ask them to "pitch" me on the spot. That is, if I were a prospect and you were delivering a presentation, what would it sound like? Here's how the conversation typically flows.

"Right now?" they reply surprisingly.

"Sure," I say. "After all, you have a choice. Either you can practice on me or you can practice on your prospects."

"Well, okay. But I never really liked to role-play." (A salesperson who doesn't like to role-play? I'm shocked.)

After several minutes, the salespeople give me their "pitch," a few examples of the types of objections they run up against, and their approach to overcoming them.

"So what do you think, Keith?"

Before responding, I asked one salesperson what he thought of his performance and if he noticed or heard any areas he felt could use some polishing or fine-tuning. Not surprisingly, the salesperson responded with a couple of generic, vague, and elusive thoughts about where he felt he needed the most assistance. In other words, he didn't know for certain. I then continued.

"I think I have great news for you," I replied confidently.

"The good news is, there are some things that you can do immediately that will result in tremendous improvements in your productivity. We're going to fine-tune some of the things you're doing and develop more compelling language to use

> **Closing Thoughts**
>
> Don't blame the game; blame the player—or, at least, the player's approach.

in your presentation, which will eliminate the initial objections you're hearing and help convert more prospects into customers. So if you're ready, I'd be happy to share with you in more detail what I'm hearing and some of the areas I see that we can work on. Are you ready to create some new possibilities?"

"Sure."

"Great. Now, one thing you mentioned earlier was that you feel the approach you take when attempting to close the sale is not working for you. Is that correct?"

"Yes, that's right. I see how the other salespeople in my company have changed their approach over the last year or so, but it doesn't seem to be as effective for me. With the approach I'm taking now, I'm certainly not generating any worthwhile results, or, I should say, I'm not getting the results I got last year when I was performing. Besides, let's face it. There are more and more companies popping up every day, and we're all competing for the same business. Plus, many of them are priced at such an advantage over us that it sometimes makes it impossible to even compete."

"Oh, so there was a time when you did experience some positive results from the way you are currently selling and closing?"

"Oh, yes."

"So, what's changed?"

"Other than the marketplace, I'm not sure. That's why I'm calling you."

"You mentioned your industry has changed over the last year or so. What have you adjusted to or changed in your selling strategy and approach in response to these new market conditions?

"Nothing I can think of."

"Have you ever been trained or coached in how to sell and close effectively?"

"No."

"So when you were selling, how did you learn?"

"I've seen some other people do it—some seasoned salespeople, my manager—but that's it, other than my own personal experiences that I hope to learn from. Maybe I'm just not cut out for this type of position."

"Okay. Now I want you to consider that it's less about the changes in your industry and more about the way you have responded to these changes that's causing you all the trouble. That is, while your market has changed, you have stayed the same. You're still asking for the sale and attempting to close the sale the way you did in the past, hoping for similar results. If the selling landscape and your industry have evolved, then it's critical for you to adjust accordingly. And that adjustment isn't limited to your tactical approach; it also includes your mind-set and attitude. In other words, it's not only the changes in your industry that are preventing you from selling.

"Let me explain," I continued. "If I asked you to go outside and dig a 10-foot-deep hole with a spoon, would you learn the lesson "Well, I guess I can't dig holes very well," or is the real lesson "If I had the right tools, I would be able to accomplish this goal faster, with less effort"? You see, it's all about the tools you're using when selling and closing. However, you can't see this if you've learned the wrong lesson (such as "It's the industry, economy," and so on).

"That's why you first need to upgrade your outlook and attitude before you can attempt to change your strategy. After all, if you learn the wrong lesson, you are bound to implement the wrong solution or come to the wrong or disempowering conclusion ("I'm not cut out for sales"). It's not that you're not cut out for a career in selling. It's realizing that change is the only constant—both the changes we can't control, such as the ones occurring in your industry, and the changes we can control, which we discussed in Chapter 2. This, in turn, would provide you with the new tools to sell in a new economy.

"Even if you handed Tiger Woods, the greatest golfer in the world, a pair of lefty clubs, while he still may outperform most golfers, he would not be able to operate at his best, at the pinnacle of his potential. He's using the wrong tools, and that's causing him to change how he plays the game. The same philosophy applies to your career and to the approach you take when asking the prospect to purchase from you and then closing the sale."

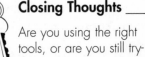 **Closing Thoughts**

Are you using the right tools, or are you still trying to drive your sales forward using four square wheels? Doing more of the wrong thing moves you farther from where you want to be.

"That makes perfect sense," the salesperson responded. "I really never considered that as much."

"Well, as you mentioned, that's the reason you called me, right?" I reminded him playfully.

"Indeed!" He chuckled. "Let's get started." We concluded our conversation by scheduling our first coaching call.

When managers call me wanting to learn how they can boost their sales and the productivity of their sales team, I ask them if they have ever provided their sales team with any specific training and coaching regarding how to close a sale.

Most say "No" or "Not as much as they should get," yet they still expect their sales team to continually produce better results in less time. (Oh, I'm sorry. I didn't count those often empowering and highly enlightening weekly sales meetings.) That's the same thing as expecting to shoot a 72 your first month as a new golfer without any lessons, practice, or coaching.

As many of the chapters in this book have reinforced, although you need the right tactical approach to close more sales, it's just as essential to have the right attitude and mind-set when approaching each sale as well as the close. But before you change what you do, you first need to change how you think.

# Get Back to the Basics

A client I worked with about a year ago recently e-mailed me, requesting some time to talk. When we finally got on the phone together, it was apparent why.

Miki was a seasoned executive recruiter. She hired me initially because her sales were down and she thought a coach might be able to give her the extra guidance and motivation she needed to get out of this slump. (She was right.)

After 3 months of coaching, Miki was back on top, the fifth top recruiter out of about 200.

Well, recently it seems as if Miki's numbers were sliding again, and instead of waiting, she immediately reached out for help.

"Keith, I don't know what's going on. I mean, I know we haven't worked together in about a year, and for a while I was doing great! But for some reason, I'm feeling stuck again."

"I'm glad you reached out as soon as you noticed that something was off. Let's do a quick diagnostic and see how things are running."

"Sure."

"So if you were standing on a 100-foot balcony looking down onto your entire sales process, where do you feel the breakdown is occurring: when attempting to get the appointment, when presenting, when closing, or when following up?"

"Well, I'm using your template for cold-calling, and that continually works great, so the leads are pretty consistent. And the presentation seems to go just fine. So I guess closing the sale is where I'm stumbling. If I were to look at what's taking up my time now, I have a handful of proposals out there waiting to be closed. And the prospects I'm meeting with are just not closing, for whatever reason or excuse they give me. The proposal stage and their decision-making process seem to drag on indefinitely."

"So you're getting in front of the right people, you feel that your presentation flows well, and you are doing a good job establishing a rapport and relationship with your prospects. However, you feel that these prospects should be able to make their decision faster as it relates to buying from you or not, is that what I'm hearing?"

"Yes, Keith, that's right."

"Miki, in the spirit of exploring every possibility, and not to step over anything, are you still using the sales process that we put together?"

"Oh yes, of course!"

"You are. Good. Then let's take a quick look at a few things you're currently doing. Miki, do you remember when we developed your pre-closing and reconfirmation approach to include at the end of your presentation?"

"Um, yes."

"Are you still asking those prequalifying questions before you discuss your pricing? You know, those questions that ensure you've addressed every concern prospects have, while confirming that your service is something they can clearly benefit from?" (If you need a friendly reminder, these questions are in Chapter 8.)

Silence. Then Miki responded quietly with, "Hmm. No, I forgot about those."

"Well, that's good news! At least we've uncovered one critical step in your process that you're not currently doing that has proven to be very effective. Once you start asking these questions again, you will notice a big difference in your performance. In addition, you won't be wasting your time drafting proposals and following up with unqualified prospects who you shouldn't be following up with in the first place.

"And what about the questions we developed to defuse the objections you hear? I know that you were running into the 'Send me a proposal' and the 'I have to talk this over with my board' and the infamous 'That's a lot of money' objection. The rebuttals we developed were squashing and preventing these objections consistently, remember?"

"Yes, I most certainly do remember, Keith. I especially remember that when I used them, these objections weren't getting in my way! The problem is, I totally forgot about those rebuttals as well! How weird is that?"

We ended our call a few minutes later after I coached Miki and her memory on what she needed to reconnect with in her selling approach. Not surprisingly, she e-mailed me a week later about a few sales she was able to close as a result of doing what she needed to do again: the basics. Miki got back to the basics of what made her successful.

Interestingly, while I identified certain things that Miki clearly needed to change for the better, it was nothing she hasn't tried, created, or done successfully before. Her real enemies were success, complacency, and time.

Whether we're in a slump or selling like a pro, when something is always going on, we become blind to it. That includes becoming complacent or often blind to the good things in our life as well as the bad. Of course, this does not exclude the productive behavior and actions we take in addition to the unproductive ones. We sometimes forget what has worked for us and what has specifically contributed to our success—the things that have become habitual. And when something becomes a habit, it's now working in the background of our lives, being done without conscious attention. We no longer have to think about doing these things. Therein lies the danger.

When coaching someone out of a slump who has all of the right components to succeed, most of the time, it's the basics that have been ignored or forgotten that contributed to the breakdown. The basic questions we ask, the presentation we deliver, the process we've developed that has successfully worked time and time again. Somehow, some way, we get sidetracked, distracted, or seduced by something we perceive to be better (or worse), like a new selling strategy or approach, the status quo, even our attitude. Consequently, we mistakenly change what was clearly identified as an approach or mind-set that was working well.

The next time you experience a selling slump or you feel that sales aren't coming to you as easily as they once did, go back to the basics. Instead of doubting yourself and your abilities, see what you need to be reminded to do consistently in your selling approach. Look at the engine that drives your sales. You may notice that the only thing needed is a quick tune-up to enhance your performance.

 **Closing Thoughts**

"I've forgotten more than you'll ever know," were the wise words of a former manager. If you continually forget everything you've learned, then you can always claim that you have adopted and utilized what you've learned. And if you continually feel that you're using everything you've read, heard, or seen and nothing is working, what a wonderful opportunity to look outside yourself and blame your poor performance on everything except you. After all, you've tried and done everything, right? In your mind, you have the validation to support such a claim, which is really an excuse in disguise. So if you forget about it, then you are always right (and never accountable). Get it?

It's all in your control—at least, the things you can control, right? After all, you can't control how competitive your industry is getting. Or can you?

# Your Only Real Competitor

At some point, I hear from practically every person I've ever worked with about the competition in their market. Companies spend so much time trying to outsell, outwit, and outprice their competition without realizing who their greatest competitor truly is. As such, they focus all of their energy on trying to beat out the wrong competitor.

Consider this. You have no external competition. No, I haven't fully lost my mind as of yet, so just try this on for a moment. I'm certainly not disputing the fact that there are other companies selling similar products that you are.

What I am suggesting is that the only competition you truly have is you—in other words, your current beliefs or outlook, your current mind-set, and your current way of doing things. Now, you may already embrace this notion. However, let's explore it on a deeper level.

Several words are synonymous with *competition: struggle, resistance, disagreement*, and *conflict. Competition* implies one side working against the other.

The two competing sides that I'm referring to in this context are as follows: that which you are comfortable doing, and that which you haven't done or tried consistently as of yet.

In truth, you are really competing against what you did yesterday. You're competing against the status quo; you're competing against feeling comfortable and doing what's predictable, with feeling uncomfortable and doing what hasn't been proven yet.

To illustrate this point, let me share a story about Dave. Dave was the owner of a small insurance company. He had a hard time managing and motivating his team. Like many small business owners, he was also responsible for selling. He didn't really have a specific management or sales process laid out. He wasn't organized and didn't adhere to any type of daily routine.

"Sales were tough," as he said. Dave felt his product was a commodity. As such, his typical approach was to try to sell on price, making it even more challenging to produce the results he wanted, especially since he wasn't the least expensive option.

Dave and I spent the first few weeks working together crafting a selling strategy and approach he was comfortable with. We developed his MVP (Most Valuable Proposition). He upgraded his mind-set and removed some mental barriers that were preventing him from engaging in the activities that yield the greatest return.

We crafted questions that enabled him to uncover new selling opportunities. Dave put together a routine that outlined the measurable activities he needed to engage in on a daily basis. He made one-on-one time with each member of his team non-negotiable and put a process in place to track their productivity and goals. He even interviewed his team, investing the time in asking them how he could improve, what additional tools or resources they felt they needed, and how he could best manage and coach each of them.

The result? Dave doubled his personal sales volume by the third month of our work together. By the fifth month, his salespeople had increased their volume by 40 percent.

So the question is, did his external competition change during this period of time or disappear from his market? Did the economy dramatically turn around? Did his product's demand suddenly skyrocket or become more effective and unique? It did not.

Dave accelerated to a higher level of productivity because of the work he did and the things that he can control, which is the path he chose to take as it relates to his development, his attitude, and his daily activities.

Dave embraced his biggest competitor, which was himself! He turned this adversary into his greatest ally.

Here's a mind-set that exemplifies full accountability. If you are responsible for bringing in new business, instead of thinking that every prospect you meet with is a potential sale for you to win, consider that every sale is already yours for the taking. Therefore, each sale is yours for you to lose—not to your competition, but to yourself, based on how well you develop and manage your selling process and yourself.

> ### Closer's Corner
>
> Consider that every selling opportunity you create is already a sale that you've won. How well you develop your core selling skills, your strategy, and the right mind-set determines whether it is another sale that you will lose.

The next time you run up against some resistance when managing or selling, remember Dave. Remember who your competition really is and embrace this as an opportunity for you to refine how you approach managing (if you do), selling, and your prospects.

Compare your progress today against what you did yesterday, not against what others are doing. This is the only accurate measurement of your growth and evolution. After all, once you get yourself out of your own way, that's when extraordinary things happen.

With today's ever-evolving market, if you are selling, managing your staff, or running your business the same way you've been running it for the last several years, you're overdue to reevaluate your philosophy. Think about what happened to Miki.

You are also making it easier for your competition to take away the new business that you're working so hard to earn.

Whether you are selling consumer goods or high-tech business applications, products, or services, companies that were once on top are closing their doors, not due to a lack of effort, but because they are still attempting to sell, manage their staff or run their business the way it was, not the way it is today.

The fact is, businesses often fail not because they lack the right product or service, pricing model, executive team, location, or marketing strategy. They fail more often because of these reasons:

1. They lack sales because they aren't consistently getting in front of enough of the right people to sell to.

2. They simply aren't prospecting, selling, or being managed effectively.

If your marketplace has changed, then you need to change with it. Anticipate the changes before they occur, in order to get ahead of your future.

> **Closing Bell**
>
> Something to consider .... Do you have a step-by-step (selling, prospecting, leadership, time management) strategy in place to ensure that you're continually increasing your income and staying on top, while actually enjoying the process? If not, the right coach can help you generate these measurable results without the costly learning curve. But finding an experienced, authentic, and credentialized coach is tricky. Send me an e-mail, and I'll be happy to help find you a few good ones to choose from.

# In Closing ... Final Thoughts from Your Coach

Training to become a master at closing the sale requires the same time, commitment, patience, practice, and diligence that would be required to become a professional athlete, entertainer, or musician. So give yourself some time to get comfortable with your new approach. Remember, it's the repetition of consistent, productive actions that will generate the consistent results you want.

This guide has opened your eyes to the changes you need to make so that you can perform like a champion. Awareness is the first step. Now that we have brought that which you need to be aware of to the surface, implementing the strategies you have learned is up to you.

As always, I'm going to continue being as up front with you as I can. That is, there's a strong chance you may get frustrated when learning and trying out these new techniques. You may go out today and try some of your new strategies, only to find that they didn't work the way you wanted. You must give it time and stay true to your commitment to lifelong learning and continuous improvement.

While we all would love to believe it's true, no magic formula is going to give you what you want overnight. Instead, use this as a leverage point: a high percentage of your competitors who are looking for that magic formula are going to give up even before they finish the race. Therefore, in many circumstances, you will be awarded more business and more sales just by staying in the race! I promise, if you put in the time to develop the right attitude, system, and skills, your persistence will pay off exponentially.

Since you have now arrived at the end of this book, how wonderful it would be if you could retain and utilize everything you've just learned. Now that reality sets in, do not do yourself injustice and disservice by shelving this book after you've read it. The fact is, there is no way to be able to absorb and retain all of the concepts in this book after reading it just once, let alone have the opportunity to use and master each valuable strategy and technique outlined in 14 chapters!

Instead, use this book as it was designed to be, as a personal one-to-one sales-coaching guide for you to continually refer back to that will be the cornerstone for your growth as a sales professional. It's a great resource to review, reinforce, and put into practice what you have learned. And if you run into a selling situation in which you feel stuck, I'm confident that this guide can address any selling obstacle you're running up against. Besides, we don't often get the value of the entire message the first time around. We need to hear it and be ready to hear it more than once.

If you are still feeling a bit overwhelmed or not sure what to do first, keep it simple. Start with implementing just one chapter at a time. That's right, just one. You can even break it down to one strategy or mind-set you want to work on adopting. That sounds like a manageable goal, yes?

Then the following day or week, build in another strategy you've learned and start using it for another week or so until you own it and it becomes real for you, a natural part of your selling efforts. Before you know it, you will be closing everything you get your hands on. Just give yourself a break and don't feel that you have to "do it all" at the same time. Take the pieces that feel comfortable for you while respecting your relearning process so that you can begin the momentum and start moving forward to achieve breakthrough results.

 **Closing Thoughts** _____

Honor the relearning process. There's no right way or wrong way. It's your way, the way that works best for you. Regardless, it's critical to respect the fact that unlearning what you've learned that no longer works and replacing it with the right approach and mind-set that does is, in fact, a process. At this point, what separates the winners from the rest is simply a matter of taking action, doing it or not.

At some points while reading this book, you may have wished that I was right there in the room with you (or at the closing table) from time to time so that you could ask me questions or receive personalized training, coaching, and support. At certain times throughout your week, you may have gotten distracted and needed to get refocused on your goals and objectives. And sometimes, when we know what we need to do and just can't seem to do it, having an expert in your corner to coach you on removing the negative, self-sabotaging behavior and thinking gets you "unstuck," in action, and back in the game.

Maybe you're a manager who could benefit from having an outside, objective perspective and a sounding board (which you probably don't get at work). After making a new hire; developing your selling and prospecting strategy, including your sales letters, voice mails, and cold-calling approach; or creating your marketing campaign, mailers, and collateral material, you may have thought, "How great it would be if a pro could critique what I've done or do some role-playing with me so that I don't have to practice on my prospects," or "I wish I could delegate some training and management responsibilities to someone I could trust so that I can free up my time," or "I know I'm supposed to coach my team, but how exactly do you develop an internal coaching program?"

Maybe you just need a quick sales or leadership performance tune-up or want the reassurance that you are, in fact, doing it the "right way." Or maybe you need to start by setting bigger goals, getting organized, reducing your stress, creating a daily routine, or eliminating distractions.

If you are ready to play a bigger game, become a sales superstar, make more money, master time management, leverage every selling opportunity, and create an even better, more balanced life, give me a call anytime and I would

> **Closing Bell**
>
> Fact: Your competition is getting tougher. Don't wait until you hear this from your customers.

be happy to discuss how we can work together to achieve your goals quickly, efficiently, and in half the time it would take if you were to do it on your own. (Say this sentence 10 times fast.)

Remember our friend Dave? Look at what he accomplished. (And the coaching paid for itself after a few months!) Find out what the top producers already know: everyone does better when they have a sales and business coach in their corner supporting them.

For more information on sales and business coaching, corporate training, or my keynote presentations and workshops delivered in person or through teleconferencing, you can reach me at 1-888-262-2450, or visit my website at www.profitbuilders.com. If you would like to receive my free newsletter, *The Winner's Path*, or some other valuable resources that I'd be happy to share with you, e-mail me anytime at info@profitbuilders.com.

**Closing Thoughts**

When training new salespeople, managers often remind them of the ABC's of selling. They are, according to them, Always Be Closing. Based on the newer model we've established, let's now give the proper meaning to the ABC's of selling, which they deserve. That is, Always Be Creating!

Now, you may be wondering, "How can a best-selling author put the time aside to have a one-to-one personal coaching practice? It must cost a fortune." Shall we not forget Chapter 2? I do what I do by choice. It is what I am deeply passionate about. Besides, if I can't help you, I'll find you someone I trust who can.

# Exclusive Resources for CIG Closers

If you read this book in its entirety and successfully implemented some of the strategies you've learned here, then I think you're entitled to a hearty acknowledgment of a job well done. As a token of my unconditional commitment to your success, I invite you to a very special resource center designed exclusively for you, my dear reader. Here's what you get simply for purchasing my book and wanting to live your fullest potential!

- Free subscription to *The Winner's Path* newsletter
- Helpful articles on sales, business, and leadership
- The time-management assessment

- The success diagnostic

- The prospecting tune-up

- The adrenaline index

- Free membership to send your own marketing campaign

- Virtual book tours, signings, prereleased book excerpts, and access to material that won't be available to anyone else

To access this resource center and take advantage of these tools, here's all you need to do.

1. Visit www.guidetoclosingthesale.com/cigclosers.php.

2. Type in the following user name and password. (They are case and space sensitive.)

   Username: KeithRosen

   Password: cigclosers

Finally, thank you for the opportunity to do what I love most—that is, contributing to your future success. I'm fortunate to live my passion and share my greatest gift and wisdom with others. You have given me my greatest gift.

I'd love to hear about the successes you've had as a result of utilizing this book, so please feel free to contact me anytime. I know with your continued commitment and effort combined with the strategies outlined in this book, it's only a matter of time until you start realizing the measurable results that follow. So until the next time, or until my next book, may your selling efforts become effortless, and I wish you extreme success.

## The Least You Need to Know

- Every sale is yours to lose to your greatest competitor: yourself.

- Schedule an ongoing maintenance program with a sales coach to continually fine-tune your selling engine to maintain peak performance.

- Your selling strategy must stay ahead of the inherent and imminent changes in your industry.

- No matter what you sell, regardless of industry or experience, the basic skills of questioning and listening will ensure your continued success.

- Remember the ABC's of closing the sale: Always Be Creating.

- Success is a choice. So is shutting this book and putting it on your shelf, or keeping it handy as a daily reference guide that you use to bring in more sales.

- Master the basics!

# Glossary

**clarifier**   This is typically a response to something said during the course of a conversation, where you rephrase in your own words what the other person said, to assure the person that you not only heard, but also understood him.

**closing**   The natural evolution of your selling process when your prospect becomes your customer. Closing is the art of creating new possibilities and solutions that may not have been presented before, while recognizing the right opportunity to ask if the prospect is ready to become a client. By this new definition, the word *closing* is synonymous with *opening*.

**confidence**   An unwavering faith or belief not only in yourself, but in each experience you have that it will all work out positively in the end, even though you don't have the evidence to support it. It's trusting in yourself without any proof to back up your conviction.

**entheos**   The Greek word meaning "possessed by a god or other superhuman power." The root of the word *enthusiasm*.

**filters**   When you listen through a filter, you are listening based on a past experience or belief or a certain expectation of the future. When you pass judgment on people by their age, success, or how they look, or when you invalidate people based on what you see or based on a similar situation with another client, you build a wall between yourself and the other person. This prevents clear and unrestricted communication and understanding of the message being received.

**mirroring**   Mirroring refers to acting subtly similar to the other person in physical ways. There is a difference between this and mimicking. As opposed to copying every gesture, which would come across as annoying and phony, follow the other person's lead in relation to their disposition, their body language, and their verbal acuity. Aligning how you speak as well as the physical gestures and disposition with that of each prospect enables you to establish more common ground with people.

**objection**   A concern, a question, or a feeling that the prospect either shares, implies, or is not saying that must be acknowledged, discussed, and satisfied so that the natural conclusion of your selling process, the sale, can occur. What the prospect is not saying is, "No, I don't want to and never will use your product or service." The prospect is really saying, "I'm saying 'No' or a form of 'No' because you haven't given me enough of a compelling reason to explore what you have in more detail." That is why an objection is often a sign of interest or a request for more information.

**reflecting**   The form and timing for discussing information. This can be based upon which method of communication the prospect utilizes to process information (whether visually, auditory, kinesthetically, or a combination) before making a decision. Reflecting allows you to better align your style of communication to that of the prospect's. As such, it makes your prospects more comfortable doing business with someone who appears to share similarities in both speech and action.

**repeat questions**   Questions that someone asks you to suggest that he or she needs more reassurance in making the right purchase this time around. The prospect may simply want to hear the answer more than once. It can also mean the prospect hasn't fully grasped all of the information you have laid out and needs to hear it once more.

**segue**   The verbal bridge you build to smoothly transition from one thought, topic, or conversation to another. Segues can come in the form of a question or a statement that seamlessly brings one topic to its apparent conclusion while simultaneously opening up the possibility to explore another topic or conversation.

**support-building questions**   Questions about problems from past experiences that let you know the prospect may be a bit timid or skeptical, and may have had a bad experience. These questions suggest that the prospect is looking for reassurance that this is the right decision and wants to avoid any past unfavorable experiences.

# Index

## A

ABC's (Always Be Creating) of
selling, 268
accountable closers, 174-175
active listening, 87-90
adapting to surroundings, 60-61
adrenalized closers, 171-174
Always Be Creating (ABC's) of
selling, 268
appearance, 57
asking for referrals, 249-250
author website, 268
awareness, 265

## B

bait and switch, 40
barriers to listening, 91-92
filters, 92-97
reactive assumptions/
judgments, 99-101
selling the same way as buying,
82-87
talking too much, 87-88
basics of selling, 260-261
blamer closers, 161-164
body language, 63
book website, 269
budget close, 191-192
building value, 220-221
business failures, 264
buttoning-up sales, 250
buyer's remorse, 234
buying signs, 74-77

## C

cancellations
buyer's remorse, 234
call for help, 235-236
keeping customer's eyes on
value, 235
reasons for, 236-237
saving, 240-242, 250
asking for referrals, 249-250
creating new possibilities,
248
exit interviews, 245-246
offering solutions, 248-249
precall preparation, 243-245
questions, 241-242
rediscovery, 246-248
removing emotions, 243
taking responsibility for, 238
changing with marketplace, 264
characteristics of salespeople
confidence, 22-24
choosing, 26-28
self-doubt, 24-26
control, 28-30
compared to creation, 31-32
fear-based, 30
risks, 30
creativity, 33-35
enthusiasm, 35-37
sincerity, 37-40
sales mojo, 254
clarifiers, 111
clarifying presentations, 143-148
preclosing, 145-148
summarizing, 143

taking prospect's pulse, 144
yes person, 168-171
closing, 12
  death of traditional, 10
  defined, 4
  hybrid system
    budget, 191-192
    control freak, 194
    exclusivity, 181-182
    fear of change, 192-194
    going out of business,
      183-185
    negative reversal, 197-198
    overview, 180
    price increase, 185-188
    pride of work, 198-199
    risk reward, 188-190
    sentence completion, 197
    shopping list, 195-196
    why, 194
    with your permission,
      199-201
  new definition, 12-13
  new school of possibility, 18
  overview, 7
  presentations, 149-152
  should not be, 9-10
  synonym for sold, 8
  types
    accountable, 174-175
    adrenalized, 171-174
    blamers, 161-164
    friendship-based, 159-160
    hopeful/fearful, 156-158
    methodological, 164-165
    perfectionists, 165-168
    pontificating, 158-159
    pressure, 160-161
competitors, 262-264
confidence, 22-24
  choosing, 26-28
  self-doubt, 24-26

consumer role of salespeople,
  51-52
contradiction, 29
control, 28-30
  compared to creation, 31-32
  fear-based, 30
  risks, 30
control freak close, 194
controlling price, 218-219
creation compared to control,
  31-32
creativity, 33-35

# D

defusing objections
  getting permission to continue,
    209-211
  hybrid closing system
    budget close, 191-192
    control freak close, 194
    exclusivity close, 181-182
    fear of change close, 192-194
    going out of business close,
      183-185
    negative reversal close,
      197-198
    overview, 180
    price increase close, 185-188
    pride of work close, 198-199
    risk reward close, 188-190
    sentence completion close,
      197
    shopping list close, 195-196
    why close, 194
    with your permission close,
      199-201
  "if" questions, 210
  isolating objections, 207-209
  no objections, 209
  offering solutions, 211-212
  practicing for, 212-213
  responding with questions,
    206-207

turning objections into new
  selling opportunities, 213-214
delivering presentations
  objectives, 126-128
  overview, 118-119
  permission-based
    clarifying, 143-148
    closing, 149-152
    discovery, 136-140
    introduction, 132-134
    Knowledge Gap, 135-136
    relationships with prospects,
      134-135
    solutions, 148
  questions, 119-120
  skipping the questions, 124-125
  turning statements into ques-
    tions, 121-124
desired state, 66
developing sales mojo, 254
discovery in permission-based
  presentations, 136-140
  emotional trigger questions,
    139
  fact-finding questions, 137
  segue questions, 140-143
disposition, 63
dropping prices, 219-220

**E**

emotions
  making purchasing decisions,
    49-51
  saving cancellations, 243
  trigger questions, 139
empathy compared to sympathy,
  52-54
encouraging silence, 105-107
enthusiasm, 35-37
evolving roles of salespeople, 11
exclusivity close, 181-182
exit interviews, 245-246

expectations, 175
eyes off value, 235

**F**

fact-finding questions, 137
failures
  reasons for, 176-178
  reasons why businesses fail,
    264
fears
  change close, 192-194
  control, 30
  purchasing decisions, 47-49
filters for listening, 92-97
finding coaches, 265
first impressions, 57
friendship-based closers, 159-160
fueling self-doubt, 24-26

**G**

getting permission to offer
  solutions, 209-211
giving value, 15-16
going out of business close,
  183-185

**H**

hopeful closers, 156-158
hybrid closing system
  budget close, 191-192
  control freak close, 194
  exclusivity close, 181-182
  fear of change close, 192-194
  going out of business close,
    183-185
  negative reversal close, 197-198
  overview, 180
  price increase close, 185-188
  pride of work close, 198-199
  risk reward close, 188-190

sentence completion close, 197
shopping list close, 195-196
why close, 194
with your permission close,
199-201

# I

identifying competitors, 262-264
"if" questions, 210
improving listening
focusing on the message,
107-108
listening for information,
108-110
making people feel heard,
110-111
paraphrasing, 112-114
reflective listening, 111-112
silence, 105-107
internal competition, 262-264
introduction of permission-based
presentations, 132-134
isolating objections, 207-209

# J–K–L

justifying price drops, 222-223

Knowledge Gap, 135-136

learning the wrong lessons,
255-258
listening
active, 87-90
barriers, 91-92
filters, 92-97
reactive assumptions/
judgments, 99-101
selling the same way as
buying, 82-87
talking too much, 87-88
filters, 92

for information, 108-110
improving
focusing on the message,
107-108
listening for information,
108-110
making people feel heard,
110-111
paraphrasing, 112-114
reflective listening, 111-112
silence, 105-107
paraphrase, 112-114
reasons people stop listening,
97-98
reflective, 111-112
selective, 92-97
to someone, 108-110
logic in making purchasing
decisions, 49-51

# M

marketplace changes, 264
message focus, 107-108
methodological closers, 164-165
mirroring, 55, 62-66
movies about salespeople, 18

# N

needs
causing action, 73
compared to wants, 68-74
negative reversal close, 197-198
new definition of closing, 12-13
new school of possibility, 18
no objections, 209

# O

objections
common, 205
created by salespeople, 229-231

defined, 205
defusing
   getting permission to
      continue, 209-211
   "if" questions, 210
   isolating objections, 207-209
   no objections, 209
   offering solutions, 211-212
overcoming, 19, 204-206
practicing for, 212-213
price
   being tested by prospects,
      223-224
   building value, 220-221
   controlling, 218-219
   dropping prices, 219-220
   justifying price drops,
      222-223
   responding with questions,
      222
   splitting the difference,
      224-227
responding with questions,
   206-207
turning into new selling
   opportunities, 213-214
objectives for presentations,
126-128
obstacles
   common, 205
   created by salespeople, 229-231
   defusing
      getting permission to
         continue, 209-211
      "if" questions, 210
      isolating objections, 207-209
      no objections, 209
      offering solutions, 211-212
   overcoming, 204-206
   practicing for, 212-213
   price
      being tested by prospects,
         223-224

building value, 220-221
controlling, 218-219
dropping prices, 219-220
justifying price drops,
   222-223
responding with questions,
   222
splitting the difference,
   224-227
   responding with questions,
   206-207
   turning into new selling
   opportunities, 213-214
offering solutions, 211-212,
248-249
overcoming objections, 19,
204-206

**P**

painful current states, 67-68
paraphrase listening, 112-114
perceptions of salespeople, 54-57
perfectionist closers, 165-168
permission-based presentations,
130-131
   clarifying, 143-148
      preclosing, 145-148
      summarizing, 143
      taking prospect's pulse, 144
   closing, 149-152
   discovery, 136-140
      emotional trigger questions,
         139
      fact-finding, 137
      segue questions, 140-143
   introduction, 132-134
   Knowledge Gap, 135-136
   relationships with prospects,
      134-135
   solutions, 148
personalities adapting to
   surroundings, 60-61

pontificating closers, 158-159

power of sincerity, 39

practicing responses to objections, 212-213

precall preparations for saving cancellations, 243-245

preclosing, 145-148

prejudging prospects, 104

prequalifying prospects, 104

prescripted closes
  budget, 191-192
  control freak change, 194
  exclusivity, 181-182
  fear of change, 192-194
  going out of business, 183-185
  negative reversal, 197-198
  overview, 180
  price increase, 185-188
  pride of work, 198-199
  risk reward, 188-190
  sentence completion, 197
  shopping list, 195-196
  why, 194
  with your permission, 199-201

presentations
  objectives, 126-128
  overview, 118-119
  permission-based, 130-131
    clarifying, 143-148
    closing, 149-152
    discovery, 136-143
    introduction, 132-134
    Knowledge Gap, 135-136
    relationships with prospects, 134-135
    solutions, 148
  questions, 119-120
  reconfirmation sequences, 238-240
  skipping the questions, 124-125
  turning statements into questions, 121-124

pressure closers, 160-161

price increase close, 185-188

price objections
  being tested by prospects, 223-224
  building value, 220-221
  controlling, 218-219
  dropping prices, 219-220
  justifying price drops, 222-223
  responding with questions, 222
  splitting the difference, 224-227

pride of work close, 198-199

ProfitBuilders website, 268

prospects
  buying signs, 74-77
  call for help, 235-236
  desired state, 66
  listening to, 87-88
  painful current state, 67-68
  prejudging, 104
  prequalifying, 104
  price testing, 223-224
  purchasing decisions
    basing on logic versus emotions, 49-51
    fears, 47-49
    reasons for buying, 44-45
    reasons for not buying, 47
  reasons to stop listening, 97-98
  reconfirming, 238-240
  relationships with, 134-135
  remorse, 234
  wants versus needs, 68-74

purchasing decisions
  basing on logic versus emotions, 49-51
  fears, 47-49
  reasons for buying, 44-45
  reasons for not buying, 47
  reconfirming, 238-240

## Q

questions
  emotional trigger, 139
  fact-finding, 137
  if, 210
  isolating objections, 208
  Knowledge Gap identification, 136
  listening through filters, 98
  permission-based presentation introductions, 132-134
  preclosing, 146-148
  presentations, 119-120
  price dropping, 222
  reasons for cancellations, 247
  reconfirming, 239
  repeat, 77
  saving cancellations, 241-242
  segue, 140-143
  skipping during presentations, 124-125
  summarizing presentations, 144
  support-building, 75
  taking prospect's pulse, 144
  turning statements into, 121-124

## R

reactive assumptions to listening, 99-101
reconfirming prospects, 238-240
rediscovery in cancellations, 246-248
referrals, 249-250
reflecting, 55, 62-66
reflective listening, 111-112
relationships with prospects, 134-135
relearning process, 266

relearning strategies, 256-258
repeat questions, 77
resources, 268-269
risk control, 30
risk reward close, 188-190
roles of salespeople, 11

## S

sales mojo, 254
salespeople
  characteristics
    choosing confidence, 26-28
    confidence, 22-24
    control, 28-30
    creation versus control, 31-32
    creativity, 33-35
    enthusiasm, 35-37
    fear-based control, 30
    self-doubt, 24-26
    sincerity, 37-40
  consumer role, 51-52
  creating objections to sales, 229-231
  evolving roles, 11
  movies, 18
  perceptions, 54-57
  reasons for failure, 176-178
  sales mojo, 254
sales tactics, 40
sales techniques, 16, 62-66
saving cancellations, 240-242, 250
  asking for referrals, 249-250
  creating new possibilities, 248
  exit interviews, 245-246
  offering solutions, 248-249
  precall preparation, 243-245
  questions, 241-242
  rediscovery, 246-248
  removing emotions, 243
segue questions, 140-143
selective listening, 92-97

self-doubt, 24-26
self-expectations, 175
selling
    ABC's, 268
    basics, 260-261
    buttoning-up, 250
    desired state, 66
    giving value, 15-16
    painful current state, 67-68
    sales mojo, 254
    same way as buying, 82-87
    tactics, 40
    techniques, 16, 62-66
    value, 220-221
sentence completion close, 197
shopping list close, 195-196
silence, 105-107
sincerity, 37-40
solutions
    getting permission to offer,
        209-211
    offering, 211-212
    presentations, 148
    saving cancellations, 248-249
splitting price differences,
    224-227
statistics, 182
support-building questions, 75
sympathy compared to empathy,
    52-54

## T

techniques of mirroring/
    reflecting, 62-66
traditional closings, 10
training
    learning the wrong lessons,
        255-258
    relearning process, 266
turning objections into new
    selling opportunities, 213-214

types of closers
    accountable, 174-175
    adrenalized, 171-174
    blamers, 161-164
    friendship-based, 159-160
    hopeful/fearful, 156-158
    methodological, 164-165
    perfectionists, 165-168
    pontificating, 158-159
    pressure, 160-161
    yes person, 168-171

## U-V

unlearning sales techniques, 16

value
    building, 220-221
    giving, 15-16
    keeping customer's eyes on,
        235
verbal acuity, 63

## W-X-Y-Z

wants compared to needs, 68-74
websites
    author, 268
    book, 269
    ProfitBuilders, 268
why close, 194
*Winner's Path, The*, 268
with your permission close,
    199-201

yes closers, 168-171

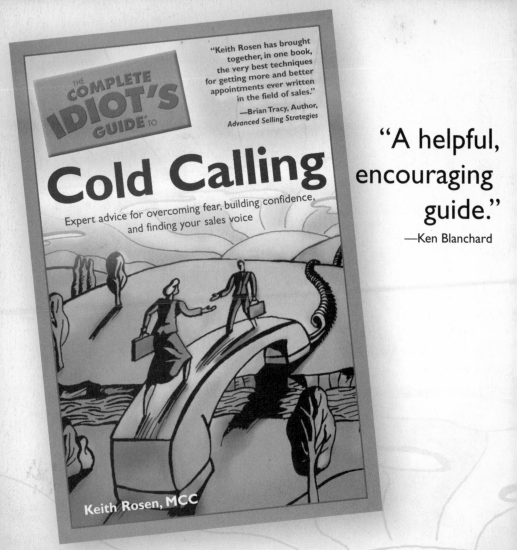